COLLEGE LIFE THROUGH THE EYES OF STUDENTS

COLLEGE LIFE
THROUGH THE EYES
OF STUDENTS

MARY GRIGSBY

Published by
State University of New York Press, Albany

© 2009 State University of New York

All rights reserved

Printed in the United States of America

For information, contact State University of New York Press, Albany, NY
www.sunypress.edu

Production by Diane Ganeles
Marketing by Fran Keneston

Library of Congress Cataloging in Publication Data

Grigsby, Mary, 1952-
    College life through the eyes of students / Mary Grigsby.
        p. cm.
    Includes bibliographical references and index.
    ISBN 978-1-4384-2619-8 (hardcover : alk. paper)
    ISBN 978-1-4384-2620-4 (pbk. : alk. paper)
    1. College students—Conduct of life. 2. College students—United
States—Attitudes. 3. College students—Family relationships—United
States. I. Title.
    LB3609.G75 2009
    378.1'98—dc22

                                                            2008033401

10 9 8 7 6 5 4 3 2 1

CONTENTS

ACKNOWLEDGMENTS

I am very grateful to the students at the Midwest State University (MSU), where this research was conducted, for sharing their lives with me. They gave generously of their time and willingly shared their stories about college life. Sometimes the things they shared were hilarious, and we laughed. Other times the experiences they spoke of were painful. Some of these students have stayed in touch with me as they have moved through college and beyond. I have learned much from them. My life has been enriched by knowing them. For this I will always be thankful.

Many thanks to Natalie Deshon, Crystal Haile, Krysta Kyd, Laura Avery, Paige Wahrenburg, and Rebekah Snyder for their contributions to this work and for their joyful spirits and inquiring minds. These undergraduate students assisted in conducting and transcribing the interviews upon which much of the analysis in this book is based. Over the year I conducted two informal qualitative research methods seminars (one in the fall and one in the winter) so that they went into the field with Institutional Review Board (IRB) certification and skills in conducting interviews and transcribing them. Natalie Deshon and Paige Wahrenburg worked with me for an entire year. Laura Avery, Crystal Haile, and Krysta Kyd worked on the research project for one semester. Rebekah Snyder became involved in the research late in the process as a transcriber, and she assisted in organizing the data in preparation for analysis.

Working with these women and participating in our lively discussions about the research at hand on Wednesday evenings, spent sitting around the large oak table in my office, are treasured memories. They are present in this book, along with the voices of the students interviewed. Barbara Barman-Julius provided editing and proofing assistance on the manuscript, and her attention to detail, combined with her good humor, is greatly appreciated.

This book represents countless acts of kindness from the people close to me. My family, friends, and colleagues have all contributed in one way or another to this book. During the years this book was being researched and written, the support from my husband, Gary Scott Grigsby, helped make the process a joyful one. My mother, Mary Elizabeth Middlebrooks Anderson, came to live with us just as the research for this book began. Her grace and down-to-earth approach to life helped me keep a balance in my daily life as the work on this book took place.

Barbara Bank, professor emeritus at the University of Missouri, helped me clarify and focus this analysis, and I cannot thank her enough. Thanks to Mary Jo Neitz, professor of sociology at the University of Missouri, for reading drafts of chapters and for her insightful questions and comments. Dr. Neitz was my dissertation advisor and has continued to play an important role in my intellectual life. Thanks also to Michael Nolan, the director of the Division of Applied Social Sciences, who steadily encouraged me in this research and helped me carve out the time needed to gather data and write.

1

INTRODUCTION

College Life through the Eyes of Students

Most undergraduates who arrive at Midwest University in the heat of August for the start of the fall semester describe feeling excited and nervous as they anticipate the challenges of college life. During their college years, most students begin the process of defining a life trajectory grounded in an individualistic ethos that moves them toward an adult identity either through choice or default.

At the level of everyday practice, they learn their way around campus. They learn how to manage their lives in the university setting; how to make friends and develop a friendship network; how to pursue varying degrees of having collegiate fun, engaging in romantic involvements, and participating in social activities; how to negotiate and change their relationships with their parents; how to study and spend time on academic work; and engage in the process of defining an adult life trajectory through the choices they make and what they emphasize during their college years. By the time they graduate, many are looking back on college with nostalgia and looking forward to the next phase in a life trajectory that has been shaped, at least in part, by how they negotiated their way and spent their time and energy while in college.

This book describes how college students at a large public Midwestern university made meaning of their lives in the early years of the twenty-first century, and how their paths through college took shape and unfolded. It describes the different paths that they took through college and reveals that class, gender, race, and ethnicity shaped their experiences and influenced the activities and types of relationships that they gravitated toward and emphasized while in college. Choices that students made in the highly individualistic and choice-based culture of Midwest State University are also found to be very central in the experiences they reported having in college.

As a college teacher, the more time I spent with undergraduate students, the more I became aware that I did not really know much about their daily lives. I noticed that they were often curious about my daily life and delighted in learning little things about what I did during the time I was not "working." Sponsoring a student club; visiting freshmen interest groups (FIGs) in the residence halls; attending events at fraternity and sorority houses; having coffee, lunch, and dinner with students; serving as a faculty sponsor for students studying abroad, first for a month in Ireland and then over winter break for two weeks in Europe; and writing literally hundreds of recommendation letters as well as support letters for awards I had contact. Interacting with many of the almost 700 students a year who are in my classes outside of class during office hours, I began to have a sense that in many respects faculty and students inhabit different worlds, and that I had little understanding of their lives beyond the classroom. I also gathered that the classroom and, more generally, even the academic side of the college experience were for many students only a small part of their college lives.

This research has confirmed my suspicions that while faculty may read the National Survey of Student Engagement (NSSE) (2005, 2006) reports and focus on the level of academic challenge provided in their classes, the active and collaborative learning opportunities they provide, the quality of their interactions with students, and how to enrich educational experiences and contribute to a campus environment that is supportive for students, each of which is considered an important performance measure for institutions of higher education (NSSE 2006), many students are likely to be much more focused on their social learning experiences with peers outside of what they consider the academic sphere in college, in settings where they experience themselves having higher levels of choice, control, and the ability to be authentic. Seventy percent of Midwest students interviewed for this study said that, for them, social learning is more important than academics. Twenty-three percent reported that learning was balanced between social activities unrelated to academics and academic activities. Observation of their daily activities provides support for their assertions.

In part this book came out of my desire to be a more effective teacher, advisor, and mentor by understanding more deeply students' interests, concerns, and everyday lives, thereby being better able to connect with them. Another motivation for writing this book was my curiosity about how students make meaning of the college experience, and what it is like for them. The people who inhabited my classes and visited me during office hours or over a cup of coffee often seemed to be travelers from a distant culture, a place as unknown and little understood by me as that of the distant exotic "natives" whose cultural beliefs and practices were the focus of much inquiry in the social sciences of past eras. I wanted to know what students believe college is about for them, how they spend their time, and what matters to them.

This book is not an exposé of hedonistic practices of students or a discourse on the further deterioration of American culture exemplified by the values and behaviors of college students. Nor is it a critique of the Greek system (Robbins 2004), an expose of student cheating (Callahan 2004), or dating and sexuality (Holland and Eisenhart 1990; Moffatt 1989), though some of these aspects of college life are touched upon as students talk about them. This book is about what college means for a snapshot of a generation of students coming of age and finding their way in the new millennium at a large Midwestern state university, in what is increasingly a fast-paced, technologically stratified, and globalizing world.

This book provides an analysis of college student culture at a large Midwestern state university, of what students say about their lives as college students, and of what we can learn from them about our culture and our own lives. Doing the research for this book has led me to empathize with the students' struggles to come of age and to find fulfillment within the context of the present-day culture and economy. The tenacity and energy that many students put into the project are awe inspiring, and I am very grateful to them for teaching me so much about college student life.

THE SETTING

The Midwest State University main campus occupies over 1,300 acres and is situated centrally in Midwest City. The campus has pleasantly landscaped grounds and well-maintained facilities. Shade gardens and beds of wildflowers greet passersby. New residence halls that provide suites and single rooms with baths have been constructed recently, as well as a new state-of-the-art recreation center and a major biotechnology research facility. A football stadium and fairly new basketball arena, along with an older sports arena and remote parking with a shuttle service to the center of campus, dominate the scenery to the south of the campus. A golf course is a short drive to the southwest.

The downtown area lies to the north of campus, with restaurants, clubs and bars, and coffeehouses, as well as specialty shops. Students flood into downtown in the evenings, particularly Thursday, Friday, and

Saturday nights. Neighborhoods on two sides of the campus have small apartment and rental houses inhabited by students intermingled with single-family homes. Fraternity and sorority houses flank the central campus on the east and west sides, with most being on the western side of the campus and close together. Major streets frame the campus and provide ready access to apartment and condo housing in the suburbs.

The campus spaces that students talk most about are the residence halls, fraternity and sorority houses, the recreation center, computer labs, the common area that houses the bookstore, food court, craft studio, and student organizations, and the student union, where student events are often held and where a cafeteria and coffee shop are housed. The main library is centrally located, as is the student success center. Two theaters, an art museum, an archeology museum, and a fine arts gallery are all centrally located.

When the freshmen arrive for fall semester their high spirits and lively interactions create a buzz of energy in the air on campus and in the downtown street life. Groups of freshmen talking and laughing walk the streets getting their bearings and getting to know each other. The recreation center is filled to capacity, and the shared-room residence halls are bustling and noisy as people get settled and get to know each other. Move-in day is more muted in the new suite and single-room residence halls that attract fewer freshmen. A long line of students, talking animatedly in the sweltering August heat, stretches down the street from a local pizza place near campus that offers free pizza to new freshman students at a welcoming event. Many students sport T-shirts or hats emblazoned with the Midwest mascot or logo worn with jeans or shorts and sandals. Undergraduates make up the majority of the population at Midwest and give the campus much of its character and high-energy feel when the university is in session.

Midwest is a public comprehensive doctoral-granting research institution with medical and veterinary programs. It is the top-ranked public institution of higher education in the state. Midwest is a member of the Association of American Universities comprising sixty-two leading research universities in the U.S. and Canada and appears in *U.S. News and World Report's* list of the top national universities. Most students in attendance are from within the state, with particularly high numbers from the two large cities in the state. Undergraduate enrollment grew steadily during the time this research was conducted. At the time this research began, in 2003, according to data provided by the registrar's office, Midwest enrolled just over 20,000 on-campus undergraduates, with a total on-campus student enrollment of about 25,500. By 2006, when the research concluded, on-campus undergraduates numbered close to 21,400, and the total on-campus student population was almost 27,000.

In 2003, close to 52 percent of the undergraduate enrollment was female. Men comprised 48 percent of the undergraduate population. A higher number of women than men enrolled at Midwest is typical of national trends and of patterns found in many other industrialized countries in higher education. "Currently, women are more likely than men to enroll in [a] 4-year college, earn a bachelor's degree, and enroll in graduate school" (Buchman and DiPrete 2006, 536).

In the undergraduate on-campus population of Midwest in 2003, when the research began, just under 85 percent of U.S. students were white, between 10 and 11 percent [1] were U.S. racial and ethnic minority students, race and ethnicity were unreported for just over 3 percent, and 1.6 percent of students were international students (nonresident aliens). In 2003, about 24 percent of on-campus undergraduate students were first-generation college students.[2] By 2005, the percentage had increased to over 27 percent. And in 2006, first-generation college students made up about 28 percent of first-time enrollments.[3] Thirteen percent of the on-campus undergraduate student population at Midwest was from out of state in 2003, rising to a little over 14 percent by 2006. About 21 percent of undergraduates at Midwest were in fraternities or sororities in 2003. Twenty-two percent of the undergraduate female students at Midwest were in sororities, while just over 20 percent of undergraduate men were in fraternities.

The use of the pseudonym of Midwest State University for the university where the research for this book was conducted invites the reader to focus on the generalized knowledge and understanding of college student culture that can be derived from the particular case and from understanding how the students make meaning of their college experience at this type of university in the Midwestern United States today. Readers who would like to know the name of the university on which the research for this book was based will be able to find out quite easily, but I suspect it will have little value beyond satisfying their curiosity, since this book aims to offer readers a deeper understanding of the lives of college students rather than understandings derived from institutionally specific details.

THE SCOPE OF THE BOOK

Looking closely at college life through the eyes of undergraduate students is important because it offers the opportunity to understand the meaning making of students regarding their experiences. The symbolic expressions, values, and practices of students and their detailed accounts provide insight into how the meanings of modern society about college and "coming of age" (Mead 1928) more generally are contested and negotiated. The sketching of the relationships among students, how status and belonging are established, how difference is addressed, how and what kinds of communities are formed, and identity work by college students will provide a lens through which to view the larger culture. It raises questions about what broad cultural and economic forces students are responding to as they seek to define what constitutes being a college student, and what it means to become a college-educated "adult" in twenty-first-century America.

Students draw from many sources, including family, peers, popular culture, institutional structures, academic traditions, teachers, advisors, and any number of others in constructing their understanding of what college is all about. Their thinking about college and experiences shapes their choices and behaviors as college students. The generalized college student culture at Midwest is constructed as college students engage in interpreting and responding to versions of what college is all about and draw from the cultural tool kit (Swidler 1986) available to them in order to solve the problems of life. The generalized culture is the one into which they are thrust, through which they learn and negotiate their way as college students, and it is at the same time the culture in which they engage in constructing. Students engage in a struggle to "use" college to serve their interests and meet their needs as human beings coming of age in the United States in the early twenty-first century. The generalized culture is, on the one hand, the culture of Midwest State University that students come into as freshmen within which they must learn to operate in order to be successful students, and at the same time it is the culture that they construct, enact, and change through their participation in it.

Most of the students engage in identity work[4] aimed at constructing a college-educated middle-class self. But they do this in quite distinctive and patterned ways that are reflected in the different patterns found in their relationships with their parents, in the different types of activities and relationships they emphasize during the college years, and in differing "blueprints" of individualism they draw on in their struggles toward adulthood and construction of fulfilling lives.

Most students whose experiences are discussed in this book were engaged in very intense identity work as they struggled not only to complete a college degree but to move toward an identity consistent with the individualist ethos that most embrace, of a competent individual moving, at a pace they deemed appropriate, toward adulthood. Students are aware that the dominant culture in the United States associates going to college with "coming of age" (Mead 1928) and social status. The variety of paths that students take in their struggle to achieve autonomy and move toward adulthood emerges in the interplay between strategies of action (Swidler 1986, 273) available to them and structural factors that may support or constrain given strategies. Students interpret, draw from, and use the dominant or shared more generalized college student culture and at the same time resist some of its dictates. The cultural work is done in the context of the institutional structure of Midwest State University within the framework of processes of economic and cultural change taking place in the world.

Four levels of analysis inform this book (Grigsby 2004). The first level focuses on students as carriers of culture. The second focuses on the ideas and practices that make up the culture (Hall and Neitz 1993). The third explores the group participation, networks, and institutionally structured activities in which students participate. And the fourth focuses on the broader cultural and economic forces that constrain, support, and shape the lives of college students. All four levels are important throughout the book but chapter 2 highlights the first and fourth levels, chapter 3 the second level, chapter 4 the third level, and chapter 5 the first and fourth levels of analysis.

THE STUDY

Qualitative research methods of intensive interviews with sixty undergraduate college students and participant observation of the everyday activities of students were employed. Each respondent also completed a basic demographic data sheet, usually at the time of written consent. Interviews and participant observations were conducted between 2003 and 2006. Most of the interviews were conducted in 2003 and 2004, with selective follow-up interviews done in 2005 and 2006. Participant observation was conducted throughout the data-gathering period but was used intensively in 2005 and 2006. Observations were conducted in residence halls, sororities, fraternities, students' off-campus homes, classes, and at campus events such as welcoming events for undergraduates, homecoming, football and basketball games, student club meetings, fund-raisers, and social gatherings. During the winter semester of 2006 I spent several full days with a subset of the students selected from the larger sample based on their emphasis of different college student cultural orientations and their descriptions of different blueprints of individualism guiding their identity work.

The goal in selecting students to participate in the study was to create a sample that would represent the overall on-campus undergraduate student population fairly closely while at the same time ensuring that adequate numbers of racial and ethnic minority students were included in the sample, despite the relatively low enrollments of racial and ethnic minority students at Midwest. Consideration also was given to making sure that students from all socioeconomic backgrounds were included in the sample. Parental educational levels, occupations, family structure, and student descriptions of family lifestyle were used to locate the class backgrounds of students. Additionally, attention was given to making sure that all colleges and schools granting undergraduate degrees were represented with consideration to the numbers of degrees granted by program. The sample was constructed to make sure that it included in- and out-of-state fraternity and sorority members, first-generation college students (FGC), and those whose parents graduated college (PGC) in fairly representative numbers. Students were interviewed at different stages in their progress through college and were then followed through the course of their college education, with some being followed more closely than others. Appendix 1.1 provides detailed information about the sample.

Pseudonyms are used for all respondents. In cases where students would be easily identified due to some very visible role they played on campus, and where there were other respondents with similar characteristics and experiences, I synthesized them into composites consistent with those employed by Goldman (1999). These instances are noted in the text. "This form is grounded in postmodern approaches that move beyond the confining structures of traditional ethnographic narratives (Denzin and Lincoln [1994] 2005, 575–86)" (Goldman 1999, 45). And, like Goldman (1999), I can assure readers that these "quotations are all taken directly from the respondents, and everything I describe actually happened to them in one way or another. I changed some details, however, in order to protect their anonymity" (Goldman 1999, 45).

THEORETICAL ROOTS AND CONTRIBUTIONS

I employ "grounded theory" (Glaser and Strauss 1967) in which theoretical understandings are built inductively from the data gathered in combination with theory elaboration that involves moving back and forth from the data to existing theoretical work that may contribute to understanding some aspect of the situation being studied (Burawoy,

Buton, Ferguson, et al. 1991). This process leads to the synthesis, integration, and refinement of existing theories as the process of better understanding the data takes place but mostly leads to theoretical insights that become evident through interaction with the data and patterns that emerge as the researcher immerses herself or himself in the data and looks for patterns (Grigsby 2004).

The analysis in the book is also linked to feminist standpoint epistemology in which there is recognition that the position in the social hierarchy and the historical location of the knower shapes what we know and how we know it (Collins 1990, 1993; Harding 1986, 1987). In conducting this research I have tried to be sensitive to the age cohort difference between myself and students and to my relative power in my role as a faculty member in the institutional structure of Midwest. By having a team of undergraduate students, as well as myself, identify subjects and conduct interviews I was able to reduce the possible influence of my status as a faculty member on the quality of the interview data. Overall, students appear to have reported as openly to me as to the undergraduate student interviewers.

Throughout the process of conducting the research, I have also tried to acknowledge my feelings of attachment and commitment to Midwest and to the undergraduate students who shared their lives as part of the research process for this book. I believe this has strengthened this research, because the strong connection with students helped me come to understand that the challenges college students face today are intimately connected to the challenges I face as a faculty member, wife, daughter, friend, colleague, and community member living in a rapidly changing economy and globalizing world and working in a large, rationalized institution. I am at a different point in the life course, and situated differently in the university, but I feel the same forces at work in my life that they do. I also struggle for the same things, at root, that they describe struggling for—meaning, belonging, and fulfillment.

I have also tried to be sensitive to the similarities I share with some students and the differences I have relative to others. I am white, like most of the students at Midwest. And, like the majority of students at Midwest, I come from a middle-class background, and both my parents were college educated. The college experience for FGC students, racial and ethnic minority students, and international students is quite different from that of the white, middle-class, PGC majority at Midwest, and throughout the data gathering and analysis I recognized the need for me to be sensitive to the influence of my own class, race, and gender location in the research process.

RELATED LITERATURE

Six bodies of literature are elaborated against and inform the analysis of the patterns that emerged from the data upon which this book is based. They include recent ethnographic studies of undergraduate college student life (Moffatt 1989; Nathan 2005); research related to college student culture and subcultures (Clark and Trow 1966; Horowitz 1987; Bank 2003); literature dealing with the separation and individuation of college-age people (Côté 2002; Arnett 2000); literature describing changing patterns in college completion rates (Buchmann and Diprete 2006); literature that theorizes connections between childhood psychological development, identity, changes in intimate relationships, and broader patterns of social change (Cancian [1987] 1990; Bellah, Madsen, Sullivan, et al. 1985; Lasch 1978); and related studies aimed at understanding changing patterns in individualization and identity development (Bauman 2001; Giddens 1991) as products of late modernity. Appendix 1.2 provides a literature review of the key works of related literature.

CHAPTER OUTLINE

Chapter 2, "Parent Politics: The Intersections of Class, Gender, and Race/Ethnicity in Student and Parent Relationships," discusses the centrality of parent(s) in the lives of college students at Midwest and outlines the different types of student and parent relationships described by students. The analysis explores the intersections of class, gender, and racial and ethnic heritage in constituting these relationships. Literature that describes distinctive features of this cohort of college students, referred to as Generation Y or the "new Millennials" (Howe and Strauss 2000), is discussed as it pertains to understanding the patterns in student-parent relationships. Relevant literature is used to elaborate and frame the patterns found in the accounts given by students and is contextualized within broader cultural and economic structural change.

Chapter 3, "Generalized College Student Culture," describes the things students say are important to them as college students and builds a picture of the generalized college student culture that freshmen enter, interpret, and play a role in constructing. Virtually all of the students, once they become acclimated on campus, recognize and describe the key features of this culture. The generalized college student culture privileges an individualistic ethos and a self-development project aimed at finding self-fulfillment. The most visible large-scale cultural events at Midwest, homecoming and football and basketball games, privilege leisure pursuits and the private sphere of collegiate fun, and most students identify these activities with the dominant or shared culture at Midwest.

The ways students interpret and act within this culture vary and are influenced by gender, class, and race/ethnicity. Gender is particularly important in the ways students interpret and make use of the generalized college student culture to fulfill the cultural expectation that during their college years they will become competent individuals making appropriate progress toward becoming adults. The things students discuss as being important to them in the generalized college student culture can in one way be viewed as aspects of culture that they must understand and deal with in their long-term life project aimed at finding meaning and self-fulfillment within a highly individualistic culture and rapidly changing economy in which they see themselves, to varying degrees, as individuals responsible for their own choices, self-development, and happiness.

Chapter 4, "Using the Cultural Tool Kit: College Student Cultural Orientations," focuses on the college student cultural orientations found at Midwest and the different ways students make use of the cultural tool kit (Swidler 1986) available at Midwest and, in the culture more generally, in constructing identity, making their way through college, and establishing life trajectory projects. The eagerness with which students who are differently situated at the intersections of class, gender, and race/ethnicity embrace the life project of their own self-development varies significantly and is found to play a role in their cultural orientations. The choices students make about how to spend their time and energy and what resources to make use of while in college also are found to be central in shaping their experiences. This chapter links to literature on college student subcultures (Clark and Trow 1966; Horowitz 1987; Bank 2003) but focuses on the dynamic quality of the selective use by students of the things available to them in the cultural tool kit and the patterns in the orientations of students toward activities, relationships, and behaviors.

Chapter 5, "Blueprints of Individualism and Life Trajectories in Late Modernity," integrates the findings in earlier chapters and explores what these findings tell us about contemporary American forms of individualism and "blueprints" (Cancian [1987] 1990) for achieving fulfillment and meaning that are reflected in the lives of college students. Some patterns in the postcollege lives of students who graduated while this book was being researched are discussed with attention to their employment, entry into graduate programs, living situations, partnerships or marriages, satisfaction with college, and confidence about their ability to have a fulfilling future through their present path.

In this chapter I assert that the importance of friendship networks and the subcultures they participate in to college students are responses to the conditions of late modernity (Bauman 2001; Giddens 1991; Beck and Beck-Gernsheim [2001] 2002) representing ways students struggle to create interdependence and connection in the face of the highly rationalized institutional setting in which they find themselves and the individualistic student-as-consumer choice maker that provides the generalized culture framework for their attendance and participation in the university. Students reassert themselves as meaning makers in the college setting, and rather than making meaning of the symbolic material made available by institutional players in the way it is presented, they interpret it in patterned ways that generally acknowledge the generalized dominant culture but construct meanings that to one degree or another are distinct from it. Through their college student cultural orientations, and the types of relationships they privilege as they seek security and an adult identity, students reveal the particular meanings the university "community" and college experience have for them.

They choose to create friendship groups, what Nathan (2005) calls "ego-centered networks," and they highly value the sense of membership in these groups. They talk about how these groups are based on similarity and common interests and also indirectly describe a level of intimacy within the group that is based on shared experiences and setting boundaries in order to create a comfort zone. It is in these nonkinship groups that students continue to learn how to be social and to acquire the cultural tools for expressing and managing close social relationships.

Students at Midwest describe three different types of orientation or "blueprints" of individualism that link to different patterns in the ways they conceive of themselves, construct their identities, relate to others, participate in the community, and seek to achieve fulfillment and meaning in life. These blueprints exist on a continuum rather than being clear-cut orientations. The blueprints are seen as forms of response to the economic and cultural demands of late modernity felt by these students. The approaches students adopt are shown to be shaped by gender, family structure, and experiences of mobility and change more generally, with patterned variations based, for instance, on rural versus suburban upbringing. The occupational status or graduate programs entered, satisfaction with college, and confidence in and comfort with their life trajectory, though influenced by class, gender, and race/ethnicity, are also found to be linked to subculture orientations they adopted while in college and their orientation blueprint for achieving individualization and relating to others as adults.

The first ideal type of blueprint is traditionalist, in which the person adopts a prepackaged identity and life trajectory model linked to traditional roles and forms of collective belonging. This contemporary form of traditionalism shifts gender traditionalist roles toward less patriarchal practices in production and reproductive work in response to changes in the capitalist labor market, and women's ability to redefine these relations to some degree, but continues to embrace patriarchal ideology and status linked to fulfilling the roles of husband/wife, father/mother, and participation in church, other community organizations, and occupation.

The second blueprint is an approach to identity work and a life trajectory model that is based in independent individualism in which the person aspires to a high degree of autonomy aimed at achieving individual desires; will seek self-fulfillment through consumerism; and will participate in leisure activities, intimate relationships, and perhaps work as a calling, with the self at the center of the life plan and others viewed primarily as playing supporting roles in meeting the needs of the person. This blueprint is linked to emphasis on private sphere pleasures, a split between the public and private self, and a view that privileges independent self-development that was found to be supported by the generalized college student culture (see chapter 3).

The third blueprint relies on individualism ideologically but combines it with a strong element of interdependence with others and commitment to them in constructing an adult identity. Interdependent individualism assumes a flexible form of individualism linked to a life project aimed at self-development and the ongoing remaking of the self through participation in interest-based collectives, shared experiences, and maintenance of a complex and varied network of relationships, many of which are transient but many of which students assume will endure through changes over time.

CONCLUSION

This book extends knowledge of college student life and culture by following students through their college years to explore student relationships with their parents, peers, and faculty; how students perceive, adjust to, and participate in constructing the generalized college student culture at Midwest; patterned variations in college student goals and behaviors during the college years; and variations in identity work and life trajectory orientations that demonstrate varied blueprints of individualism among students. It looks at how the experiences of college students and their orientations are influenced by class, race/ethnicity, and gender and by the choices that students make about how to spend their time in college.

2

PARENT POLITICS

The Intersections of Class, Gender, and Race/Ethnicity in Student and Parent Relationships

The importance of parents in the daily lives of most students at Midwest University became apparent early in the research process. Respondents often went into rich detail and spent considerable time describing their relationships and interactions with their parents. Clearly the identity work in which students engage as part of the "coming-of-age" process in college involves their parents in significant ways.

> "I'm really, really lucky to have such a wonderful family!"
> (Jane, biology major)[1]

Family was the most favorably described of all the institutions touched on by students in interviews. Fifty-five of the sixty students interviewed said that they value their relationships with their parent(s). From freshman to senior, the majority of students spoke of their parent(s) as being important in their lives.[2] Jane has blue eyes and wears her sandy-blond hair parted on the side and shoulder length, with tiny diamond earrings twinkling next to gold studs in her pierced ears. She is wearing a short, pleated skirt and matching sweater with a faux leather pink flower pin near the neckline. She is animated and smiling as she describes her family "We're like very cheerful! And we just love each other so much! And I like, I'm really, really lucky to have such a wonderful family!" Jane's attitude toward her parents is typical among Midwest students.

This chapter examines the types of relationships students describe having with their parents and explores the ways in which these relationships are constituted by broader patterns of social change taking place within the intersecting systems of capitalism, patriarchy, and racial and ethnic stratification (Walby 1990; Collins 1993). The "parent politics" analyzed in this chapter is based on a definition of "politics" in keeping with the way Chinua Achebe, political activist and author, defined it when he said politics is "the way people treat each other" (Henderson 1999, E1). Politics is understood "as a contested symbolic, material, and institutional terrain . . . intrinsically linked to public policy formation and individual identity and action" (Morrow and Torres 1995, 196) that is not limited to government, state, politics, or voting but includes virtually all dimensions of human interaction and experience, including relationships between college students and their parents.

Many of the students interviewed expressed gratitude toward their parent(s) for emotional and/or financial support. Some said it was very important for them to know that their parent(s) will be there when they need them. Some told of times in college when turning to their parents for advice and support was very important to them. Other students described frustration and sadness because their parents did not understand their struggles and how hard college really is. These students often believed that their parents were not able to give them relevant advice for success in college but still appreciated their emotional support.[3]

Three themes emerged as being significant in the ways students described their relationships with their parents. For some students the issue of gaining more autonomy in their relationship with their parents was primary. Some students emphasized being comfortable in their relationship with their parents, while some emphasized a desire for their parents to better understand the challenges they face as college students at Midwest. Appendix 2.1 includes a table that locates students by the theme that was most salient in their descriptions of their relationships with their parents by parental educational level, gender, and racial/ethnic minority and white status.

AUTONOMY

Twenty of the sixty students in the sample (fifteen women and five men, one FGC and nineteen PGC, one racial and ethnic minority, and nineteen white) emphasized a desire to have more autonomy in their relationships with their parents and expressed a desire for their parents to be less controlling in their interactions with them. Of the fifteen women who voiced a desire for more independence and autonomy from their parents, there were thirteen white and one African American PGC women and one white FGC woman. The five men who expressed a desire for greater autonomy from their parents were white PGC students.

Jane's parents both attended college. Her father is a college professor, and her mother is a schoolteacher. They are very involved in her college experience. They come for football and basketball games and take an active interest in her academic performance and sorority activities. Jane is from out of state and, like most out-of-state students at Midwest, she comes from an adjoining state. Jane feels very fortunate that her parents are able to give her "advantages" by paying for her college and all of her needs. She is among an estimated 24 percent of students at Midwest whose parents pay the cost of their college educations.[4] Jane says:

> My parents have given me the opportunity to make school my work. And I get an allowance every month. I think, it's a little high. Honestly, like, I don't think I deserve that much. But seriously, I don't understand how I go through this money. Because I don't pay out of this money for gas, I use a credit card for that, and they pay for my credit cards . . . I hope I can give my children the same advantages they have given me.

She does not know how some of her friends who have to work while in school manage it. She says that she is just very glad she does not have to work and can take full advantage of being in school. Jane goes home only during some major holidays and breaks. She does volunteer work, participates in student government, and is headed for the career she says her parents believe is best for her. She is a junior majoring in biology and initially planned to go on to medical school and become a doctor. Her older sister is in medical school. But during the course of her college career Jane's plans changed. For a time she considered becoming a pharmacist, a dentist, and eventually settled on becoming a physician's assistant.

Because Jane's parents attended college, she says they understand the challenges she faces as a student, and they often give her advice on things that come up. While Jane clearly appreciates all her parents do for her, she says that she wants more independence and autonomy in relation to them.

The source of the complaints by the women wanting more autonomy is usually that their parents are trying to tell them what to major
in, which courses to take, and how to manage their finances and social
lives. Two women also said that their parents were trying to influence
their dating choices.

Angela's comments are typical of white, middle-class, female students whose parents are college educated and who focus their complaints against their fathers. About half of the women who expressed a
desire for more autonomy focus their complaints directly against their
fathers. The other half are more irritated with their mothers. Angela, a
junior, is majoring in communications. She has curly red hair that is just
below shoulder length. It bounces slightly as she leans forward, her
bright blue eyes wide, her freckled cheeks taking on a peachy glow as
she prepares to describe her relationship with her parents. Angela goes
home on holidays and major breaks. She begins with emphasis, saying
"[I'd like to say] I love you and thank you for all of your guidance!
Because there has been a lot of advice!" She continues in a half humor-
ous but emphatic way, raising her eyebrows as she makes her points:

> Thanks for the advice! I hope someday I'm mature enough to
> understand it. I'm a very mature person, but I'm not at the
> point where I have to be worried about saving for a mortgage. I
> don't have a house! (laughs) You know, I'm not at the point
> where I have to be worried about putting aside money for my
> children's college education. I'm not at the point where I have
> to be worried about some of the things that I think they want
> me to be worried about. So thank you for the advice. I appreci-
> ate it, and someday I'll be at the point where I will take advan-
> tage of it. But for now, you know, a lot of this I just need to
> figure out on my own!
>
> And the other thing is, I'm not as naïve and stupid as I used
> to be. I think because I used to be so naïve they felt the need to
> give me a lot of advice, like they needed to guide me. But they
> still feel the need to do that and I sometimes chafe under that.
> I'm kind of like "No, I can figure this out on my own. And in
> fact it will mean more when I figure it out on my own."
>
> That was a great thing, for example, having a bank account
> on my own that I had to be responsible for. My dad still feels
> the need to ask me constantly, "Are you making sure you are
> balancing your checkbook? Are you checking your bank state-
> ments? Are you doing this?" "Yes dad, I know. If I make mis-
> takes I want them to be something that I figure out how to

correct because that's a learning experience." That's a true teachable moment! I tease my dad because he has what he calls "teachable moments" so like we'll be doing something as a family and we'll have to all stop so dad can teach us something. For his birthday I got him a card and it was a chimpanzee (that said) "I listened to all of the advice you gave me over the years and I wasn't really listening" and he (the monkey) has his fingers in his ears. My dad thought it was funny. So thanks for the advice, and I hope someday I can use it, but for now just kind of let me figure it out on my own.

Angela's struggle for autonomy clearly focuses on gaining independence from her father and the family dynamics she feels are keeping her from becoming fully independent. She plans to marry after graduation and to move where her husband goes. She says her main goal in life is to be a wife and mother, and that her career will come second.

Those whose struggles are primarily with their mothers often express anger that stems from a wish that their mothers would help them stand up against patriarchal control, though they do not articulate it this way and often avoid criticizing their fathers directly.

Jane throws up her hands in seeming disbelief as she explains her situation. This is at the point where she was planning on becoming a pharmacist.

I've just set my sights on being a pharmacist. I will own the building. My sister is in medical school. She is brilliant. I always had so much to live up to. Why can't you (my parents) just, like support me (in) struggling with what I want to be, like how about letting me . . . I sometimes just feel like, "support me!" And I really do want to do this, and I don't want to be a doctor! You have Ellen (her sister), you know, you've got free medical care or whatever right there. You know? You've got free visits. You don't need me to be a pharmacist! So I just sometimes wish they just kind of like (say) "hey, it's okay, she (Jane) will make something of it." And I'm kind of scared too. They want so much for me, and sometimes I feel like they go a little over . . . overbearing.

Jane says she is closer to her father, and that he advises her frequently. She is more irritated with her mother, the person she wishes would stand up for her and help her in choosing the career she thinks she is really suited to. Jane wants to be an event planner. She played a key role in planning a major university event during her junior year in college and realized she is very good at it and loves it. Jane looks out the window. It is early spring and the trees are just starting to bud. Sunlight streams in and catches light in a small tear that rolls down her cheek. She looks up, her eyes full, and she speaks rapidly, the words coming so quickly that not all of her thoughts are fully completed before the next one is spoken.

> I know my mom wanted to be a lawyer, and my dad or my mom's mom was like "no, you'd be good with kids. Be a teacher." And so my mom was a teacher. And so that's why I kind of don't know why she is doing this. I don't know if I've expressed enough what I want to do! I don't think I'm going for that career. And I've talked to my mom a lot about that. I'm like "Mom I've got to get a career where I'm around people." And I just put things together. And right now I'm going to be a pharmacist and my friends are looking at me like "why?" And I go, well, honestly "cause my parents know I want the two houses, like one in Vail, and one in the Hamptons . . . , I'm beginning to realize that I don't need that."

It is telling that Jane feels confusion about who forced her mother to become a teacher rather than a lawyer, Jane's father, or her mother's mother? (See Johnson 1988.) She wishes her mother would support her in doing what she wants to do instead of aligning with her father.

The source of irritation for the five men who said they want more independence in their relationships with their parents was related to their parents wanting them to perform better academically and/or their feelings that their parents were trying to interfere in their "fun time" while in college. Two of the five also said that their parents were trying to find out about their social lives, in particular the people they were dating, and that they did not want to share this type of information with them. Four of these five men voiced much more irritation with their mothers than their fathers. One has a troubled relationship with his father, described as an "abusive alcoholic."

Chip, a sophomore journalism major, is one of the five PGC men who said they are uncomfortable with the level of involvement their parents have in their lives. Chip's is one of the more forceful complaints I heard from this group. He especially views his mother as being problematic. He has the following to say about the level of parental involvement in his college experience.

Their active interest is an understatement! My parents are all over me about it, to the point I wish they weren't! But, you know, what are you going to do? It's negative to a point where, like the thing I should be worried about in college should be my grades. And so a lot of times, when I get something that comes back as really crappy, *I'm* not the person that it comes to my mind, oh, how am I going to fix this in class, how am I going to get my grade back up. It's my parents! My parents have a problem with what they don't see me doing, work! It means I'm not doing anything. So to them, not seeing me means I'm just on this nine-month vacation a year. So therefore I go home for break, breaks *suck*! I go home for break, and instantly my mom will have a schedule, and she'll write it out. Like stuff for me to do, starting [at] 6 [in the morning]. And this is not a break for me. [I'd like to say], "Look I really am working my ass off here!"

Chip is engaged in the academic aspects of school and plans to go on to graduate school. He is also largely economically dependent on his parents and does not work at all during the school year. Unlike most of the men who go home more frequently, Chip goes home only on breaks and major holidays. Much of the tension that exists between him and his parents seems to be linked to his parents' concerns about how well their investment is being used. Chip seems to have more issues with his mother than his father, as she is the one who appears to communicate these concerns more frequently. At one point Chip blurted out in an angry tone, "She was a sorority girl at Midwest and we never would have met if she were here now! She doesn't understand my situation at all!" Chip says his mother also is constantly asking him about the women he is dating, and he says he is not dating that much and would not want to share it with her if he was.

The distinct developmental experiences that boys and girls from white, middle-class, and upper-middle-class families go through in contemporary Western societies may play a role in the irritation of these young men being focused on their mothers. Chodorow (1978) and Johnson (1988) describe relationship dynamics within nuclear families in contemporary Western cultures in which boys must make a painful break with their mothers, who usually have been the parent most present in their lives and with whom they have emotionally bonded, in order to establish their masculine identities. Fathers, they say, are mostly emotionally absent from the lives of their children, engaged in the breadwinner role, and have relational styles that are more distant. Girls, on the other hand, do not have to make the same kind of break with their mothers to establish feminine identities and maintain a relationship style that extends from the relationship with their mothers into the close relationships they have throughout their lives. This leads the men to have styles of relating that are focused on remaining in control, distant, and independent, while women focus on establishing emotional intimacy and relationships.

Chodorow's (1978) work has been criticized for applying only to white, middle-class people, which may explain why her approach to understanding behavior seems to fit best the subset of men who are middle- and upper-middle-class whites. Four of the PGC men from middle- and upper-middle-class families expressed irritation with their mothers in keeping with the identity work necessary to establish an independent masculine identity as middle-class, white men raised in nuclear families. None of the racial and ethnic minority men did, and only one of the white, first-generation college students did. The majority of the men did not complain about relationship issues with their parents but described boundary setting with them, and most frequently with their mothers.

COMFORT

"Basically, anything I want to do they are there to support me!"
(Jeff, business major)

Twenty-nine students, in the sample of sixty (twenty men and nine women; twenty-two PGC and seven FGC; five racial and ethnic minority and twenty-four white students), described being quite comfortable in their relationships with their parents in terms of the level of autonomy and the tone of interactions with them.

Jeff, a white man whose parents attended college, is a junior. He plans on a career in business, either running his own company or being the CEO of a corporation. He is majoring in business at Midwest University. Jeff sits comfortably in an oak chair, his forearms laid out on the oak table at which he is sitting. His hands are open, palms up. He wears blue jeans and a Midwest University T-shirt. His brown eyes, close in color to his hair, grow thoughtful, and a softening of his features takes place as he prepares to speak. His clean-shaven jaw relaxes, and a smile plays across his whole face as he says the following:

My family, at home, is very loving. I attribute everything I have to my family. I mean, I can't say enough. I wish, I hope, that in the future I have as great a family as I do now. I mean, that I can provide for my family with what they've provided me. They provide for me, actually, to come to college. I don't pay to go to college. They help me out with that. Basically, anything I want to do they are there to support me!

Jeff, like Jane, is among the students at Midwest whose parents pay for the bulk of their college educational costs, and like most students, he expresses how important family is to him but feels that, far from trying to control him, his parents support him in anything he chooses to do, and he is comfortable with the type of relationship he has with his parents.

Bruce, a sophomore majoring in biology, provides a typical description of the middle- and upper-middle-class white males who say they are comfortable in their relationships with their parents. His father was a doctor but retired early. Bruce is a sophomore and plans to go on to medical school. He says he is balancing his parents' desire to be involved in his college life with his priority of focusing on his academic goals. Bruce manages his parents based on the idea that his desires should be given priority.

[My parents are] not as active [in my college experience] as I think they would like to be. Dad is kind of just letting me go, because he realized the college experience is kind of a personal thing. Mom would still like to be actively involved, but they have to have a limited experience, for me [because that is what I want]. I'm the one going to college, not them! I'm the one learning. I think they're, Mom's having a hard time letting go of her first-born. But they don't really have an active experience. I involve them as much as I can. . . . The point of coming here is to do well, and succeed where others have failed, and go on to something greater after that. And they know that's what I'm doing.

Bruce goes home every Friday night for a visit and then goes to work at a nearby hospital on Saturday. After establishing that he is setting limits with the level of involvement of his parents in his life as a college student, he notes his perception that his mother would like to be more involved than he allows.

Typically those who emphasized being comfortable in their relationships with parents were not as concerned with negotiating more autonomy with their parents but with managing and controlling their relationships with them. Thirteen of the eighteen PGC white men in the sample and two of the three PGC racial/ethnic minority males expressed comfort with their relationships with their parents. Some of these men described their parents as readily giving them the independence they wanted, but most described how they set limits on parental involvement in their lives.[5] Five of the FGC males (four white and one racial/ethnic minority) also expressed comfort in relating to their parents but did not emphasize having to set limits or negotiating their independence relative to their parents.

Howe and Strauss (2000) suggest that the parents of this cohort of middle- and upper-middle-class students spend a good deal of time with them throughout their lives, and that their fathers are more involved than previous cohorts, and this may have a bearing on the high comfort levels most of the men report having with both parents. One man even mentioned that his father had worked from home and was always available to him and his brother and how important this had been in their development. He was one of the men who described his relationship with both his parents as ideal.

Jeff, who was quoted earlier in this chapter as an example of the importance this cohort places on relationships with parent(s), is one of the few men who adamantly voiced a high level of gratitude for the financial and emotional support his parents provide him. Most of the PGC white men expect or take for granted that their parents will support them financially and emotionally. One man even said, "I told them, you know, flat out. I want you to support me now because I don't want to have to get a job or have to work! So they pretty much take care of all my expenses."

In *Millennials Rising: The Next Generation* (2000), Neil Howe, a political scientist, and William Strauss, an economist, theorize that the cohort that entered college in 2000, and for some years to come after that, has distinct characteristics that set them apart from those who attended college in previous decades. One of the characteristics found in this millennial cohort, which is also referred to as Generation Y by some, is that their parents are "intruding" in nature, where the Generation X parent was "distant" (Howe and Strauss 2000).[6] Their work has been used by many as a framework for thinking about changes that college administrators, student services personnel, and faculty are observing in the current student population.

According to Howe and Strauss (2000) the parents of this cohort of students are putting their children's needs at the center of their lives, often working more and delaying personal fulfillment in order to give them the best opportunities possible. The focus of their book and the broad generalizations they make about cohort differences fit best with the interview accounts of the white, middle-, and upper-middle-class students whose parents attended college.

The basic argument Howe and Strauss make is that, fearful that the family is threatened, boomer parents have put tremendous energy into maintaining and strengthening it. They maintain that the "American family" has been reestablished by this group of parents and children as the central institution in their lives, which is consistent with the feelings that students expressed in the interviews for this book.

Howe and Strauss say that in the face of what they perceive to be "weak or discredited public institutions," these parents have developed a "fixation on control, and a cooler style of nurture," by which they mean a less overtly authoritarian form of parenting (2000, 141). Based on the accounts of the middle- and upper-middle-class college students in this study, particularly the women and men who emphasized wanting more autonomy from their parents, the involvement of their parents in their lives is often intense and even invasive but is most often not overtly authoritarian. The popular press and college and university administrations have noted the increasing involvement of college student parents such as these, calling them "helicopter parents" (Shellenbarger 2005).

Not surprisingly, the intense relationships between Generation Y college students and their parents have led to the publication of an abundance of self-help literature for college students who want to establish independence and maintain a "healthy" relationship and their parents who need to "let go."[7] Implicit in the messages of this literature is the idea that college students should want to become more independent or, from another angle, should want to reduce their own dependency on their parents, and that parents should not try to control the decisions and actions of their college-going children.

It is telling that a brief search for resources on the Internet for parents of college-bound students resulted in screen after screen of Web pages dealing with resources to help parents of new college students "let go." Many of these Web pages are made available by colleges and universities where personnel are reporting more invasive parental involvement than ever before. Lists of self-help books are also prevalent. Some colleges are even giving workshops for parents to encourage them to become less intensely involved in the daily lives of their college-going offspring (Freedman 2004). The advice in these books suggests that at least some parents have difficulty dealing with the departure of children for college and even more difficulty with change in the level of dependency between themselves and their college student children.

Letting Go: A Parent's Guide to Understanding the College Years (2003), first published in 1988, authored by Karen Levin Coburn, Assistant Vice Chancellor for Students and Associate Dean for the Freshman Transition at Washington University in St. Louis, Missouri, and Madge Lawrence Treeger, a member of the Washington University Counseling Service, and a psychotherapist in private practice in St. Louis, is one of the most popular titles in this genre on the market. Treeger confirmed the results of my review of this literature, indicating that the self-help literature aimed at parents of college students began to proliferate in the 1980s but really came into its own in the decades following.

The self-help literature for college students and parents generally focuses on the emotional aspects of dependence and is consistent with the dominant cultural norms associated with the expectation that young people who go to college will have a coming-of-age experience that shifts them into independent adulthood. It states that most parents will willingly "let go" if they are communicated with clearly and witness developing maturity and responsible independent decision making on the part of their college-age offspring. It assumes that most college-age people will develop a clear sense of direction and will become comfortable and confident in making independent decisions without being guided or strongly influenced by their parents if they are given emotional support by parents and encouraged to make their own decisions about things such as what to major in and how to allocate their time. It is solidly embedded in the expectations that were socially constructed out of the period of the "great transformation" and the economic industrialization process (Polanyi 1944; Thompson 1963).

This literature largely addresses the concerns of middle- and upper-middle-class parents and students. It suggests that parents in this cohort are engaged in identity work that constructs them as successful in the child-rearing project based on their high level of involvement in every aspect of the life of their college-age offspring. These are the parents described by Howe and Strauss (2000) who have scheduled themselves and their children tightly throughout the lives of their children. They have transported them and organized them, and their social and leisure activities have been intimately intertwined with those of their children.

Mothers and fathers have participated in these activities, but mothers more than fathers.

Jane and Jeff, like the majority in this group, with parents who are financially supporting them and guiding their choices, look to having high-status and high-income occupations, nice homes, and happy families. And yet both couch these expectations in the tentative language of hope rather than certainty. And each reports quite different relationship dynamics with their parents. Jane is struggling to achieve more autonomy, while Jeff is quite comfortable with the boundaries he has established.

The accounts of students show that, overall, men appear to have an easier time negotiating a comfortable level of autonomy in their relationships with their parents than do women. The majority of men, including racial and ethnic minorities and whites and PGC and FGC students, described being comfortable in relating to their parents. The men have a stronger sense of entitlement to resources of their parent(s), where the women more frequently describe being very grateful for, and even guilty about, the use of their parents' resources for their college educations. Underlying cultural expectations associated with patriarchal production relations within the household (Walby 1990), in which men are dominant and "entitled" to have a higher amount of household reproductive work done for them and to have a higher degree of control over the household income, appear to be shaping student and parent relationship dynamics, even as women are attending college in higher numbers than men (Buchmann and DiPrete 2006).

The important role parents play in the socialization of their children is well known, as are the strong emotional attachments between many parents and their children. The types of emotional attachments that develop between parents and their children and the shape the relationship takes are influenced by many cultural, social, and economic factors that change over time. Interwoven with these norms of emotional attachment, central in the focus of the self-help literature, are broader cultural and economic relationships embedded in institutional structures that change over time (Walby 1990).

Though Howe and Strauss (2000) briefly acknowledge that less economically fortunate students exist, they do not focus their analysis on the experiences of these students or their parents or consider how cultural capital and economic capital are interconnected in shaping somewhat different student and parent relations for first-generation students—nor do they focus on the variations in experiences of different racial and ethnic groups.

UNDERSTANDING

I just wish you understood! (Talisha, a prejournalism freshmen)

The common theme in the accounts of students who emphasized wanting more understanding from their parents is not a frustrated plea for more independence and autonomy but a desire to have their present situation better understood by their parents. These students (seven women and four men; nine FGC and three PGC; five racial and ethnic minority; and six white) say that their parents do not understand the demands being placed on them in college and often note that their parents are pressuring them to excel academically without understanding how hard it is to do so.

Talisha, who is black, was first interviewed as a freshman. At that time she was a prejournalism major. Now she is in the journalism program, focusing on magazine writing. Talisha was raised by her mother and grandmother. She goes home to visit on some major holidays. During her college years she spent one summer with her brother, another near home doing an internship for a local newspaper, and one on study abroad to Italy. She sits back in her chair, petite in frame, with gentle eyes framed by long lashes. She wears jeans and an ivory wool sweater. Her earrings sway as she moves her head and looks into the distance, takes a breath, and begins. She describes her feelings about her mother this way:

> [I'd like to tell my mom] I wish you would give me more money! I wish you understood that there's a lot more that goes on in college than you think. Like, studying! Like, you could, anyone can pass by with a C just about, but sometimes in some classes it's hard to get, like, a B, a B–. (laughs) And that's really hard, and sometimes they don't understand that. They think cause you're getting an A in one class that, you know, you should be getting an A in all your classes then, but some classes are way more difficult than others.

Talisha believes her mother does not understand the demands of college or the challenge to get all As. She is one of three African American women, an Asian American woman, and three white women interviewed who express similar feelings. Their parents, they say, expect them to get all As without understanding that in college it just is not as easy as it was for them in high school.

Like a number of first-generation college students, Talisha expresses concern about maintaining a connection with her family as she changes social status through gaining a higher education. She notes that some family members are "jealous" of her brother who received his college degree at Midwest. She says she tries to be "low key" when she visits because she wants to get along with them and enjoys seeing them. Her older brother graduated from Midwest University ahead of her and has maintained close connections with the extended family. He was living with their grandfather for part of the time Talisha was in college. Talisha clearly gains strength from her family, in particular her brother, whom she says is "very calm, very wise, always thinking of like theoretical, like state of mind. Everything has a purpose." She also was very close to her grandmother, who died while she was in college. In describing her grandmother, she says:

> She is an old wise teacher for twenty-five years, got her Ph.D. from a small Mississippi town. My grandma and I are close. We're not as close (as we used to be), because on the telephone she can't hardly hear what I'm saying so she's just like, "Okay baby, I'm gonna go," and I know she doesn't understand what I'm saying, but when we (are together) we just have a close relationship because she helped raise me a lot.

Talisha makes sure it is understood that she values the wisdom of her grandmother. On the other hand, she says:

> My mom is a basic [Taurus], I don't get along with her too well. She's very nice when you're distant from her, like in college, when I don't see her every day. She's really sweet on the phone, you know, she says, "Hey baby,' but if you live with her, she's just psycho, just crazy. My mom's just like the black sheep of the family. . . . Me and my mom don't have that great of a relationship, and so that's kind of difficult because when I need advice, sometimes she's there and other times, like you can't rely on her.

Talisha says she hides the fact that she is working from her mother because it will anger her. She says her mother does not really understand what college is like.

> She thinks she does, but she really doesn't. I haven't even told her I've gotten a job because every time she calls I'm studying

somewhere and I was telling her about "I think I might get a job." She's like, "you better not get a job! Every time I talk to you you're studying. You don't have time, blah blah blah." But I have a job anyway, but I just haven't told her. I don't think she knows what having a job is, like, actually good for me because it keeps me on track with my studies instead of slacking off.

Talisha's brother has helped her adjust to the demands of college. She points out, "My brother is another part of my parenting because he kind of helped raise me. He has, he's like the father figure in my life, so a lot of what he says really connects with me. Especially since he always says 'you know, I've been through that. I went to Midwest too, and this is what you have to do.'" Talisha's brother offers her essential support. His success in college and his knowledge of how to manage it have been very important to her.

The themes in her description of her relationship with her mother of discomfort with demands that she get excellent grades, combined with the sense that her mother does not really understand what Midwest is like for her, are touched upon in the accounts of five of the seven women desiring understanding. Her discomfort in her relationship with her mother at least in part, is because of the constant demands by her mother that she focus on studying and getting excellent grades. Woven throughout Talisha's story as a freshman is the underlying need she has for connections with people who can give her the type of advice she craves, someone to rely on, as she faces the challenges of attending a "white" university (Feagin, Vera, and Imani 1996).

Taylor, an African American woman from a single-father household, said that her college-educated father's expectations for her to excel when she came to college were extremely high. From her perspective he has unrealistic expectations about her academic performance and does not understand how hard the courses she is taking are. Taylor said that she had resigned herself to being unable to fully share her situation with him, because the gap between her experiences and his understanding of them was so big it was impossible to bridge. Taylor eventually turned to peers for support. Now a junior, she says that her social life is very important to her. She noted jokingly that she finds it difficult to focus on academics at times because of the many opportunities for social learning, which she views as being at least as important as her studies.

Concerns about aspirational pressures from family were mentioned the most by students who emphasized wanting their parents to better understand the demands of Midwest. Literature suggests that among racial and ethnic minorities who have suffered oppression and marginalization, parental aspirations may take on a "continuing familial dimension" (Feagin, Vera, and Imani 1996, 25) that places heavy pressures on those who make it into a university such as Midwest to achieve at a high level. For most the pressures of family aspirations appear to be balanced with the sense of emotional support they receive from their families.

Abbot, a black PGC student, who is a junior majoring in music education, described having a loving and close family that he missed greatly due to the distance of Midwest from his hometown in Alabama. Abbot is quite comfortable in his relationship with his parents, a relationship he describes from the perspective of believing he has already achieved adult status and is on his own to figure out how to succeed in college and life. He feels little pressure from his parents about his performance in college but says he wishes they could be more involved in his college life. Both of Abbot's parents are college educated, but he says that his experience as a college athlete is unfamiliar to them, and that he has to turn elsewhere for guidance in how to succeed in college. Because he is a college athlete, he does not get to go home on breaks very often. Abbot did not express any desire for more independence from his parents. He is clearly independent and, if anything, he wishes that they could be closer and more involved in his life. Far from home on an athletic scholarship, Abbot mentioned with sadness that his parents could not come for his matches due to the travel distance from his hometown in the South. Abbot maintains that his parents provided the upbringing that is the foundation for his life, including involvement in church, which continues to be important to him.

Tan, an Asian American male, describes his relationship with his parents very calmly and does not suggest that there is any overt conflict with them. A senior in psychology, he reported that he visited home monthly because "the Asian family ties require me to go home frequently. I'm also expected to help with the business." Tan says that when he visits his parents, he opens and manages several bars owned by his family, oversees several apartment buildings, including mowing the lawns, and checks on the quick shop they own, collecting the income for deposit.

Like the majority of students, Tan is enjoying his new freedom at college, yet he senses tension between his enjoyment and the expectations of his parents. Hesitatingly and with some doubt in his voice he says, "I'm free, I guess, in a way, being away from home. That's the main thing. Meeting new friends and making sure I keep in touch with them, hanging out with them, enjoying myself, going out." Like a number of the students defined by Midwest University as racial and ethnic minority students in the sample, Tan describes parental expectations and pressures that have their own particular cultural nuances. His parents, and extended family members who have immigrated to the same community as his parents, pressure him to focus on academics and to achieve upward economic and social mobility. He is very aware of the importance of his success to the perceived success of his parents by other family members. At the same time he has grown up in the United States and participates in the dominant culture, particularly peer culture, in a way that distances him from family members who grew up in Korea. He says:

> I'm the only one [in my family] that grew up in the United States. Like everyone else, like, immigrated. They came here after being born in Korea, and they had trouble with the language. So I think that's why they chose to become doctors or engineers because they just studied all the time. But since I was born here I have more of a social life, stuff like that. So it seems like I'm the black sheep of the family right now. (laughs) Everyone's just looking at me right now, like, hey, "So what are you going to become when you grow up?"

Tan says that his parents and extended family have high expectations that he will earn a degree that provides him with a high-status occupational future. He has not chosen a career path that they view as high status, and he senses that he is a disappointment to them, the "black sheep" of the family. Tan plans to go on for a master's degree and pursue "a career in psychology." He makes meaning of this by calling up his higher level of assimilation to the dominant culture in the United States, specifically linguistically. Tan is bridging cultures as he negotiates trying to fulfill his parents' expectations and participates in the dominant culture of college life at Midwest that specifies that college is all about making friends, hanging out, and having fun, which according to the popular ideology of the college student culture (which will be explored in chapter 3) is most important in having the coming-of-age experience that college is supposed to be. Tan does not express the desire that his family will understand him and his choices; instead, he focuses on the validity of his own meaning making about his choices and how his family's perceptions of them are a product of their life experiences and Korean upbringing and cultural heritage. Still, his belief that they do not understand is central in his relationship with them and in his life as a college student.

Like Tan, Mia, who is of Taiwanese descent, says that her mother has high expectations of her academically. She says she wishes her mother understood her situation better and grasped how challenging Midwest is for pre-med students. Mia's mother owns a Chinese restaurant in a small tourist town in the state, and Mia is expected to help out. She says her mother expects a strong commitment to the well-being of their family. She describes wanting college to be a time when she finally is able to be free to have an active social life and to enjoy herself.

Racial and ethnic minority student accounts reveal that though there are nuanced differences in the challenges described by those whose parent(s) earned college degrees and first-generation college students, some of the basic tensions that are salient for them are similar. In the cases of Tan and Mia, their desire to approach college as a "coming-of-age" experience in keeping with dominant cultural images of college life is not consistent with parental desires to focus primarily on academic achievement. For some students the sense of inability to convey to their parents how difficult it is to operate in the environment at Midwest is linked to an element of frustration that is related to the "whiteness" of the university, its bureaucracy, its size, where they become "just a number." This type of discourse has been shown by other studies focused on the experiences of racial minority students to be linked to a sense of invisibility or lack of being recognized. Feagin, Vera, and Imani (1996), for instance, find this is caused by the inability or unwillingness of the white majority in such institutions to "recognize" black students as "full human beings with distinctive talents, virtues, interests, and problems" (1996, 14).

James, a freshman first-generation college student from a small town in state, is walking with me from class to my office. He is white. He has on jeans, a T-shirt, and flip-flops. His hair is spiked, blond on the tips and dark at the roots. Only a few weeks ago he was a red-head—pink-red. The weather is warm, with a hint that rain is on the way. He is crying, ignoring or unaware of the curious looks he is getting from other students. Between sobs he tells me that he is not making the grades his parents expect from him in college. I am aware that he made an A on the first exam in my course, and I ask him if he is concerned about his performance in my course or other courses. Both, he says. He says he feels badly about his performance in my class, because the A he is earning is not as high an A as some of his FIG companions are making in the course. In other classes, he has mostly As and Bs. He says he may be making a C in one class.

Back in my office he describes how he feels. His parents, who did not attend college, do not understand why he is not making straight A pluses as a first-semester freshman. "They just don't understand!" he wails. "Every time we talk on the phone, they tell me I have to make As, and that I need to work harder." James's reaction to the pressure from his parents and from the demands of college is more intense than most first-generation college students, but a number in the sample express similar, though less intense, feelings of pressure in their relationships with their parents since they came to college. A year later, after he had gotten counseling, James said he was doing better though still feeling very pressured to do well academically.

Many of these students feel they are largely on their own to figure out how to do well in college. Being pressured by parents to excel in college, but finding their parents unable to provide much concrete advice or even to understand the college landscape, is a frequently discussed issue for white and ethnic and racial minority first-generation students. During their college years most create a support system at college and come to accept and understand the level of understanding their parents have of their experience as college students. By graduation most say they are grateful for the encouragement their families gave them during college, even though they were not able to give them detailed advice on how to succeed in the university setting.

Kathy is an FGC college student aiming to be a doctor. Her plans include marrying her high school sweetheart and settling down in her hometown to raise a family and practice medicine. She is close to her parents and siblings and frequently returns to her hometown, which is not far from Midwest City to help on the farm and attend church. She says that her parents give her emotional support and have provided her with the values that make her want to become a doctor, but that "sometimes they don't understand why I can't come home to help out on the farm more. I tell them I have to study ,and they don't really get it! They are really supportive, but they don't understand how much time it takes." Concerns about parental understanding were centered on negotiating how she used her time as a college student and involved her educating them about the time demands of her studies. She maintained a very close relationship with her parents throughout college, and when her younger brother followed her to Midwest, she had laid the path for them to understand the demands he faced.

Some students, focused on the issue of understanding, also say that they feel they may give their parents the impression that they are rejecting them as they obtain educational credentials that their parents do not have and attain a lifestyle that is very different from the one with which they grew up. Some also voice fears that their parents will somehow reject them as this change takes place. At the same time they say that if they do not succeed, then they will disappoint their parents.

Roy's leg is twitching as he talks. He is wearing cowboy boots, jeans, and a T-shirt with the name of a farm equipment manufacturer on the front. He is studying agricultural business management and plans to work for a firm in the agricultural sector of the economy. Lean, with short blond hair and blue eyes, he does not sit still easily. Roy is describing the death of his mother, and his father's remarriage to a woman who is a strong disciplinarian. The reconstituted family of which he is now a part is chaotic, and he finds his new stepsister very irritating. He sighs and says:

> It seems like once I got down here, seems like I do a lot of the calling back home. They call every once in awhile. But I thought dad would try to call more often. I think he's just kind of shy, kind of embarrassed. I guess he probably doesn't want me to think he's kind of sissy to call all the time or something. It's a lot different down here, a lot different from home. He just started farming once he got out of high school. . . . My mom [was] a really shy lady. She taught preschool and [was] uh, just definitely one of the nicest people I'll ever know. I could talk to her about anything . . . I'd talk to mom first. Uh, stepmom, she's like totally different from mom. She's more, kind of, strict. I get along with her, but it is quite a change I've had to deal with.

Roy is dealing with the process of blending a family made up of his father, stepmother, himself, his two brothers, a stepsister, and new half sister. He notes, "When I left for college I was nineteen years old, and she (my half sister) was nineteen months old." The primary emotional support he had growing up was from his birth mother. She attended college, while his father did not. Losing her support has been very difficult for Roy, and it is clear that he continues to grieve her death. In Roy's case, even though one parent attended college, he finds himself experiencing college more like a first-generation college student due to the death of his mother prior to his college years.

College is leading Roy into another type of life than the one his father and stepmother have on the farm. Feelings of tension and concern about making his family comfortable and continuing to be accepted by them with the changes he wants to make in social status are on his mind. Especially poignant is the gulf he feels developing between him and his father. Roy wants to "better" himself without having his family perceive that he is "getting above his raising" or moving away from a close connection with them.

At the same time, according to Roy and other students in a similar position, new sources of support and guidance are needed to make it through college successfully. Roy joined a fraternity and has found it helpful as a source of knowledge about how to manage the demands of college. Negotiating his family situation presents quite a different set of challenges than that faced by students whose parents have remained married for the duration of their lives and are focused on their college-age child's success.

Family structure, as Roy's story suggests, is intertwined with other factors in shaping variations in the types of relationships with parents reported by students. Appendix 2.2 provides detailed data on the family structure of the households of origin of the students in the sample.

Much of the research literature that compares first-generation college students to other students reports that there are significant differences between students whose parent(s) attended college and those who do not have a parent who graduated from college (Pascarella, Pierson, Wolniak, and Terenzini 2004; Terenzini, Springer, Yaeger, et al. 1996). Pascarella and others (2004) summarize the literature as follows:

> The weight of evidence from this research indicates that, compared to their peers, first-generation college students tend to be at a distinct disadvantage with respect to basic knowledge about postsecondary education (e.g., costs and application process), level of family income and support, educational degree expectations and plans, and academic preparation in high school. (250)

Quantitative research has shown that in two-parent households, where both parents have at least some college education, gender parity exists between sons and daughters in transition into college, though for the most recent cohorts daughters are privileged in college completion over sons in virtually all family types (DiPrete and Buchmann 2006). For the more recent cohort of college students, gender-specific effects on college completion when only one parent with a college education is present are not significant for the overall population (Kalmijn 1994). The education and occupation of mothers have been found to be equally important for sons as for daughters in college completion (Korupp, Ganzeboom, and Van Der Lippe 2002).

For cohorts born before 1965, sons were privileged in college completion in all but households with a college-educated father. Today in households where fathers have a high school education or less or are absent there has been a reversal from earlier cohorts where this family type privileged sons over daughters in college completion to a situation in which daughters from these family types have increased their college graduation rates, and the graduation rates of sons have dropped, regardless of the mothers' education (DiPrete and Buchmann 2006). However, racial and ethnic minority sons are advantaged relative to other household types by having a college-educated father. Still, racial and ethnic minority women, overall, have higher college completion rates than males.

The most disadvantaged group for college completion is males from households where the father does not have a college education or is absent (Buchmann and DiPrete 2006). Two of the three students in this study who dropped out were white male FGC students from single-mother households. The third was also a white male but came from a two-parent, PGC household. He did not gain entry into the professional program that he came to Midwest to attend and moved home to attend college because his parents were not willing to continue to pay the higher cost of attending Midwest.

HOME TIES

Students who say they have established comfortable relationships with their parents in terms of autonomy and those who anticipate living in their hometowns after college report more frequent visits home. This pattern is offset in cases where "home" is in a distant state rather than within easy driving distance. Students who are struggling for more autonomy or understanding in their relationships with their parents, more of whom do not anticipate returning to their hometowns to live after college, visit less frequently.

Jeff goes home every three weeks. Like most of the men in this group he goes home more frequently than do the women. It is important to note that ten of the thirty-one women in the sample are from out of state, while only one of the men is,[9] but of those who are from out of state, only one woman and one man are from states that do not border Midwest. This means that most of the students could go home for visits fairly easily. Yet even among the in-state women and in-state men, men report more frequent visits home.[10]

Women whose parents attended college visit home less frequently than women who are first-generation college students. In part this may be because more of the women with parents who attended college are from out of state, but the accounts of the women suggest it is more complex than that. Jane's earlier description of her relationships with her parents exemplifies the tensions that make the women, particularly those who are middle and upper middle class, with college-educated parents reluctant to visit them too frequently.

The more frequent visits home by women who are first-generation students are in keeping with the account of Kathy, who was mentioned earlier in this chapter. Kathy has curly blond hair and blue eyes. She is very direct in her communication. A top student who performs very well on standardized exams and in critical thinking tasks, she is goal oriented in her approach to college. She is from a small town that is about a two-hour drive from Midwest City, where she plans to live and work as a doctor after she completes her education. She gave an account, as an FGC daughter, that became familiar as the interviews proceeded. She described in painful detail how alone she felt her first semester in college. She lived on a residence hall floor that was primarily inhabited by women who were pledging sororities, and she was not. Her high school boyfriend, a year behind her in school, was still at home. She said she lived week to week just looking forward to being able to go home for the weekend to be around people with whom she had something in common. Her sophomore year was different, because her boyfriend came to Midwest that year, plus her parents bought a house for her and her brother, also a student at Midwest. They shared the house and rented to other students. This meant she no longer had to live in the residence hall.

Kathy said she did not fit in with other students because of her strong orientation toward academic achievement and focus on a career as a doctor, which she felt most of the students she encountered did not share. She observed that the women on her residence hall floor were oriented toward social life on campus, in her view almost exclusively. One of her comments was about how they were "constantly polishing their nails and talking about going out." She disapproves of their emphasis on appearance, plus she is a devout Baptist and was brought up in a culture where drinking alcohol and dancing are frowned upon. She believes that the dominant student culture of the university is one steeped in behavior that is at best a waste of time. She noted that her involvement in the Baptist Student Union on campus during her freshman year helped her "survive" until she could get out of the residence hall. Kathy's visits home were a comfort to her because she was not comfortable in the culture of the residence hall. She remained closely linked to her family, her high school boyfriend, her friends from home, and the values and behaviors that she perceived as the norms in her hometown.

The ideal of moving away from home, which became the norm in an earlier era as a survival necessity when the shift from an agrarian to an industrialized economic base took place, continues to be prevalent in the college students' expectations. Most do not plan to return home to live with their parents upon graduation from college. But a lifelong, very close relationship with parents is anticipated and desired by many. Twenty-three of the thirty-one women interviewed (74 percent of the sample) and sixteen (55 percent) of the men said they do not plan to live in the same town as their parents upon graduation. Most of this group indicated that they will need to go where jobs are available. Some said they would like to live closer, but they do not think that they can find jobs closer than a two-to-four-hour drive from home. The majority say that ideally they hope to live within easy driving distance of their parents. Appendix 2.3 provides a table of students orientations toward returning home after college by gender, race/ethnicity, and parental college educational attainment.

Twelve of the PGC men, ten white and two racial and ethnic minority men, say they will not return home. Four white FGC males definitely do not plan to ever return to live near their parents. Among the twenty-three women who do not plan to live near their parents, thirteen are white and two are racial/ethnic minority PGC women and four are white and four are racial/ethnic minority FGC women. Three of the twenty-three women who do not plan to live near their parents are planning to marry very soon after graduation and say that they will move wherever their husbands' careers take them. Five are uncertain what they will do upon graduation. Most, like Talisha, plan to follow their own careers and to go geographically where they need to go in order to succeed in their profession.

Contrary to the assumed norms in the self-help literature for students and parents, and the values and expectations of the dominant culture that children will leave home to go to college and move where the job market takes them after college, 35 percent of Midwest students in the sample said that they hoped to return home to live after graduation. These students expressed a sense of commitment to place and to family ties that influenced their plans and hopes. Twenty-one students, thirteen men (45 percent of the sample of men) and eight women (26 percent of women), say they plan or hope to move "home" to live, either immediately after college or eventually. Of course, whether this will actually be the case is uncertain, but the desires and expectations of this kind of close connection with parents in adulthood are significant.

Of the thirteen men who hope to locate near their parents after college, nine are PGC and four are FGC. None of the men who want to return home to live are from single-parent or reconstituted families. Eight of the PGC men who hope or plan to live near their parents are white and one is minority. Among the four first-generation men who want or plan to return home, three are white and one is a minority. Three of this group plan to go home eventually, and one indicated he would like to but is not certain it will work out because of the job market there, and he may have to locate in a town nearby the one in which he grew up. One man in the marines said he is studying education so that when he completes his career in the marines he can locate back near his home and get a job teaching.

Men who describe being comfortable with their relationships with their parents who are from the relatively affluent, two-parent, never divorced, PGC and FGC families frequently say that they want to return near home to live after college. This is particularly true for PGC men whose parents have a high financial investment in their college educations. Jeff, who says he does not plan to live near his parents after graduation, offers some insights into what may motivate these men to return to live near their parents after college if it is possible. He says:

> I'm learning to live on my own. . . . The simplest things it's like my roommates don't know how to start a dishwasher just from looking at it, or don't know how to make macaroni and cheese. It's like their moms have always done these little, stupid things for them, you know, laundry, stuff like that. They shrink their clothes all the time and I, I never would have expected that this would sound like bragging, but I am actually better than them at stupid stuff like that. What I thought would be a nonissue is apparently a part of life that a lot of guys my age have to get past. They have to learn how to take care of themselves basically. . . . My one roommate makes me sick, like his connection with his mom. She's always like taking care of him. She's done everything for him, and she's never let him learn on his own, and that's taught me something about how I want to raise my kids. I'm going to let them make their own mistakes and learn from them. I'm going to be there to guide them, but I'm definitely not going to do everything for them, like a lot of my roommates' parents. You really can be ignorant of stuff like that if your parents have made it that easy for you your whole life, just given you everything.

The desire on the part of these men to return home to live after college may in part be connected to the dynamic described by Jeff of caretaking by mothers and the accompanying freedom- and autonomy-gendered parenting styles that became evident in which parents allow college-going sons a good deal of autonomy. It also is connected to the class and status of their families in their hometowns and to the ties they have there, beyond their families.

Relatively affluent students who enter the university generally already hold an identity that is closely linked to their parents' social status and to a peer culture identity based on the display of consumer goods and the consumption of experiences, distinguishing them as being upper-middle class. Cruises such as the one Jane went on with her parents and trips to Europe during the summer are good examples. These students' status upon entering college is tightly linked to their parents' ability to pay and largely remains so during the course of college, though the choices they make while in college can enhance or detract from this status.

College peer culture is discussed in chapters 3 and 4, but for the present it is sufficient to note that in order to play the peer status game and build on it, this group of students prefers to remain tightly connected to their parents, but students may try to give the impression to peers that they are independent and have autonomy, or are struggling to attain it. Masculine identity work in particular is linked to claiming this model of behavior among peers. Meanwhile, women describe struggles to achieve autonomy. The title of one of the books to help parents in the letting-go process, *Don't Tell Me What to Do, Just Send Money*, by Johnson and Schelhas-Miller (2000), sums up quite well the feelings of many students, particularly some of the men, in this category.

Howe and Strauss found that half of all parents (56 percent of fathers and 44 percent of mothers) believe that their children would like them to spend more time together, but only fifteen percent of children agreed. They drew on research by Galinsky (1999) that found that what millennials really want is for their parents to be less tired and stressed (30 percent) or to make more money (23 percent). Howe and Strauss (2000, 135) assume that wanting their parents to make more money comes from the belief that more income will result in lower stress levels for their parents. Based on this research, there is a more simple reason that some college-age students want their parents to make more money—they want to have access to more money from their parents in order to reduce their own stress while in college. Most men in this group say that they do not want their fathers' stressful lifestyles which they link to demands of work, and several male students mentioned telling their parents that they needed more financial support in order to focus on college.

Jeff, like a number of the people whose parents provide a high level of financial support, says he is grateful to his parents for their overall support, especially the financial support they are giving him. "I would definitely say that the money, they see it as such a financial, um strain, and I guess I would just reassure them that the money that it costs to go to this university is worth it, and the cost of just college in general I think is worth it." Jeff's recognition that his parents, though they are fairly well off, are sacrificing to send him to Midwest attests to the fact that even middle- and upper-middle-class families experience the costs of Midwest University as significant.

With the increasing costs of higher education, the rising debt loads being assumed by parents and students to pay for college, and a competitive job market for those with undergraduate degrees, it is not surprising that parents who pay also want to have a high degree of input into decisions regarding where their children go to school, what they major in, and even what courses they take. Angry Internet postings from self-avowed "helicopter parents" (Shellenbarger 2005) focus on the high cost of college education and the unresponsive bureaucracies in universities and colleges as the motivating factors in their management of their college-age students' daily activities and needs. They say they want to make sure they get their money's worth from the investment. These attitudes are in part influenced by the perception that their child is living in an era of extreme competition for the "good" opportunities society has to offer. The steady downward mobility of all but the top quintile in net income of people in the United States over the past three decades points to the fact that all but the most affluent of people in the United States are likely to experience the rising relative costs of higher education as a significant economic burden and view themselves to be sacrificing in order to send their children to school.

To understand what is shaping the student-parent relationship dynamic of students at Midwest and to understand the full range of student-parent relationships, it is helpful to examine changes in the economy and economic policies that impact educational institutions and shape employment opportunities, which are leading the relatively more affluent PGC parents to want to micro-manage their children's college careers to make sure they get their money's worth and encourage minority and FGC parents to view this as the key to upward mobility in a narrowing opportunity structure that leads them to emphasize to children the need to do well academically.

From the students' perspective, doing well at Midwest University requires them to focus on school and to forego the full-time job market for much of the year. It is very difficult to do well at Midwest and to work enough to pay for school and support oneself and very few students do so. Rising costs of higher education make it more difficult than ever for students to put themselves through Midwest University without financial assistance of some sort. Student loans and working are the two most common methods students use to finance college beyond parental investments, unless they have academic or athletic scholarships.

There is an inherent contradiction in a cultural coming-of-age norm that demands independence and autonomy when one is financially dependent on the very people one is encouraged to gain autonomy from. For many PGC students and some FGC students, parental investment in their educations is relatively high. When students perceive this to be the case, they tend to rely more heavily on their parents for advice about their decisions in college. This research suggests that, overall, women experience parental involvement as being more controlling than do the men. This is especially true for students who make educational choices that lead to occupations in which they are unlikely to be able to achieve a social status equal to that of their family when they enter the job market. This situation tends to encourage men in particular to orient toward moving close to their family after college. This research suggests that, overall, women, and some men, in this group experience parental involvement in their college educations as being more controlling than they would like and are more likely to plan to pursue careers and go where their graduate education and/or work takes them after college.

First-generation college students tend to be less affluent than those with college-educated parents and to have less knowledge about university education, what to expect, and the institutional norms of behavior in college than those whose parents attended college. Students who come from disadvantaged or working-class backgrounds often take out substantial student loans that they will pay back once they enter the job market. These students also often have to work more than their colleagues who have higher levels of parental financial support. The earnings of these students go not for consumer goods or going out to have fun, over and above the basics, but to meet their basic needs. Some in this group receive scholarships that enable them to attend college at a relatively low cost, but often the scholarships involve unique demands and stressors of their own, for example, those experienced by college athletes or those on academic scholarships that require them to maintain relatively high grade-point averages in order to remain eligible for the support.

Not surprisingly, this group of students' struggles with their families are not about getting more independence or autonomy to make decisions while in college but about needing their families to understand how hard it is for them to succeed with the level of institutional support they get and the complexity of dealing with the bureaucracy while they are in college. They also are concerned with managing high parental expectations and extended expectation to excel in college. In most cases, they turn to other people for understanding and guidance to give them confidence as college students. Connections to faculty mentors and peers are particularly important to these students.

The shift toward meeting student financial need with loans ends up saddling students, such as Jim, a first-generation college student with no parental financial investment in his college education, with large loans to pay back. Even though Jim has been highly motivated toward academic achievement and is eager to move into a career as a physical therapist, he will begin his career with close to $50,000 in debt. This has produced an increasing ambivalence in him about his decision to come to college and about graduating and beginning to work, because he knows it will take him years to pay back the debt. Jim says, "I hope I'll find the work fulfilling, otherwise college will have been a bad choice for me."

The dominant cultural ideology of the United States emphasizes the ability of capable and hardworking individuals to attain upward mobility facilitated by educational achievement. However, governmental policies over the last three decades have steadily undercut the ability of the less privileged to have equal access to the benefits of education, because middle-class affordability rather than meritocracy and egalitarian access has become the focus of financial support methods (Brown 1997; St. John and Parsons 2005). This encourages parents of less privileged students to press them to excel in college as a means to achieve upward mobility. At the same time, rising costs and the perceived competition in admission and in the job market by parents have encouraged parents with resources and knowledge of college to become very involved in the college careers of their children because they view it as an investment that they intend to see lead to a career. Near graduation Jane commented that her father had told her she had to succeed in getting into a professional school, because he and her mother had "invested too much in you for you to fail."

EMERGING OR DELAYED ADULTHOOD?

There has been considerable media coverage about the delayed adulthood of American young people of college age and beyond. Scholarly work points to this trend as well. Arnett (2000) maintains that this period is best called a period of "emerging adulthood" (469) (ages eighteen to twenty-five) and is a distinct period demographically, subjectively, and in terms of identity explorations. Arnett claims that the period of development of emerging adulthood exists only in cultures that allow young people a prolonged period of independent role exploration during their late teens and twenties. He writes:

> Emerging adulthood is distinguished by relative independence from social roles and from normative expectations. Having left the dependency of childhood and adolescence, and having not yet entered the enduring responsibilities that are normative in adulthood, emerging adults often explore a variety of possible life directions in love, work, and worldviews. (Arnett 2000, 469)

According to Arnett, "About one third of emerging adults go off to college after high school and spend the next several years in some combination of independent living and continued reliance on adults, for example, in a college dormitory or a fraternity or sorority house (Goldscheider and Goldscheider 1994)" (Arnett 2000, 471). His description of college-going emerging adults fits well with the attitudes and beliefs described by white middle- and upper-middle-class students in the sample whose parents went to college. "For them, this is a period of semiautonomy (Goldscheider and Davanzo 1986) as they take on some of the responsibilities of independent living but leave others to their parents, college authorities, or other adults" (471). Arnett finds that "in a variety of studies with young people in their teens and twenties, demographic transitions such as finishing education, settling into a career, marriage, and parenthood rank at the bottom in importance" (Arnett 2000, 472). Arnett maintains:

> The characteristics that matter most to emerging adults in their subjective sense of attaining adulthood are not demographic transitions but individualistic *qualities of character* (Arnett 1998; emphasis in original). Specifically, the two top criteria for the transition to adulthood in a variety of studies have been *accepting responsibility for one's self* and *making independent decisions* (Arnett 1997, 1998; Greene et al. 1992; emphases in original). A third criterion, also individualistic but more tangible, becoming *financially independent*, also ranks consistently near the top. (Arnett 2000, 472–73; emphasis in original)

At Midwest, the middle- and upper-middle-class white college students and a few of the more affluent racial and ethnic minority students whose parents attended college can accurately be described as being in a period of life that is demographically and subjectively consistent with the emerging adulthood period of development theorized by Arnett (2000). A number of these students view themselves as being dependent on their parents during college, even as seniors. Most women who fit Arnett's description of emerging adults stressed wanting more autonomy from their parents, while more of the men described being comfortable in relating to their parents. Several voiced concerns about being able to make it on their own after college, suggesting that at least some of the students feel more dependent than semi-autonomous. These students also frequently mentioned that they do not want to have the stress and long hours of work that their parents do, and that they are in no hurry to graduate from college and enter the demands of a career. More men than women expressed ambivalence about the demands of real life. Many focus their descriptions of the type of jobs they want in contrast to what see in their parents' work life, and they say that they want to enjoy the pleasures of college life before they have to enter the real world.

It is not, however, as easy to locate white, first-generation college students or most of the racial and ethnic minority students' accounts in the same way. First, they tend to view themselves in less dependent terms, especially if they are attending college on academic or athletic scholarships. Many also are working to help put themselves through college. These students, in keeping with their parents' high expectations for them, are eager to complete college and get jobs. They described little hesitation about entering the adult work world, and when they did it was linked to the challenges they think they face and uncertainty about their abilities to meet those challenges, not their reluctance to work long hours or fear of being stressed. Instead, they view getting a good job as a way to reduce their stress and have an enjoyable life. Their relationships with their parents are based on a college life that already involves taking responsibility for themselves and making more independent decisions than do their peers whose parents are college graduates and who are making higher levels of financial investment in their children's college educations.

Acknowledging that most studies of emerging adults had focused primarily on white samples, Arnett (2003) undertook a survey of African American, Latino, Asian American, and white students. He hypothesized that racial and ethnic minority students "would be less

likely to support individualistic criteria for adulthood and more likely
to support more collectivist criteria" (Arnett 2003, 64) as criteria for
adulthood. He anticipated finding that, overall, African Americans,
Latinos, and Asian Americans would "have a subjective sense of reach-
ing adulthood earlier" (64) than white Americans because of "higher
collectivism, specifically of having greater responsibilities within their
families of origin" (64).

He found that the "conception of the transition to adulthood held
by emerging adults in American ethnic minority groups differed in
important ways from the conception held by white emerging adults"
(71). For the purposes of elaboration against the findings of this
research, the most relevant subscale measure Arnett used in his study is
a "role transitions subscale" that focuses on the perceived importance
of transitions such as getting married, finishing education, and becoming employed full time as criteria for achieving adulthood. Arnett confirmed his hypothesis that these transitions would be more important
for racial and ethnic minorities. For instance, he found that "the proportion of emerging adults supporting 'become employed full time" was
43 percent for African Americans, 50 percent for Latinos, and 35 percent for Asian Americans but only 19 percent for whites" (72). This
finding is quite consistent with the accounts of the majority of racial
and ethnic minority students and also a number of the white FGC students in this study who are eager to complete school and get good jobs
as quickly as possible.

Arnett found that African Americans and Latinos were the most
likely to feel that they had reached adulthood, with 59 percent of
African Americans and 48 percent of Latinos indicating that they had
achieved adulthood. One possible contributing factor to the difference
in perceptions of adulthood according to Arnett is that living in "a relatively low-SES family may mean having more family responsibilities in
childhood and adolescence than whites do (Fuligni, Tseng, and Lam
1999; Phinney et al. 2000), which may contribute to an earlier sense of
having reached adulthood" (73). This research suggests that beyond the
experience in their family home, some first-generation college students,
both racial and ethnic minority students and white students, take fairly
high levels of responsibility for their decisions, activities, and finances as
college students and perceive themselves more as adults because of this.

Sociologist James E. Côté (2002) contextualizes observed changes
in the transition to adulthood by synthesizing the individualization
thesis found in theories of the life course with a social change perspective that includes social structural factors. He maintains:

> The societal context in which this new transition to adulthood
> is taking place is sometimes referred to as late modernity . . . ,
> an era in which market-oriented policies and consumption-
> based lifestyles are replacing community-oriented policies and
> production-based lifestyles (for example, Furlong and Cartmel
> 1997). Consequently, problems and issues that were once
> addressed with collective solutions are increasingly left to indi-
> viduals to resolve on their own (Beck 1992). (Côté 2002, 117)

Côté begins his examination of the influence of structural factors versus
individual agency with the assumption that the population he is studying, Canadian university students, has already been "roughly but not
absolutely" sorted by social class, with "the secondary educational level
constituting a structural barrier separating the (lower income) working
and (higher income) middle classes (Andres et al. 1999)" (Côté 2002,
118). Within the population of university students, Côté tries to learn:

> (1) how their various individualized trajectories to adulthood
> work out; (2) what effects factors like gender and differing
> parental financial support for their trajectory choices have on
> later occupational attainments and personal fulfillment; and (3)
> how they deal with the middle-class competition for career
> advantage (e.g., many Canadian university graduates report dif-
> ficulties in finding rewarding employment and/or feel they are
> overqualified for the jobs they obtain with the degree (Norbert,
> McDowell, and Goulet 1992; Kelly, Howatson-Leo, and Clark
> 1997; Frenette 2000; Krahn and Bowlby 2000). (Côté 2002,
> 118–19)

Côté finds within the college student population that there "seem to be
weak 'structural' effects," but he did not find that "gender and parental
financing were highly predictive, such that males with the greatest
parental financial support should have the best long-term outcomes. . . .
Instead, with respect to financial support, females who received high
levels of financial support and males who received low levels of support
(from parents) appear to benefit the most, and agency seems to play a
role in long-term outcomes regardless of structural factors" (131).

Côté's findings, while counterintuitive to simple class reproductive
theories, link well with patterns found at Midwest among high financial
investment PGC students. The majority of high-investment PGC males
are comfortable in their current situation and are not highly motivated
to strive academically or rush to embrace careers beyond college, and a

number of them are looking forward to futures living near their parents after college. The majority of high-investment PGC women, both white and racial and ethnic minority, are motivated to do well academically in college and move into careers. This research reveals that the tensions these women report experiencing as they try to gain autonomy and reduce parental control play a role in their orientations.

CONCLUSION

Parents are very central in the daily lives of most students at Midwest. Many students expressed gratitude toward their parent(s) for emotional and/or financial support. Some noted it was reassuring to know that their parent(s) are there when they need them.

Drawing on Sylvia Walby's (1990) conceptualization of patriarchy as a system of social relations that is composed of six structures, "the patriarchal mode of production, patriarchal relations in paid work, patriarchal relations in the state, male violence, patriarchal relations in sexuality, and patriarchal relations in cultural institutions," (20) we can link the gendered patterns found in student and parent relationships to structures of patriarchy that intersect with the class locations of men and women in shaping their relationships with their parents. We can also see that these relationships are negotiated within the structures of patriarchy, and by focusing on the students' ideas and behaviors, we can see that they are responding to these structures to achieve their desires.

Many of the women from middle- and upper middle-class families engage in discourse that affirms the importance of their parent(s) to them while they also describe struggling to establish more autonomy. Patriarchal relations in the cultural institution of the family, while less important than current patriarchal relations in paid work, still clearly are significant for these women, especially the women from two-parent, male-headed households, a higher percentage of whom complained about wanting more independence from their parents. In addition, the women tend to feel their parents are trying to control them, more so than do the men.

Parental concerns about their daughters' social involvements, in particular with men, came up in several of the interviews and are the source of tensions. This represents an intersection of patriarchal relations in the family and in sexuality, exerting institutionally legitimated control over female autonomy. One woman said when she broke up with her boyfriend and then got back together with him her parents were very upset with her. They wanted her to end the relationship permanently and exhorted her to do so. She said she was angry with them about it. She said, "I wish they would trust me to make my own decisions and treat me as a mature person!" For the most part, the men in this group did not talk about their parents trying to regulate their intimate relationships with dating partners.

The women, overall, visit home less frequently while in college, and fewer of them plan to return home to live after they graduate. When they are able, most of these women want to establish autonomy, and they look to the time when they have a job and can support themselves, or, as in the case of three of the women who plan to marry after college, a time when they are married and can achieve that goal.

The women express more distress about negotiating autonomy and/or the lack of understanding from their parents than do the men. This, at least in part, stems from gendered patterns of relating found in the contemporary United States, in which relationality based on mutual understandings arrived at through verbal communication is very central for women, while shared time together is more central for men (Cancian [1987] 1990). This also may link to the comments from Abbot about wishing his parents could visit and be near him more and may have a bearing on the higher frequency of visits home by men than by women overall.

The men, on the other hand, are much less likely to complain about needing more independence or autonomy from their parents while in college. Patriarchy, as Walby (1990) shows, relies in part on male dominance in the family as its structural base. For this reason it is not surprising that the families of college men give them independence more readily than they do their daughters. It is the men who are expected to play the dominant role in carrying out patriarchal social relations, and in this role they are expected to be independent and in control.

More of the men than women plan or want to return to their home to live either upon graduation or in the future. This could be because they are comfortable in their relationships with their parents since they experience fewer parental attempts to dominate their decision making. It may also be that men, more so than women, expect to benefit in tangible ways from their proximity to their parents through shared economic activities and inheritance. Chapters 4 and 5 will describe the lower levels of motivation academically and toward professionalism among some of the men at Midwest, especially among those men who perceive the level of financial support provided by their parents as significant and whose parents hold high status in their home communities. These men also are centrally concerned with masculine identity work while in college.

In terms of the reproduction of racial and ethnic inequality, we know that racial and ethnic minority students enter Midwest University in very small numbers compared to the percentage of the general population who are ethnic or racial minorities. And in this chapter we have learned that some in the sample describe facing a unique set of challenges in negotiating their relationships with their parents and managing these relationships to help achieve their goals. For black, Latino, and Asian American students at Midwest, the "whiteness" of Midwest is a key feature of their college experience. Feagin, Vera, and Imani (1996) offered a clear insight into the experiences of African American students with which accounts of most of the black students interviewed for this book are consistent. Family for racial and ethnic minority students at Midwest is a basis for solidarity (hooks 1984) in the face of entering a culture at Midwest that most of the racial and ethnic minority students perceive as "white."

Some students described the challenge of coming to realize, deal with, and accept that their parents, though well intentioned, were not able to give them advice they considered relevant for helping them succeed in college. These students often said that they really wished their parents could better understand their struggles and how hard college is. Most students said they had to turn to peers, faculty, or other mentors for practical advice on how to manage college, because their parents did not understand what college is like. But by the end of college, most also said that they were happy with the support their parents had given them emotionally and expressed gratitude for the encouragement they provided. Over the course of college most had come to understand their parents better and to appreciate the type of support they had given them.

Seven minority students and five white FGC students interviewed described familial aspiration pressure as central in their college experience though there were nuanced differences in the form it took and their responses to it varied. This is consistent with the findings of Feagin, Vera, and Imani (1996) and Bui (2002). Feagin, Vera, and Imani (1996) noted that "this familial pressure is common in many American families, but it takes on an added dimension for those who are members of an oppressed group that has faced major racial barriers to education" (23). Bui found that first-generation college students ranked gaining respect and status, bringing honor to their family, and helping their family out financially as key reasons they came to college. Students who were not first-generation college students ranked most highly having college-going siblings or other relatives and a desire to get out of their parents' home (Bui 2002). This pattern is consistent with the attitudes of many of the PGC students at Midwest.

The "coming-of-age" experience that college continues to represent in the dominant culture of the United States begins at home for most students. Instead of one type of parental involvement in the lives of their college-age students, accounts of differently situated students tell us that the ways students experience their parents' involvement are gendered and shaped by broader cultural and economic forces. The role of college as a place where people "come of age" is changing in the face of broad economic and cultural patterns of change in the global political economy. The relatively affluent students and parents are drawing on their cultural "tool kits" (Swidler 1986) to attempt to reproduce the family social status, if not to improve it. Attending college is one tool for gaining cultural capital that may convert into social and economic capital (Bourdieu 1984, 1986). Students and parents believe that gaining admission to a good college or university is very competitive, and college-educated parents in particular have a strong sense of the rank and quality of program they want their progeny to attend.

Structural factors and agency intersect in parental politics, both influencing how class and gender relations are reproduced or changed. Certainly we know that class, race/ethnicity, and gender shape the experiences of college students before and after their arrival on campus. When students arrive at Midwest they enter an educational setting that the dominant cultural ideology of our society tells us opens up a range of opportunities that those who do not come to college will not have and offers a wide range of choices to those who enter. Chapter 3 focuses on the ways students describe the norms, values, and practices of the generalized college student culture at Midwest, and their responses to it. For some students this culture is described as a "shared" culture, while for others it is described as a "dominant" culture. Regardless of how they make meaning of it, students understand that to make their way as college students they must learn the culture and how to operate within it.

3

GENERALIZED COLLEGE STUDENT CULTURE

"Don't take life too seriously, you'll never get out alive." (Van Wilder, in *National Lampoon's Van Wilder* [2002])

This chapter outlines the key elements of the generalized college student culture at Midwest University by exploring what students say they focus on as they enter and acclimate to the university setting. Students at Midwest University describe a generalized college student culture that values four things highly: (1) Knowing how to "take care" of yourself; (2) Knowing how to cultivate and manage relationships (this includes being able to "get along" with others, which includes making new friends, cultivating "close" friends, building friendship networks, seeking similar others for support, and having romantic involvements; (3) Developing as a unique individual; and (4) Knowing how to balance "having fun" with academics. Social learning is said to be "fun." Classroom learning, on the other hand, is "work."

Virtually all students at Midwest are aware of this generalized culture that has at its core an individualistic ethos that invites and challenges them to make lifestyle choices and to engage in activities that express their unique identity and ability to manage their lives and thus to affirm a sense of ontological security and stable life trajectory aimed at coming of age and finding fulfillment in the "real" world beyond college. Most students want to claim that they are having a "real" college experience, describe these common elements, and work to make sure that they have some version of these experiences during their time in college.

The expectation that people will leave their parents' home and make their way in the world is deeply ingrained in contemporary American culture (Bellah, Madsen, Sullivan, et al. 1985). When students come to Midwest State University, they have most often literally left

"home" and are embarking on the next phase in individuation and separation from parents, as described in chapter 2, and they are challenged
with the self-development project of finding their way in new relationships and activities.

> Leaving home in a sense involves a kind of second birth in
> which we give birth to ourselves. And if that is the case with
> respect to families, it is even more so with our ultimate defining
> beliefs. The irony is that here, too, just where we think we are
> most free, we are most coerced by the dominant beliefs of our
> own culture. For it is a powerful cultural fiction that we not
> only can, but must, make up our deepest beliefs in the isolation
> of our private selves. (Bellah, Madsen, Sullivan, et al. 1985, 65)

Students faced with this challenge describe a generalized college student culture that is in part centered in the individualistic ethos of self-
sufficiency and developing as autonomous unique individuals and at the
same time focused on finding a sense of belonging through making new
friends and developing a friendship network in their new setting as
quickly as possible.

The language of independent individualism is accompanied by
behavior that demonstrates a strong need for social bonds. These
"new" connections are, from the perspective of students, their responsibility to make and maintain. They generally say that their friends are
people to whom they were drawn, and that they chose to become
friends with them because they shared common interests. Most students
establish a small group of networked friends. The sense of collective
belonging that they find in these groups is very important to them.
Friends are described by most students as being the most important part
of college life. The choice of friends, like the choice of living arrangements and what to major in, is a very important "lifestyle" (Giddens
1991) choice they face as college students.

About 70 percent of the students in the sample feel that social
learning in college is more significant for them than academics. Twenty
women (62.5 percent of women) and twenty-two men (78.5 percent of
men) expressed this view. Angela, a junior majoring in communications,
sums up her ideas about balancing work and "fun" this way.

> I don't think college should be about drifting . . . not really
> caring. I definitely think there should be investment, you know,
> work for whatever it is that you want to do, but most impor-
> tantly, more than anything else, in college, you should have fun.

It shouldn't necessarily come at the expense of your studies (or) the overall goal of graduating, but if you're finding yourself at a point where this is no longer enjoyable, then something is wrong. Take this time to have fun and enjoy your youth! Try not to take it too seriously.

Most students do not say that academics do not matter, but they believe that the social learning they do with peers in college is more important. The types of social learning that the students in this group value vary, with some focusing on more traditional, institutionally supported social activities such as making new friends through church and religious student organizations, joining fraternities and sororities, and becoming involved in formal student organizations and student government, while others value informal socializing as central for them. Very few students say that their academic learning is the most significant part of their learning while in college. Only two women and two men said that the academics in college were most central to their learning experiences in college. Ten women and four men, about 23 percent of the students in the sample, felt that their significant learning was taking place in a relatively balanced way, maintaining that academic and social activities were equally important.

Much of the learning engaged in by college students involves gaining the skills needed to traverse the cultural boundaries between public, semipublic, semiprivate, and private spaces that often appear unbounded and unmarked to the uninitiated arrival on campus. Appropriate behavior in the shared cultural space of the campus is generally approved of, while inappropriate behavior, for a given context, is harshly judged. Observe the way that students act toward the student who asks frequent content-related or intellectually challenging questions in class versus the one who asks what is going to be covered on the exam. The first type of student will be viewed as breaking the generalized student culture's norm of subordinating academics to peer fun and shunned by most students, the second as savy. The ability to move across cultural spaces and navigate them well is highly valued and is practiced as students learn to get along with others, make friends, and balance social and academic activities.

The college student shared culture is learned, constructed, carried, and contested by students in interaction with each other within the institutional structures of the university and the larger culture that surrounds the institution. Parents, peers, and others from their home communities, popular culture images, and the interactions they have with college student peers and university personnel, framed by the institutional structures of the university, all play a role in forming the sense of what the college student culture at Midwest is like for students, how they fit into it, and the ways that they make use of it as college students.

Popular images of what college life is like, as portrayed in movies and on television, influence the construction of college student culture and the ways that students make meaning of their experience. The ideas about focusing on having fun and social learning that dominate the shared culture draw heavily on dominant middle-class, white, popular culture images of college fun. Popular culture images of college life depicted in movies such as *National Lampoon's Van Wilder* (2002) give the impression that a hedonistic collegiate culture is dominant. When, in the fall of 2005, I asked students in my large introductory classes to list three movies they had seen about college life, *Van Wilder* was the most frequently named movie of the last decade, with over 60 percent of the students including it on their lists. Appendix 3 provides a plot summary of the movie. It was surpassed in frequency by only one movie, the old classic in the same genre, *Animal House*. One aspect of the generalized college student culture that this type of movie is consistent with is the belief that the source of fulfillment and meaning while in college comes primarily from college social life and personal relationships rather than from academics.

While most students say this version of college student culture is not really what college ends up being like most of the time, it continues to be the most visible popular culture view of which the majority of them are aware. In fact many students describe everyday college life as boring or routine once the newness has worn off. Still, a majority of students carry popular culture images of the quintessential college life, such as in *Van Wilder* or *Animal House*, and these images are intertwined with their sense of the generalized college student culture they feel exists around them at Midwest.

Linking to the power of popular culture images that privilege nonacademic aspects of college life, such as parties and hedonistic activities like excessive drinking, having sex, and sports, is the fact that the most visible and sizeable collective gatherings where a cohesive college student culture can be acted out at Midwest are football games, homecoming, and men's basketball games. These events are notably removed from academics, are male-centered sports, and highlight traditional gender roles, with women as spectators, cheerleaders, and queens of homecoming and men as spectators, athletes, and kings of homecoming (Foley 1994).

These events, of course, do not attract all students, but they are the primary types of events that offer opportunities for a large number of students to come together and gain a sense of collective identity connected to college life at Midwest. Even if students reject participating in these cultural activities, they still must do so in the shadow that the generalized culture casts at Midwest, a culture that in many respects is institutionally supported. The generalized form of collective identity that is institutionally supported is compatible with the deeper consumerist, individualistic, choice-based culture of the campus that most students take for granted and embrace. After all, many of those who chose Midwest from a wide range of possibilities chose it so they could have lots of choices academically and socially, earn a relatively high-quality degree, enjoy a state-of-the-art recreation center and excellent information technology access, and the wins of the football and basketball teams of the university. Even the sense of collective belonging that is constructed at homecoming and at football and basketball games rests on entertainment and private enjoyment as the goal for spectators.

The generalized college student culture that students enter at Midwest University privileges peer interactions that take place in a private college student cultural space that students believe largely excludes adult authority. For most the residence hall is the first place they inhabit and share with peers at college and is very important in establishing a sense of what the shared college student culture is for them. About 85 percent of freshman students live in residence halls.

Students think of residence halls as student-dominated space and their rooms as their own private space. Despite this perception, adult institutional authority that monitors student behavior in residence halls is always present in the form of resident assistants who report to university personnel and who are responsible for monitoring the activities of students and enforcing the rules specified by the university administration. But resident assistants are not perceived by most students as adults or as having a great deal of authority over them. It is true that adults rarely visit their residence hall rooms or even traverse the hallways. Parents may be there when they move into the residence hall and for parents' day. A faculty member may come to the residence hall in her or his role as a sponsor of a learning community or to present a program at the request of a resident assistant, but most of the time adults in positions of authority are not physically present in the residence halls. The only students unlikely to live in residence halls during freshman year are men who pledge fraternities and move into their fraternity houses or fraternity annexes. The fraternity houses have relatively less adult authority from the university inserted into the day-to-day living setting than do residence halls, which may be one of the reasons for their popularity.

At Midwest University, like many universities, a new type of residence hall is being built in response to consumer demands for more
privacy by students and their parents. At Midwest, four new residence
halls housing over 1,000 students in two-bedroom suites with a shared
bathroom and single rooms with private baths have been built, and
another is under construction. The total room capacity of the residence
halls is over 5,000 so the private residence halls now make up about a
fifth of residence hall housing capacity. The types of relationships that
students build with each other in these residence halls are different
from those that develop in the shared-room residence halls with communal bathrooms, according to university personnel and resident assistants who have worked in both types of facilities. The impact that
these new residence halls will have on the shared culture of the university overall remains to be seen but, as this chapter will show, there are
early signs that it is consistent with a general shift toward an even
more consumer-driven, institutionally mediated, and individualistic
shared student culture.

In my visits to shared-room residence halls what stood out was the
flow of people up and down the halls, the open doors and the visiting
taking place, the knowledge students have of one another's activities,
interests, and quirks, and the openness with which students express
their views to each other in that setting as compared to the classroom.

In contrast to the shared-room residence halls with communal bathrooms, the private-suite residence halls foster less visiting from room to
room, giving the first impression that they are little different from an
apartment building. Gabriel, a resident assistant in a shared-room residence hall where I had given a fairly well-attended session on race and
identity, had told me how hard it is to get students to attend such ses-
sions. He had gone door to door right before the event, drumming up
attendance. At the time he mentioned to me that he had a friend who
was a resident assistant in one of the new residence halls, where students could choose a two-bedroom suite with a shared bath, a two-bedroom suite with a shared living room and bath, or a private room and
bath, where building community was even harder. He offered to put me
in touch with her.

Amy had first worked as a resident assistant in a shared-room residence hall and was then recruited to work in Integrity Hall, one of the
new private-suite residence halls. Her experience gave her the ability to
compare the student cultures fostered by each. She summed up the contrast this way. "Where students in the other dorms (with shared rooms
and communal baths) resented my enforcing rules because they said I
was 'just one of them,' in this dorm they complain because I'm just 'the

hired help' and have no right to tell them what to do, since they are paying for their privacy and have a right to do what they want in their rooms." According to Amy and others working there, the suite and single-room residence halls attract more affluent students, and their parents display a sense of what Amy referred to as "entitlement." She noted, "They expect us to cater to their needs and to be available twenty-four hours a day, even though we are taking classes and their parents treated us the same way, like hired help, on move-in day." She goes on to describe how difficult it is to get students in the new residence halls to participate in organized events or programs. "We've just about given up. We have given up!" She went on to describe how a student living on her floor agreed to plan a program for the residents once she learned it could go on her resume, but that she didn't even come to the event she had planned. No one did. Amy explained, "The only reason she did it was to get it on her resume." "Most recently," she says, "we organized a progressive dinner at the homes of faculty members. It was really fun. But only two students showed up. It was disappointing. I don't think they will build any more of this type of dorm after the one already under construction is completed. It's a disaster! It doesn't work."

The suites are much more expensive than shared-room and communal-bathroom residence halls and are a new development at Midwest that mirrors similar trends across the country at comparable schools. They have only recently opened. The private-suite residence halls have created a housing stratification system that had not previously been as pronounced in residence hall options at Midwest. The least expensive shared-room residence halls without meals are $3,225, while the cost of a shared suite is $5,080 in FY 2006. The cheapest residence hall has shared rooms, communal baths, and no air conditioning and is referred to by many students as "the ghetto." Competition for students by universities and perceptions on the part of decision makers that parent and student consumers want upscale facilities, along with beautiful grounds, up-to-date recreation centers, and glamorous sports stadiums, have led Midwest to invest heavily in such construction.

Sororities and fraternities, contrary to popular belief, are no longer the most expensive living arrangements and are instead in a range comparable to and at times even less costly than some residence halls with meal plans. It is easier to make friends in the ghetto or the fraternity or sorority house than it is in private-suite residence halls. Pledging a fraternity or sorority provides housing, parking, computer and study facilities, and meals and, like the high-end residence-hall rooms, is usually an option for those whose parents can afford the costs and who value participation in the Greek system. Those without parental financial support can sometimes afford them, but they have to work and/or go into substantial debt to do so. One woman who did have to work to pay for college said that she quit the sorority as it was too difficult to keep up her academics while living in the sorority house and working. She ended up living in low-cost housing with several roommates.

Walking down the hall in one of the new residence halls with suites and private rooms, I feel like I am in a large hotel hallway. It is quiet and clean. All of the doors are closed. Someone sits in the commons watching a program on the large-screen television. There are very few decorated doors in Integrity Hall and those that have been are sparse. The difference between Integrity Hall and the ghetto is startling. The ghetto doors were heavily decorated, and bulletin boards were filled with announcements. Integrity Hall seems sterile and empty in comparison. When I asked Amy, the resident assistant in Integrity Hall, why there were not very many decorations on the doors in the new suite residence halls compared to the shared-room residence halls, she told me that there was a rule in the new residence halls that you had to use a particular brand of double-stick tape for mounting decorations, and that the requirement discouraged students from decorating. This explanation may have some validity, but the tape is readily available and not extremely expensive, so I suspect that the lack of decorating is also linked to the difference in the ways students perceive the space of the shared-room residence hallway and the suite and private-room residence hall hallway. The suite and private-room residence halls are more like an apartment house, inhabited by individuals who come and go, living their lives behind closed doors.

The living arrangements that students make after freshman year usually are influenced by their economic situation and reflect their goals and orientations toward academics and social life upon entering college. The choices they make throughout college are shaped by this beginning, both the economic and cultural resources they have, and the orientations toward academics and social life with which they enter college are central in shaping how they make meaning of college and how they choose to use it. Most students will move off campus and live with small groups of similar friends. Some will opt to live close to campus. Not surprisingly, many of these students will be those who do not own a car. Though Midwest City has public transportation, and some apartment complexes have shuttles, students without cars often like the flexibility of walking to campus and downtown. The type of housing and furnishings they have will depend on what they, and/or their parents, can afford or can borrow. It is common practice for parents with adequate resources to buy suburban homes in Midwest City for their college-age children and to manage them as rental property. The student will select several other student friends to live with them as renters, and the parents will make the house payments on the property with the rental income. Some students will live in a fraternity or sorority house for at least some of their college years where they have a network of sisters and brothers with whom to sit in classes and socialize intensely. The most expensive option of the private-room residence halls will be chosen by students who want the convenience of being close to campus, having meals provided, and having a high degree of privacy.

While it is much less likely, for instance, that a first-generation college student who is taking out student loans to finance college will choose the most expensive living arrangement offered in residence halls, that of a single room with a private bath, some do. None of the students in this sample who worked to support themselves through college opted to live in the more expensive residence halls, preferring to limit their student loan debt.

Living arrangements, along with other formal institutional structures designed to manage and organize the process of educating students in the large rationalized bureaucracy of Midwest University, play a significant role in what students learn both inside and outside of the classroom. How students are situated, for instance, which residence hall they live in, shapes what they learn about college student culture. Deciding to live in a residence hall with shared rooms and communal baths or in one with two-room suites and a shared bath, or opting for a single room with a totally private bath will shape the experience a student will have and is often dictated by parental economic status and willingness to pay. The more privacy one has, the more expensive the cost of living in a residence hall. It is from their locations in residence halls and fraternities, where they live and do most of their socializing, that college freshmen at Midwest begin their lives as college students. They move in before classes start and find themselves in a setting that privileges peer relations and requires what many say seems like a long walk to get to classes.

KNOWING HOW TO TAKE CARE OF YOURSELF

"I had a lot of anxiety about being able to care for myself. My mother had always done everything for me." (Iris, sophomore, prejournalism major, 2003)

Once freshmen are situated in a residence hall or fraternity house, the first big concern for many of them is taking care of themselves in basic ways. While it might seem as if they would be well equipped for doing this, many have anxiety and struggle during the first months of college to work out the basics of taking care of themselves on a daily basis. Some students also describe basic skills such as doing their own laundry, managing their time, and figuring out how to eat a healthy diet as challenges.

Iris, a sophomore, describes her struggles to do this when she was a freshman. She is among the 12 percent of students at Midwest who continue to live in a residence hall after their freshman year. This morning she has her blond hair pulled back in a ponytail. Her eyes are wide and intensely focused on mine as she starts to describe the most meaningful learning experiences she has had in college. She wears jeans and a blue sweater, topped with a grey knit jacket and tennis shoes. She has a fair complexion with rosy cheeks, and a light sprinkling of freckles graces the bridge of her slightly upturned nose and out over her cheeks. Iris is a sophomore from out of state. She came to Midwest to study journalism. Like most out-of-state students at Midwest she is from a neighboring state. She relied heavily on her mother to do laundry, plan her schedule, and cook healthy meals. Iris's parents both graduated from college, and she says her mother anticipated the kind of adjustment it would be for her in terms of taking care of herself while living in the residence hall.

> I had a lot of anxiety about being able to care [of] myself. My mother had always done everything for me. On the way to [Midwest], while we were in the car, she gave me detailed directions about doing laundry and she wrote them down for me. . . . I didn't know how to eat! My mother had always prepared really nutritious and healthy food. It was hard to find that balance in all the options in the cafeteria. I gained weight living in the dorm, even though I tried to eat healthy. It was really hard not being able to rely on my mom for food.

Iris describes in rich detail the challenge of doing laundry when she first came to college.

> There is the whole aspect of learning how to take care of yourself, learning to do laundry! As we were driving over to Midwest for move-in day last year my mother wrote out a whole page of laundry directions on how she does laundry, because she is very specific, so I never had to do laundry at home, because she always wanted it done a certain way. We would

throw in a load of towels or sheets or something so I knew how to do that. But she has specific ways of doing colors, color knits, color cottons, dark knits, dark cottons, and so she wrote all of that out for me. Laundry was very important. Learning to feed yourself, learning that you have to take care of yourself, do all that important stuff cause mom is not there to make you dinner, which was very upsetting for me the first few weeks last year.

Iris connected the notorious "freshman fifteen," or fifteen pounds or more that many freshman gain, to her not having had to pay attention to her diet prior to coming to college because her mother took care of managing it for her.

Todd, a sophomore in health professions, who is hoping to be admitted into the physical therapy program, is from a big city in the state. He is slim with brown hair and eyes and wears black shorts and a T-shirt that features a local restaurant-bar. He pledged a fraternity and lived in the fraternity annex his freshman year. He explains:

I'm the baby of the family. I don't have to wash my own clothes. I don't have to clean up after myself. I had trouble with that for awhile (in the fraternity), and after awhile I shut my mouth and did my stuff and did really good as a pledge. I grew into the person, well I grew as a man because they (my fraternity brothers) taught me (what) life was really like and the responsibility.

Todd, Iris, and many students at Midwest found that college was an adjustment, not only socially but in terms of the basics of taking care of themselves. Todd was not used to doing his own laundry or cleaning up after himself and had to learn to do these things. His description, like many of the descriptions by men of the different aspects of coming of age while in college, is linked to masculine identity work and becoming a man. Women did not make similar explicit connections to feminine identity work or becoming women.

Being able to take care of themselves is more often discussed as a concern by students from college-educated, two-parent, middle- or upper-middle-class families in which their mothers took care of the laundry, cooking, and errands for them while they lived at home. It was less frequently discussed as an issue by first-generation college students and students from single-parent or reconstituted families.

CULTIVATING AND MANAGING RELATIONSHIPS

Getting Along With Others

> "I think the major thing is learning how to get along with people, especially living in the residence halls here." (Iris, sophomore)

Concern with learning to get along with a wide range of people is most central for students during their first semester and generally through the first year of college. Most student described how important it is to be able to get along with others and to be tolerant of differences, and how their experiences in college helped them get along better with all types of people. Most of the white students believe that Midwest is very diverse with respect to race, ethnicity, and religion. Most racial and ethnic minority students do not think Midwest is racially or ethnically very diverse but recognize some diversity in rural and urban backgrounds. The students who are not from metropolitan suburbs sometimes claim that Midwest University is really a university for people from the two big cities in the state, and that people from those cities in the state dominate the scene.

Unstated directly, but embedded within the shared culture, is also a value for the presentation of self in public and quasiprivate/public cultural spaces of the university that is easygoing and tolerant. The easygoing self is presented in places such as classrooms and in standing in line to buy books at the bookstore. It is honored in common rooms and in other public spaces. This self is based in a polite, tolerant, superficial approach to interactions and requires little from the authentic person beyond conforming to a polite form of interaction with others. Opinions of students that would lead to conflict are left beneath the surface in these settings, cloaked in a high value for easygoing tolerance of difference that quickly leads to a cordial detachment on the part of most students. Institutional interests often coincide with and play a role in constructing this dynamic. After all, heated discussions about sensitive issues can result in problems for the institution.[1]

The college student shared-culture norms mirror this approach, strongly emphasizing the value of being able to get along with others. This often leads to the attitude on the part of individual students that it is necessary to accept intolerance and lack of respect for women, racial and ethnic minorities, rural people, and others deemed "different" by some living in the residence halls, since they are viewed to be expressing just another facet of difference that needs to be accepted. The student who makes a big deal out of someone else's offensive ideas or behavior that takes place in quasiprivate cultural space is generally thought to be overacting. After all, the unique, fun-loving self needs leeway to sometimes be "politically incorrect" in private, where the majority of students describe their most significant learning experiences in college taking place.

The experiences they describe include a wide variety of relationship issues. For instance, one woman described dealing with a "redneck," who listens to nothing but country music, and gaining an appreciation for a type of music she never dreamed she would learn to like. Another described having to deal with a roommate who was having sex with someone while she was in the room trying to sleep. The negotiations about this ended in the roommate moving out. Many students described as problematic roommates who were either very messy or very neat. Many described also negotiating bedtimes, cleaning routines, and social activities with others in the residence halls.

Iris, like most students at Midwest University, emphasizes the importance of social rather than academic learning as being significant to her as a college student.

> One of my friends in the dorm said college is not all (about) academic(s), you learn other things (too). Which is true, because the whole academic aspect to further your learning academically, learn more about all of the subjects you are interested in, (and) somehow end up getting a job with that learning (is only part of it.) There is also the whole aspect of learning to get along with people, learning how to take care of your self. . . . I think the major thing is learning how to get along with people, especially living in the residence halls here.

The centrality of being able to get along with people is touched upon early in her discussion, as it is with most of the students. Iris, like most, mentions the residence hall as the place where she had to learn how to get along with people, even if they do not always act the way you are used to people acting. She lives in a residence hall that has shared rooms and communal baths. Both of her parents have college educations, and they are paying for some, but not all, of her college education. She works full time during the summer and does some part-time work at a restaurant during the school year. She also works as a resident assistant in her residence hall.

Living in the dorm, having to live on a whole floor of other people, and the dorm I live in each floor half of it is girls and half of it is guys, and I'm used to living with guys cause of my dad and my brother so I'm used to all that, but um just living with that many people and trying to get along and not hate anyone on your floor [is a learning experience]. I'm not a hateful person so that part is not hard, but having to live with people who are less neat than you and who don't care when they walk around the hallway in just a towel, but you know you have to deal with that [and] learn there are certain protocols around certain people. I think that is the most important thing to learn at college is people skills. Last year I had two really bad roommate situations. I only had one for a month before I had to leave the room the night she started yelling at me because I didn't want her boyfriend there watching football when it was time to do homework.

Here she also points out that she can stand up for herself when she needs to. She did not let a "bad" roommate run over her; instead, she confronted her and ended up moving out of the room.

Iris goes on to describe a problem she encountered in which she was tolerant of teasing that she came to view as inappropriate only because it was parents' weekend and her father saw sexually explicit comments that had been written on the white board on her door. Here she reveals that she views the residence hall as a peer student-culture space where certain behaviors that are not acceptable in the view of adults like her parents, or in the classroom, if kept private among the peers, are tolerated.

There are problems living in the dorm, social aspects. Somehow my white board on my door this year has turned into "let's leave sexual remarks to Iris" on the board (laughing). I don't know, I have no clue [why]. When my dad came to pick me up Friday there was one I did not see when I walked in the room, otherwise I would have erased it. I hadn't checked my white board and he saw it. One of my friends was like "Iris, did you know this was on your board?," and my dad was oiling our hinges so he was standing right next to it. He had seen it. I don't say the F word but it was something about screwing me or something using the F word, and I was like "What? No really come on!" And it was parents' weekend, so like what if I hadn't seen that and I had left it? Oh I was like, "That is bad, that's very bad!" Luckily I erased it before my grandparents brought me back on Sunday.

Iris assumes the sexually explicit comments made at her expense on her hallway door should be tolerated and hidden from adult authority. This suggests that the public space of hallways has an assumed dominant peer culture that is sexualized and male dominated rather than egalitarian and respectful of women. This is consistent with Moffatt's (1989) findings at Rutgers. Plus, the experiences of most women students in high school and college in academics, organizations, and professional activities are such that issues of sexism and inequality are not perceived as particularly central to them (Neitz 1985). Few of the women, a total of five, mentioned concerns about gender inequality or expressed interest in feminist concerns. Instead, most women interpreted the sexist behavior of men as "guy rudeness" that has to be tolerated as part of learning to get along with others.

Iris (like most, but not all, white students at Midwest University) says she has come into contact with more diverse people at Midwest than when growing up.

> All of my friends from my hometown are white. Here at school actually one of my really good friends is from St. Louis and she is black. I mean I really don't notice kind of race things cause I much prefer hanging out with a person I like, and it really does not depend on what race they are, but I've also come into contact with a lot of people who have had a lot of different experiences than I have, which is really nice, because on the whole in my high school we pretty much had the same experiences. I mean, there were little differences, like you get to travel more or went to a camp instead of staying home for the summer, but pretty much on the whole they are all the same. . . . One of my really good friends here actually lived in Belgium for two years, because her father is part of the navy, so she got to live on the U.S. base there, and I've come into contact with her, and she has become one of my best friends, and just people who have had different experiences than I have. It is really nice.

Iris also describes interactions with her current roommate that establish her and her roommate as people who can get along with others, are accepting of difference, have a good sense of humor, and enjoy having fun together. For Iris, having fun is hanging out with her guy friends and watching videos, without having to talk, and eating chocolate chip muffins baked by her roommate on her birthday.

Making Friends

The Importance of Friends: "I think it's the people I meet, the friends I make that really matter." (Jane, sophomore)

By far the biggest concern for most students, from day one in college, is making friends. Tim, a junior in mechanical engineering, summed it up by saying, "To survive at Midwest, you have to make friends fast! Otherwise, you'll be out there all alone. You'll crash and burn. Midwest is just too big a place not to have a network."

Most students report that their friendships develop with people who have similar interests, those they meet in residence halls or fraternity houses. Some of the choices students make, such as whether to join a club or an organization, or pledge a sorority or fraternity, do influence their friendship networks, where they make their close friendships, and how and where they meet the people with whom they have romantic relationships. About 60 percent of the freshmen at Midwest choose to participate in a freshman learning community (FLC), or a freshman interest group (FIG). Freshman interest groups, also called curriculum-based learning communities, are made up of students who take the same classes together. This gives them a ready-made friendship support group in their classes and when studying. Both types of groups usually are made up of other people who are interested in the same career or who share an intellectual interest, and those who live nearby in the same residence hall.

Some students elect to network with the people they know from high school who are also at Midwest. Some, more men than women (Purdie 2006a), arrange to room with these high school contacts. Some students accept random roommate assignments. More women than men choose single-gender floors (Purdie 2006b). The immersion in peer culture in the residence halls may include intense, even volatile, relationships, or a retreat into one's passion for computer gaming and cruising Facebook. The majority of students at Midwest establish a fairly mundane routine of study, attending classes, doing laundry, eating, exercising, and socializing with a group of friends they meet in the residence halls, based on propinquity and establishing some shared interests and values.

About 21 percent of the undergraduate students at Midwest join fraternities and sororities, and their social networks and romantic relationships are made primarily with peers in the fraternity and sorority system. Most men who pledge fraternities live in the fraternity house or annex as freshmen, but women who pledge sororities generally live in a residence hall as freshmen. Men in the Greek system generally miss out on the residence hall experience, which is the place where most students report experiencing exposure to diversity and learning to get along with those from different backgrounds and those who hold different values.

Starting during the first semester of college, most of the private daily lives of students takes place in a cultural space they experience as separated from the adult-controlled academic activities of the classroom. Behind the doors of their residence hall rooms, in off-campus places largely inhabited by peers, or where they socialize in groups of peers and later in off-campus housing or sorority and fraternity houses is where students say much of their social learning takes place. Most establish a group of closer friends with whom they have more authentic friendships, not the easygoing, more superficial relationships associated with the public-self identity work that is salient in the public spaces associated with residence hall commons and hallways, the recreation center, dining halls, libraries, student service centers, classrooms, computer labs, offices, and the lawns and benches of the campus. Most students also assume that college is a time for romantic involvements and potentially developing partnerships. Those who do not become romantically involved or even go out with potential romantic partners often describe their experiences as inconsistent with what they perceive as the norm of having involvements while in college.

You cannot miss the constant use of cell phones by students as they traverse the sidewalks of campus on their way to classes and head back to their car, residence hall, or fraternity or sorority. Listen in on several hundred of them, as I have over a two-year period, and you will hear mostly calls aimed at networking with peers to meet. Immediately after class, some students flip open the cell and begin the calls. They last until they get to the next class. Occasionally the calls are to parents, once in a while they are emotionally charged conflicts with peers, and a number are logistical calls about being picked up or meeting for lunch. The desire to network has a frantic, almost desperate, tone at times. Students describe wanting to make sure that they are not left out of anything the group is doing or planning, and that they know everything that is going on with people in the group. It is very important to be "in the know," an insider, not an outsider. Some students describe feeling as if they have to spend more time socializing than they should because they fear being left out of the group if they do not. The desperate feeling of needing to belong and the pressures when you do belong are mentioned by students fairly frequently in reference to their freshman year, but not so much later because they usually have established a core of friends that they network with through the remainder of their college years.

Iris, like a number of the women, spends time describing how she is friends with both men and women. Some of the men also specifically mention women friends, but more men mention having a "girlfriend" and go on to focus their discussion of friendships mostly on other men.

> I definitely have more guy friends than I did in high school. I mean, I hung out with guys in high school partly because I was in the music department at my high school, and we were all very close-knit because we spent a lot of time together, so you get to know everybody. You get to know everybody's pet peeves. One or two guys I was really close with. But here, there are nights where I would much rather hang out with the guys than with the girls! Just because the guys just want to watch a movie and the girls want to talk, and I don't feel like talking, so just sitting there and watching the movie is great.

Iris, like many of the students, talks about building friendships and the types of friends she has. She reveals that she is aware of differing gendered relational cultural styles and lets me know she is comfortable operating across them, and at times she even prefers the masculine form of social interaction that requires less talking. Some students, more women than men, emphasize the importance of developing friendships with both men and women in order to view themselves as well rounded. For some, developing friendships with both men and women in college is important, because they feel that they were unsuccessful in building such friendships in high school and want to have that experience.

Earlier, Iris had established that she is comfortable with men, and that living in the coed residence hall was not an issue for her because she believes she knows how to relate to men through growing up with her father and brother. The way that Iris talks about her friendships with men and women reflects her identity work aimed at establishing herself as well rounded, able to make new friends, to cultivate networks, and to have close friends of both genders.

Iris had a boyfriend at home in her early college years. During that time she was not interested in becoming romantically involved with anyone in college and focused her energies on building friendships with both men and women. They eventually broke up, and Iris became open to becoming romantically involved, but she says that she is so busy with school, dance club, and finding time for friends that she is not really available to date. She had a male friend to whom she began to feel attracted, but he graduated and moved to his first job without a romantic relationship developing. She and two women friends have visited him in the big city where he now lives, and they maintain a friendship. She described being confused about what some of his behavior meant. Did his putting his arm around her mean he was romantically interested in her, or did it mean he viewed her as a buddy he was comfortable touching? Iris spent a bit of time pondering this and would have liked him to be romantically interested in her. But she did not seriously consider asking him directly how he felt about her. Iris has as her peer reference group others who are career oriented. At this point, she is focused on her career future and has friendships with people who are similarly oriented or who are student residence hall employees. Presently she views romance and marriage to be in her future sometime after college and once her career has begun.

Each of the key components of the shared college student culture is touched upon by Iris. She outlines the challenges that the college social scene in the residence halls presents, and then she describes responses that involve being easygoing and tolerant when it is appropriate and standing up for her self in reasonable ways by objecting to a former roommate letting her boyfriend watch football in their room when she needed to study. Iris neatly integrates identity work aimed at being able to set appropriate limits and establish autonomy with an ability to balance academics and fun. She also describes herself and her roommate in terms that show they are friends and know how to balance academics with having fun. Gendered cultural content is also present in her account. For Iris, the shared-culture value for making new friends includes being friends with both men and women and valuing masculine forms of relating as well as feminine. If anything, Iris focuses on letting me know that she values masculine relational forms at least as much as feminine ones. She also notes that one of the reasons her female roommate is easy to get along with is that she is not "overly" smart, in some small way buying into the dominant cultural idea that likable people, in this case a woman, are not generally extremely intelligent.

SEEKING SIMILAR OTHERS

People Like Us (Me): "You're always drawn to people like you." (Daryl, sophomore agricultural education major)

Daryl, a sophomore, is from a small town in the state where Midwest is located. He, like Iris, continues to live in a residence hall as a sophomore. He is one of over 175 dorm resident assistants at Midwest University that make up 1.16 percent of the 12 percent who remain in the residence halls after their freshman year. He is a tall, stout man with sandy brown hair, a fair complexion, ruddy cheeks, and twinkling blue eyes. He clearly takes pleasure in describing how important living with a diverse range of people while at college has been for him. Classroom learning, he explains, is not the most important part of the college experience for him, it is the social learning.

> You learn stuff in the classroom, but I mean, you can read a book anywhere. There's just so many different life experiences that you learn coming to college just because there are so many different kinds of people and they're bringing their experiences and you are bringing your experiences, and it's just so different from each other, so I would say that would be the most significant thing that I've learned. . . . I come from a very small rural community with very little diversity. So coming to Midwest, I mean the diversity is almost overwhelming at first. Well, I shouldn't say that, but I mean it's different, just living with a diverse population. I like sports, hanging out with friends, playing video games, stuff like that. . . . I've made a lot of friends.

For Daryl and many students at Midwest, "diversity" means people who are not like themselves in background, with variations of region, metro, and nonmetro home communities. Religious upbringing, and tastes, and racial and ethnic diversity are included in the meaning of "diversity" by these students.

Daryl has dated his high school sweetheart, also a student at Midwest, all through college. His friendships in college are tightly linked to the residence hall in which he lives, friends he and his girlfriend share from home, and people he knows in his major. Daryl is among the minority of students at Midwest University who say they have met people they became friends with in class. He is in the agricultural education program, a fairly small program that he says emphasizes both in-class and extracurricular activities that build relationships among the majors. Programs with active clubs, extracurricular activities, mostly small classes, and faculty who advise students in their programs as well as teach the core courses have higher numbers of students who report making friends in their classes. Still, most students at Midwest say they rarely make friends just through meeting them in class.

Daryl has both women and men friends. Some of the women in his residence hall say he is a "sweet teddy bear." They rely on him for advice and support. He is viewed as easygoing and kind. Daryl sees himself the same way and enjoys just hanging out with other people in the residence hall or at the house of a friend who has moved off campus. He comes from a religious upbringing that frowns on drinking alcohol, and he does not participate in the drinking party culture at college. Yet he has many friends, both women and men, and he views his experiences of getting to know new people in college, hanging out with them, watching rented movies, listening to music, talking and joking, and eating snacks together as the fun he expected to have in college. Daryl's participation in the generalized culture of Midwest is largely through being a sports fan and the social life he enjoys with peers.

Daryl, like most of the white students at Midwest, feels there is great diversity in the student population. He acknowledges that most people seem to hang out with people more like themselves but believes that coming into contact with people who have had different life experiences is beneficial for him.

> You're always drawn to people like you, so there's a lot of times a tendency that if somebody's different, not to include them in your group. . . . There are definitely cliques and groups that some people are allowed to join and other people aren't. It might not even be a conscious decision a lot of times.

Talisha came to Midwest University from out of state and had gone to high school in a city in the northwestern United States where she experienced much more diversity than she sees at Midwest University. Unlike Daryl and Iris, who also lived in shared-room and communal-bathroom residence halls, she does not perceive Midwest as having a very diverse student population. Also, in contrast to Daryl and Iris, who find social learning outside the classroom more significant for them, she thinks most of her important learning in college has taken place in the classroom and some has occurred socially. Unlike many of the in-state students at Midwest, she does not have many high school peers on campus. She has come to recognize the importance of networking for her success in college and values the opportunities she has to meet people while living in the residence halls.

> A lot of them [significant learning experiences], actually surprisingly, have taken place in the classroom. I'm definitely applying stuff that I've learned in classrooms. I think learning

to communicate with other people is important, and that you learn that in college, because you're always meeting new people. It's kind of like you have to keep, and it's really hard to keep, contact with people, so you definitely learn how to, like, keep more contacts. I love the residence halls, because that's where I met all my close friends! Because you live with them like every day, so that's, you automatically have contact with these people. It's hard not to have contact. If you don't have contact with them, something is wrong.

I've enjoyed meeting new people like definitely. I met one of my really good friends in college so far, she's very interesting, very loud, (laughs) very dramatic, oh my God. I think I have had more dramatic experiences with her than with anyone in my whole entire life. I like to go to poetry readings a lot. Going out to dinner is our main thing, but since I'm broke now I've gotta stop that. I love listening to music, so in the beginning of the semester I would always go to places that had live music. I love doing that, but now I hate this semester, because I've found that I don't have time to do anything that I enjoy.

Talisha has found that to give the amount of time she wants to give to academics, she sometimes cannot socialize as much as she would like to. She enjoys her friends, but she balances work and play by devoting a higher percentage of her time to academics. Talisha also expresses disappointment over the lack of diversity at Midwest University.

Socially I expected it was going to be more diverse. I thought it was going to be way more, like, out-of-state people, and I didn't like the fact that it's not as much, it's not as diverse as most universities that I thought it was going to be. . . . All my friends are out of state, we're prejournalism. And I didn't know the history of Midwest, so coming in I thought everyone was like, you know, "free love! Everyone loves everyone!" And all of a sudden it's just this intense hostility surrounding people, so, I don't know, I don't like that.

Talisha's close friends in the residence hall during freshman year were in a freshman interest group (FIG), and she joined in on the activities of the group even though she was not formally signed up for the FIG. It was very important to her, because she experienced some aspects of the generalized culture at Midwest as a hostile, dominant culture that she has entered and must survive in, and being part of this group gave her a sense of belonging. She welcomed having a circle of people to do things with and depend on as she got her bearings. Talisha wishes there were more people from out of state at Midwest, more diversity. She says she has no interest in getting married and plans instead to pursue her career, she notes that she would like to "go out with guys more." She says she doesn't understand why, but "guys at [Midwest] just don't seem interested in me."

She says she expected a culture where "everyone loves everyone," but what she experiences is a culture where "intense hostility" surrounds people. Because Talisha is black and also comes from a background that is not affluent, she is aware of the limits of the dominant culture. Plus, Talisha has friends who are nonheterosexual, and she says they are also marginalized at Midwest. She complains that in addition to often feeling marginalized by white students, she believes that many of the black students on campus negatively judge other blacks who socialize with whites, something she chooses to do. She says there is a split in the African American student population between those she calls traditional and conservative and those who are liberal and progressive. She says she got used to the high school culture of the big northwestern city where she lived in which blacks mixed with people from all different backgrounds, including whites, and she says that she does not like the restrictive culture at Midwest, which she says is more racially segregated in terms of socializing.

Roy, a junior majoring in agricultural business management, is from a small town in the northern part of the state. He, like most men who are involved in fraternities, did not live in a residence hall freshman year. Instead, he lived with other pledges to his fraternity in the basement of the fraternity house. He remembers feeling intimidated until he started meeting people in his fraternity and connecting them to people he already knew. The most important aspect of college, according to Roy, is his social learning that takes place through his fraternity. He has made virtually all of his close friends in the Greek system.

> Mainly meeting a lot of people [has been significant]. I have made a lot more connections, and I have, well it was a cool thing when I came down here, I came from a small town, so coming . . . here where I'll [graduate] with a thousand or so I'm not sure how many, a bunch. So it's pretty, kind of intimidating, but it was definitely a pretty good experience too, just once I started meeting people around here (in the Greek system) I found out that I knew somebody they knew, so, kind of make connections, that's probably the most fun!

For Roy, like most students at Midwest, networking is central. But unlike many students, he does not have to work that hard at it. His network is structured by the traditions of the Greek system and easily tapped into. He likes the connections he is making and likes being in an environment where the people he meets know other people he knows. Most of his friends are in the Greek system. He points out that when he first arrived on campus he was intimidated by the size and impersonality of the setting, but his involvement in a fraternity quickly changed that situation. He found the same types of dense network connections in the fraternity and sorority system that he experienced growing up in a small town, and he says that he now feels "right at home." Roy describes the part of college life he has enjoyed the most in the following way:

> Probably the biggest thing is in this (fraternity) house. I've just learned to take responsibility for a lot of things. I've grown a lot since pledgeship. I've become more of a leader as house manager. It's a pretty big job to fill sometimes. [To] keep everybody motivated, 'cause one of the things you've got to do is like cleanups and stuff, keeping people all motivated, especially like older members than you, to keep the house clean is sometimes kind of [difficult].
>
> I have a girlfriend from high school, and she's down here. Like uh, our fraternity does a pairing with sororities and like for homecoming stuff. So you do a lot of work together, like build house decs [decorations] together, and skits and everything else. You do a lot more interacting, get all, try to, you, organize and get along with them and that and also going over and serenading them and that kind of stuff. We have parties every once in a while and where we'll have it, we'll be bused out to a bar or something.

The leadership Roy has learned to assume in his fraternity with peers is an important venue for identity work that establishes a developing sense of adult autonomy and masculinity. The activities and parties that people in his fraternity and the women in sororities paired with the fraternity share are where he experiences college fun. His friends in college were made in the fraternity and sorority system primarily. Getting along with a wide range of people and experiencing diversity involve getting along with the women and men in the Greek system to do joint projects and socialize.

The roles fraternity men and sorority women play are in many ways dictated by the organization of the Greek system and the traditions of fraternities and sororities. Roy describes the activities they engage in as being predictable and patterned. Sometimes the men and women work together on joint projects such as floats for homecoming. Other times they relate in more tightly scripted ways, such as when the men go to a sorority house and serenade the women. Part of what has been most fulfilling to Roy in college is the leadership role he has been given by peers in his fraternity, and the fact that he believes he does a good job at it.

CONSTRUCTING A UNIQUE SELF

Facebook Interests: "Politics and tits"[2] (Trevor, senior political science major)

Recently the introduction of Facebook on campuses across the United States has led to it becoming a very important venue for the aspect of identity work aimed at defining oneself as a sought-after, unique personality. Popular culture provides much of the material for developing this aspect of self, along with photographs of oneself having lots of fun with peers. Facebook is a powerful social networking tool that enables students to easily maintain knowledge of and/or a connection to many people they know from high school, meet in person at college, or connect with electronically through Facebook alone. This study suggests, however, that most students do not build key relationships primarily through Facebook but instead use it to build and maintain a network of friends and as a tool for comparative identity work.

Facebook is an online directory where people register to be listed. It now provides the ability to network with people at more than 2,500 colleges and universities. High schools also are participating. Anyone with a valid educational .edu e-mail address from a school that participates can use Facebook, including not only students but faculty, staff, administrators, and alumni. In early 2006, Facebook was receiving 250 million hits daily and ranked ninth in overall traffic on the Internet (Bugeja 2006). Facebook provides a format for creating a profile of oneself that projects the image one wants. Users are invited by the format to list their name, address, cell phone number, interests, favorite books, music and movies, relationship status, employment history, class schedule, and anything else they want to disclose. Profiles often are updated daily by users, and most users check Facebook at least once a day to see if anyone has written on their wall.[3]

Facebook also allows the user to make "friend requests," inviting people they know, have met, or want to know to join their friend list. The friend list includes those with whom one is close, such as roommates, close friends, and significant others, but it also can include any number of acquaintances. Students say it has become a way to approach someone who has caught their eye, with little risk of public embarrassment. After all, an online rejection is fairly painless compared to walking up to a person you do not know after class and trying to initiate a conversation, only to have him or her blow you off in front of others. Users also can "tag" people in photos posted and link these to their Facebook profiles. The photo-sharing site Flickr is the one most used by students (Heining 2005). The friend list becomes part of the identity projected on Facebook, because visitors see the list and can check out people in their friend group with a click on their link. Comments friends make about you can be part of your profile. People can post messages on your wall, or someone can "poke" you, a way to let you know they have checked out your profile.

Facebook also offers numerous user-organized groups for people to join, or you might start your own. Many of the groups are based on consumer or leisure activity preferences, comical or outrageous concerns and preferences, shared "insider" knowledge or experiences in a given setting, and some on personal characteristics. Several students say they finally had to block Facebook on their computers because they realized that they were "addicted" to it and could not keep their grades up if they continued spending so much time on it.

Trevor[4] lives off campus with three buddies in a house his parents financed. His Facebook profile tells us his major and his date and place of birth. In the "looking for" category provided by Facebook, he has entered "friendship, dating, someone to play with, anything I can get." His entry in the "interested in" category is "women." His relationships status is "single." His political views are "moderate." His "interests" are two, "politics" and "tits." His main profile picture shows him drinking beer with a group of friends. He wears a tiara on his head. His entries in the Facebook categories for "clubs and jobs, favorite music, favorite TV shows, favorite movies, favorite books, and favorite quotes" are extensive. Trevor lists internships under jobs. Most recently he has posted a quote from one of his favorite televisions shows, the U.S. version of *The Office* on NBC. The quote he likes is "Diversity tomorrow . . . because today is almost over" said by Michael Scott in the show.

Another of his favorite quotes is, "Don't take life seriously because you can't come out of it alive." Interestingly, he credits Warren Miller, filmmaker, author, and entrepreneur, with saying it. Wikipedia, a source relied on heavily by Midwest students, notes that this is one of Warren Miller's well-known quotes. Trevor does not mention Van Wilder's use of the phrase, "Don't take life too seriously, you'll never get out alive," in *National Lampoon's Van Wilder* (2002), nor does he mention Elbert Hubbard (1856–1915), an American philosopher and writer who, according to the *Random House Webster's Quotationary* (Frank 1999) and Wikipidia, actually coined the phrase "Do not take life to seriously, you will never get out of it alive." Regardless, the general sentiment implied by the quote seems to have diffused widely in college student culture.

Linked photographs include pictures of trips he has been on, of him and others at parties with drinks in hand, and of group shots of him with peers in various settings. Trevor has established his collegiate persona as fun loving and unique through his popular culture tastes, his masculine sexuality, and his irreverence for political correctness, noting his interest in "tits" and how much he likes the humor that pokes fun at those who try too hard to be politically correct regarding racial and ethnic minorities. Extreme in nothing, not even politics, which he has focused on studying, he shows a sense of humor and a self surrounded by similar others.

The profile invites describing oneself in terms of one's major, politics, relationship status, popular culture tastes, and types of friends. Trevor makes it clear that he is heterosexual, that he is interested in politics, and that he has an irreverent sense of humor about political correctness but is also sensitive to issues of inequality and diversity. He loves sports, and he knows how to party.

The many friends, both women and men, he has linked to his profile and the comments they have written on his wall call up all kinds of good times and shared secrets of wild parties and "out-there" behavior in which they have engaged while in college and show that he has made lots of new friends in college, and that he has an extensive network of connections with peers, not only at Midwest but at other universities and colleges where he knows people.

The construction of the unique self of most students is shaped by the framework provided by the generalized college student culture and is starkly outlined by the categories Facebook provides for achieving this goal. Even establishing uniqueness has a script that must be followed. The categories that matter and the ways that communication, networking, and interaction are structured reflect a value system that is consistent with the individualistic, consumerist, cultural norms of the generalized college student culture. And Facebook makes the identities that are constructed readily available for consumption and potential acquisition as "friends."

BALANCING WORK AND PLAY

Jane, now a senior, is majoring in biology. As a freshman she lived in a residence hall where a number of other pledges to her sorority lived. Jane's friendship circle is made up mostly of sorority sisters and fraternity brothers. As a sophomore she moved into the sorority house. Jane has fond memories of her time living in the sorority house too, but she says the constant "drama" eventually grew old, and in her junior year she opted to live off campus with several of her sorority sisters. She dated the student government president for a time and has dated others throughout college. Just recently her relationship with a boyfriend who is in a fraternity ended. Jane, like Talisha and Iris and most women at Midwest, assumes a norm of dating and romantic involvements while in college. She dates and socializes with friends. She usually goes to a couple of downtown restaurant bars when she goes out with them. She describes friendships with women and men as important. Jane tries to balance academics with having fun, but she views the social learning she has done in college as the most significant and regrets the lack of time for having fun.

> Honestly I feel like nothing I've learned in the classroom will help me do what I want to do in the end. I think it's the people I meet, the friends I make, that really matter, just, just how I express myself to this university and what, what I can retain back from them.

Jane believes that social learning has been more significant for her while in college, but she has consistently tried to balance the time and energy she spends on academics and socializing so that she succeeds in her career aspirations. Her parents are very insistent that she make good grades and continue to pursue a career in one of the health-related professions. Jane, like Roy, had one of her best learning experiences while in college in connection to the leadership role she played for the Greek system, at the campus level, in planning homecoming. But, unlike Roy, she does not link these experiences to attaining adult gender identity, instead linking them to gaining interpersonal and organizational skills that she hopes will transfer to her professional career.

Alex, a senior majoring in physical therapy, like most students at Midwest, describes his friends at college as being very important in his overall college experience. He lived in a residence hall his freshman year, but his friendship circle is largely made up of people he knew in high school. He lives with two friends from high school, one of them his best friend. He describes his activities with friends being centered away from campus mostly, though they enjoy college sports together. Alex has black hair and brown eyes. He wears black slacks, a white shirt, and loafers. He's involved with his "clinicals" now and is dressed for work. Alex is Latino and he, like Talisha, says that Midwest University is not very diverse. He looks forward to settling somewhere after college where there is more diversity. Alex, a white Hispanic, socializes mostly with non-Hispanic white people. He is from the suburbs of a large city in the state where there is a larger Hispanic population. He met his girl-friend, a white woman who is also a student at Midwest, through friends while in college. She too is from the west side of the state, though from a mid-size town north of the city where Alex's family presently lives. Right after college they got married and moved to the southwestern United States.

> I have a lot of friends. I have a girlfriend that goes here. I live in a duplex with my best friend and another person I went to high school with. Oh, they can be quiet if I need to study, but at the same time they're really fun. It's a lot of fun, plenty of partying. I don't know, my first two and a half years I probably partied more than I should have, but now I'm starting to slow down. I think homework's starting to get to me. Meeting people, having fun, you get breaks in the day. It's not like an everyday job, you know, I can go home at 11:00, take a nap, be back up here at 2:00 and finish my day. I go to bars, I play intramurals, have parties a lot, go to parties, kind of just hang out, sit at home and watch TV, have buddies over.

Clearly the college coming-of-age experience for Alex was slanted toward social learning in nonacademic settings, but now he, like many seniors, has begun to pull back from full participation in some aspects of the shared college student culture in which he once was fully invested. He says he no longer parties or goes out to bars as much as he used to. Alex defines college fun primarily as time spent relating to other young men.

Roy, Alex, and Trevor describe their relationships with male peers as being central to them while in college. Though Alex is seriously involved with his girlfriend and will soon marry her, he does not talk very much about spending time with her. Roy also has a girlfriend from home who is in college at Midwest too and who socializes with him in fraternity-sponsored events and on a regular basis privately, yet he talks most about his relationships with male peers in the fraternity. Male peer expectations shape the important social learning experiences of these men and define what is most important in establishing themselves as college men. These men emphasize social learning with peers over academics and privilege time spent with other young men in their descriptions of what is most significant for them in college. For these men, committed relationships with women are linked more to their discussions of life after college when they plan to settle down to work, marry, and have a family than to having fun in college.

Roy describes experiences of social learning linked to masculine identity work typical of men in fraternities. He also describes the activities organized by the fraternity and sorority system to structure male and female relationships and to construct masculine and feminine roles within those settings. Fraternity men serenade sorority women, go to off-campus parties in rented facilities where they can drink and dance, free of the constraints of a dry campus, and pair off as boyfriend and girlfriend.

This is not the case for Daryl, who describes his friendships with men and women as being equally important and says he is very close to his girlfriend. He describes the things they do together in detail. He emphasizes his relationship with her as being central to him during his college years, but he also points out that he wanted to build new friendships and have new experiences, such as studying abroad. Daryl also has relationships with a wide age range of people outside the university. He and his girlfriend attend the same church and are active members, already assuming adult roles in their congregation. They act as sponsors for groups of younger children in the church on outings and in planned activities. These children clearly look up to them. And they take their roles as sponsors seriously, often discussing the types of issues they may face on a given outing and planning how they will operate as a team to handle them.

Daryl already sees himself as an adult, though he says he is still enjoying the fun of college. His descriptions of his friends and activities show that he has at least one foot fully in the adult world, and that his approach to friendships in college is shaped by the types of responsibilities and roles he plays in his hometown community, where he is already assuming adult male responsibilities. His need to do masculine identity work aimed at establishing himself as an adult is minimal at this point in his development. Daryl's rural upbringing linked him closely to his father in farming together and their deep involvement in church. These two aspects of his upbringing seem to have provided him with a clear role model in his father, whom he admires, and a picture of the actions and behaviors expected of him as a man, and he has begun to perform them. Daryl's approach is typical of more rural than suburban and urban men.

Iris, Talisha, and Jane all talk about their friendships with both women and men as being important to them. Iris has not dated much in college, partly because she had a boyfriend when she first arrived and partly because she has felt too busy for romantic involvements and has not pursued them. Yet she highly values her friendships with men. Talisha dates, but she says she is not interested in a serious relationship right now because she needs to focus on her class work. She cultivates both male and female friendships and seems to value these relationships equally, based on the time and energy she spends describing them and based on what I observed during participant observation. Talisha says she goes out with guys sometimes, but that men at Midwest do not seem interested in her, and she does not think there are very many men at Midwest who are "her type." She expresses some disappointment in this situation. Jane has had several romantic relationships while in college, and the last time I spoke to her during her senior year she said she was enjoying being single during her last semester of college. She also says that she values her friendships with both men and women.

CONCLUSION

Students describe a generalized culture that expects them to use their college years as a time to learn how to take care of themselves; to get along with diverse others; to make new friends, build networks, and more generally learn how to relate to others; to develop their own unique selves, personality, and direction; and to learn to balance work and play, in preparation for real life, which will require all of these capabilities. The residence halls, sororities, and fraternities are the places most students make their closest friends and begin to develop friendship networks. Some students rely on friends from high school from the start. A few students say that they make friends in clubs or organizations. Classes are the least frequent place where students report making close friends, with a few notable exceptions connected to programs that formally group students and move them through programs as a cohort. Freshman year in the shared-room and communal-bath residence halls is the time in the lives of students at Midwest where they say they encounter the most diversity and learn how to get along with other people. Though limited in depth, this is often the only such experience students have had in their lives.

The ways students focus their energies in their endeavors to acclimate and find their way in the generalized college student culture differ most dramatically along gender lines. Men tend to link their masculine identity work to this process more tightly and to emphasize their relationships with male peers at college. Women emphasize learning about men's ways of relating and work to become culturally knowledgeable in how to build real friendships with men. Most students say it is important to have both women and men as close friends. This is true for heterosexuals and nonheterosexuals in the sample. Most women talk about their friendships with women and men in more equal measures and describe spending quality time with them. A few women focus on male friends or female friends. Most men mention women friends or a girlfriend but then spend most of their time describing the fun times in college as those they spend with their male buddies. A few men come to college with established adult roles in their home community that they anticipate continuing after college. These men either embrace having the college experience and making new friends, as Daryl did, or they view college as a credentialing experience primarily and maintain strong ties to their home community and friends during college rather than immersing themselves in the new culture at Midwest.

Women and men who are involved in romantic relationships are no less likely to have a network of women and men friends than those who are not involved in romantic relationships. In some cases the friends of the person with whom they are involved become close friends of theirs too, extending their friendship networks and even remaining important if they break up with the person who introduced them to each other. The norm for the majority of students is to form friendships with people they view as being fun and interesting. Friendships also are described as sometimes being based on having similar interests or tastes. Of course, what becomes quickly apparent is that the people who are viewed as fun and interesting and who share similar interests and tastes also are often people of the same socioeconomic background, the same race, and at Midwest often even from the same hometown, especially if they are from one of the big high schools in one of the big cities in the state.

Hegemonic masculinity (Connell 1987), though muted in some settings, pervades the shared-residence hall culture, even to the extent that blatantly sexist acts, such as writing a very graphic description of sexual physical acts that are supposedly going to be inflicted on the woman on a woman's door, are considered by the women on the floor as something to be tolerated, because one needs to "get along" with other people. Though generally more subtle than popular culture depictions such as those in *Van Wilder*, the shared college student culture continues to tolerate the devaluation of women.

Women students do not complain frequently about men's behavior in the dorms and when they do it is almost apologetically, as though they are at fault for not being able to get along or take care of themselves in the face of some form of behavior they find unacceptable. One woman did report a case where women on the floor confronted some men who were behaving in a "rude manner," which resulted in voices being raised and doors being slammed, but according to her there was no change in their behavior. Some women opt for living on a women's floor in the residence hall to avoid some of what one woman referred to as "guy rudeness," but serious or angry complaints were rare in the interviews. Some men opt for living on men's floors in the residence halls too, to avoid sharing private space with women.[5]

Many, though not all, white students believe that there is a lot of diversity at Midwest, and that they have exposure to diversity that enables them to learn how to relate to and get along with people who have backgrounds, experiences, and values different from their own. Many also acknowledge that most people end up being friends with people they are similar to in some significant ways. Most racial and ethnic minority students, and a few white students, on the other hand, maintain that the campus is not very diverse, because the student population is mostly made up of white, middle- and upper-middle-class students. Some students in this group feel that minorities are marginalized by the dominant culture of the campus, and that the issues and concerns of minorities are devalued and ignored. Yet even among the students who express discomfort with the racial homogeneity found on campus generally and in individual fraternities and sororities, most say that they are uncertain whether this should be changed or not, or how it could be accomplished.

Some students, both white and racial and ethnic minority, work hard to make friends across racial and ethnic boundaries, but many opt for networking largely within their racial or ethnic group if there is a large enough population to do this, their fraternity or sorority if they belong to one,[6] their athletic team if they are an athlete, or their friendship circle they form living in the residence hall during freshman year.

The form that institutional multiculturalism has taken in the generalized college student culture at Midwest, largely supports a sanitized and superficial tolerance in public spaces rather than authentic engagement in creating recognition and understanding across differences (Eisenberg 1999; Delanty 2003, 108). When students talk about getting along with others, in a way they are talking about the cultural dictate that they manage their relationships with others so that they do not have open conflicts about serious matters of difference in public spaces of the university. A public- and private-sphere separation is the accepted norm where difference is expected and accepted in the private sphere, defined also as the sphere where differences of cultural diversity are located. Public tolerance and cool detachment in the face of conflicting views about race/ethnicity, gender, sexuality, or other issues that might provoke conflict are recognized by most students as the norm.[7]

Having fun is viewed by virtually all college students as an important responsibility that they must fulfill in order to claim the genuine college student experience. For some students, having fun involves drinking and going out to bars and parties. The emphasis on partying, drinking, and sex and the hooking up that goes along with these activities is linked to popular culture depictions of college life that most students can readily call up when asked about the dominant college student culture. For other students, having fun involves being with people with whom they are comfortable and hanging out in residence halls, watching television together, or going to a movie. Shared activities that are not things engaged in by the majority of students are important for some of these students too, since part of fulfilling the coming-of-age expectations of the generalized culture is that they will display unique lifestyle choices. For Iris, it is ballroom dance. For Roy, it is the leadership role he plays in his fraternity. For a few students, such as Talisha, fun involves making friends with people who are different from oneself, testing one's comfort zone, and basing one's friendship on shared intellectual interests and academics. Talisha enjoys parties, live music at intimate clubs downtown, poetry readings, and listening to speakers who visit the campus with her friends. She likes to engage in lively discussions about music, articles, and books.

Nathan's (2005) and Moffatt's (1989) findings about undergraduate college culture are generally consistent with the aspects of the Midwest college student shared culture that values getting along with others, making friends, and knowing how to have fun.

Nathan maintains that

the university community was experienced by most students as a relatively small, personal network of people who did things together. This "individual community" was bolstered by a university system that honors student choice, as well as a level of materialism in the larger society that, by enabling students to own their own cars, computers, TV sets, and VCRs, renders collective resources and spaces superfluous. (Nathan 2005, 54)

Drawing partly on the work of Bellah, Madsen, Sullivan, and others (1985), Moffatt (1989) also concluded that the high value placed on the friendly self among Rutgers students of the late 1970s and early 1980s came from their orientation toward private expectations and satisfactions linked to the rise of individualism in contemporary American society that pervades the real world that is experienced by students, along with most people in the society at large, as "hopelessly complex, impersonal, and bureaucratized" (Moffatt 1989, 40). This led Rutgers students, according to Moffatt, to look to the private pleasures they could have in college as the ones where they would develop their authentic selves.

Midwest students' focus on being able to get along with others, making new friends, and knowing how to have fun is most salient and pervasive early in their college life, particularly while living in residence halls. The early emphasis on getting along with others and making new friends shifts to one on balancing having fun with friends with academic activities, and cultivating a unique self through more nuanced lifestyle choices that reflect the movement toward an adult life trajectory as college progresses.

Nathan's observation that "individualism rules" (2005, 52) among the students she studied, and that "Rather than being located in its shared symbols, meetings, activities, and rituals, the university for an undergraduate was more accurately a world of self-selected people and events," (54) would hold at Midwest as well. The "ego-centered networks" that Nathan says "were the backbone of most students' social experience in the university" (55) are also at the center of the daily lives of students at Midwest. These friendships continue to be central and to form the basis for a network of peer relationships for most college students, but the ways these networks are established, the amount of time differently oriented students spend with their friends, and the types of things they do together, especially after freshman year, vary considerably. The ways students are situated within, respond to, and use the generalized college student culture vary.

Getting along with everyone is relatively more important in the residence halls, where (until the recent introduction of private suite/room residence halls) everyone is thrown together, than it is after students move off campus or into sorority houses and live with their friends. Fraternity men are likely to live in fraternities from the start, and they then may move out of the fraternity house to live in an apartment with friends where they have more privacy. Getting along with everyone, or the "friendly self," as it is called by Moffatt (1989), remains important in classes where diverse viewpoints and types of people come together. But it is less salient as a focus for students as they move into daily lives that engage them more deeply in different college student cultural orientations and form friendship groups of more like-minded people that they gravitate to as college students. Only about 12 percent of nonfreshman students live in residence halls, and many choose to stay on campus to be able to focus on academics without distractions or housekeeping demands, or to be resident assistants, rather than to prolong their freshman-year fun. The vast majority, some 85 percent, live off campus or in sorority and fraternity houses.

By the end of freshman year, most students have a core group of friends and build a friendship network from those over the course of college. By that time most have gravitated to college student subcultures and have developed a set of friends and a friendship network in which they are embedded. Ironically, the ideology of individualism that students espouse encourages them to seek a sense of belonging somewhat urgently or else face being left out of the peer college student culture. The desire to find a group with whom to share leisure time pleasures is only part of it. Another part of students' drive to find new friends as quickly as possible is aimed at proving their cultural competence as individuals beginning in a new setting. Competent college students are supposed to make new friends. The alternative is being left out of the peer culture, where friends are viewed by most as the single most important indicator of success in college, which most of them believe is more about social learning than it is about academic learning.

At the same time, students acknowledge that their college friends provide important support in figuring out how to succeed in college. Even during recruitment, students are told that Midwest offers them a cornucopia of options. The college experience, from the start, is in a way framed as a set of consumer choices. Students know that they are expected to make responsible choices, and they believe that those choices matter. Many students turn to other students more than to any other group for advice on everything from which courses to take to how they can better get along with their roommate. Part of this stems from propinquity and part from a belief in a sort of situated knowledge and the idea that other students have a better understanding of their situation than anyone else. The idea is that the people around me, who are most similar to me in experience, are the best able to advise and support me. The structure of the university reinforces this perspective, with students largely grouped together in residence halls and fraternities their freshman year, and to some extent even sorted by class, race, and gender into groups as evidenced by the stratified pricing of residence halls, and the general separation of black and white students in the Greek system, and of women into sororities and men into fraternities. It should be no surprise then that students establish "ego-centered networks" (Nathan 2005) as an initial response to the environment in which they find themselves.

Class status linked to parental levels of education and lifestyle plays a role in shaping the daily lives of college students, from where they choose to live to the types and frequency of their leisure-time activities. It is true that those without parents to pay can usually take out student loans, but then they will graduate in debt, thus many students with relatively less resources will opt for less expensive accommodations than their more affluent peers. Season tickets for football and basketball games, many bars and restaurants that cater to students, and a plethora of campus events and activities are available, most for a cost. This means that the "lifestyle" choices of students aimed at individualization and establishing an adult life trajectory project continue throughout college to be shaped by their economic conditions.

One of the key lifestyle choices of students, and one given central attention in this chapter, is where they live freshman year. The framing of this sorting as a consumer choice is at the heart of the institutional culture students learn. Still, the residence hall is the place where most students say they are exposed to people with different experiences and ideas than they hold. Being able to get along with a wide range of people means different things for differently situated students, but the most consistent exposure in private space that most students at Midwest have to diversity of class, race, sexual orientation, and region of origin is in the shared-room residence halls, a space that most students move out of as soon as they can but remember fondly as the place they faced the challenges of learning how to get along with all kinds of people, gained skills to be able to take care of themselves, and made some of their closest friends. It is during this time that they make meaning of or "learn" the generalized culture of Midwest. It is also during this time that the foundation for their significant learning at Midwest is laid, learning that many say is most significantly connected to peer social relationships rather than academics.

To understand the lives of college students at Midwest and the ways in which they participate and construct community, it is necessary to go beyond a focus on the generalized college student culture to the consideration of college student subcultures. When we do this, it becomes evident that the line between the investment of the authentic self in private pleasures and the public sphere is not so clear-cut for some students over time, while it is clearly the case for others. For some students, the ego-centered friendship groups with whom they bond become the support groups for their engagement in academics, professional development, and other public-sphere activities as well as socializing, while for others they support a focus on partying and hedonistic pleasures and peer relations aimed at figuring out how to be men and women.

Chapter 4 shifts our attention from the generalized college student culture at Midwest to varied college student cultural orientations that exist within it. It shows that students who are differently situated relative to the generalized college student culture, and at the intersections of gender, class, and to some extent race/ethnicity, choose to gravitate in patterned ways to specific college student cultural orientations. This chapter describes ideal-type college student cultural orientations that emerged in interviews and participant observation and explores the characteristics of the cultural orientations.

4

USING THE CULTURAL TOOL KIT

College Student Cultural Orientations

This chapter describes five college student cultural orientations found among students at Midwest University and develops an ideal-type model of college student cultural orientations that integrates the primary and secondary cultural orientations emphasized by students. Students were found generally to orient toward more than one of the cultures, almost always to have one cultural orientation that was primary for them, and rarely to strongly emphasize more than two of the cultural orientations in their daily lives. The patterns of participation in them by students in the sample are presented, and descriptions of the characteristics and daily lives of representative students who orient toward each of the ideal types of college student cultural orientations are included.

Individuals are placed in terms of their primary and secondary ideal-type cultural orientations. Appendix 4 provides a detailed table that outlines the primary and secondary ideal-type college student cultural orientations of students in the sample by gender, race and ethnicity, and parental educational level. Of course, individual students do not fit perfectly into any two ideal-type cultural orientations, because as individuals they are complex and unique.

The ideal types are designed as a tool for understanding the patterned variations of orientations of students to certain sets of ideas and behaviors about college and what it means to them. The ideal types were derived through coding transcriptions of interviews with attention given to what people said about their purposes for being in college, how they spent their time, their goals in college and beyond, and what they said mattered to them more generally.

The daily lives of students vary considerably based not only on their primary college student cultural orientation but also on their secondary orientation. While this typology is not identical to any other found in the literature, it draws selectively from several key studies to elaborate and compare findings with other typologies of college student culture (Clark and Trow 1966; Horowitz 1987; Bank 2003).

While some literature has described similar orientations as subcultures (Clark and Trow 1966), at Midwest these orientations are, for the most part, loosely bounded enough so that they do not conform completely to the definition of a subculture group. At Midwest these orientations do exist within the context of the generalized college student culture and share in it, to varying degrees, in keeping with subcultures, but they do not represent clearly defined or bounded groups. Instead, they are made up of constellations of behaviors, practices, values, and norms available in the college student cultural tool kit, and the patterned orientations emerge from the ways students make use of what is available to them and what they emphasize in their daily lives as college students.

THE CAREERIST COLLEGE STUDENT CULTURAL ORIENTATION IDEAL TYPE

The careerist college student cultural orientation ideal type consists of a set of ideas and behaviors that emphasizes college as the means to having a desired career and becoming a professional. Knowledge associated with the career is valued, but general knowledge that is part of the general education curriculum requirements often is considered nonessential, a waste of time. There is an eagerness to get into the course work that is directly related to the career future that is anticipated.

The relationships with faculty involve seeking mentorship in how to succeed in the profession, research related to professional development, and connections that enable students to ask faculty for recommendations when they enter the job market. These students often report having college friends who are interested in the same discipline they are studying, students they met in the residence hall in freshman interest groups (FIGS) or in classes in their program. Some also have friends they know from high school who are attending Midwest. Those who are in fraternities and sororities often have their closest friends in the fraternity or sorority but also have friends in the program with whom they socialize.

These students view other students who want to get into the professional program for which they are aiming as both competition and potential resources. Students outside of the program are often less central for those with this orientation, especially once they move out of the residence halls and beyond taking general education courses. Careerist-oriented students frequently complain about other students who are not motivated to learn the material necessary to succeed in their profession. They acknowledge that they have to display public tolerance for "slackers" within their professional program when such people are members of their cohort, and the expectation of the program faculty and administration is that peers will work together to ensure that everyone learns. Students are readily able to identify these individuals and privately say that they will not make good professionals. They sometimes chafe at the need to include them in the groups into which they are organized for some of their professional program academic work, maintaining that it is unfair that they will earn the same degree but that the slackers in the program will not have the knowledge base and skills they need to have in order to be fully competent. The academic slackers among them, often are very blatant about their lack of application to learning and do not make excuses for depending heavily on the knowledge base of peers in group learning situations. Careerist-oriented students sometimes complain about the pressure to make good grades but generally accept the institutional framework that requires them to "make the grade" (Becker, Greer, and Hughes 1995) or be eliminated from the professional program to which they aspire and the career they seek.

THE CREDENTIALIST COLLEGE STUDENT CULTURAL ORIENTATION IDEAL TYPE

The credentialist, ideal-type college student cultural orientation emphasizes earning a degree, for itself, as a means to obtaining status security (Collins 1979). The credentialist ideal type is tied to a primary emphasis on getting a university degree without a strong professional or career orientation, or a serious interest in learning, as a necessary credential for maintaining or gaining social status in the workforce and culture more generally. The orientation here is toward doing the least work necessary to obtain the credential. College academics are viewed as hoops that must be jumped through to get the desired object, the diploma for the wall, and the status it represents.

Credentialist students often complain that some faculty members assign too much work because they do not understand the overall load students have. These students also value very highly faculty organization and predictability. While all students appear to value well-organized courses with clear learning goals and predictable evaluation methods, this group is particularly vehement in its dissatisfaction when a teacher falls short, because students say it hinders them in calculating what they have to do in order to get the grade they need in the class. Students with this orientation often openly acknowledge that they do only the minimum work necessary to get the grade they want. Those with a credentialist orientation do not tend to develop close relationships with faculty or with students they meet in class. Their friendships are generally with people from home and contacts they make through home ties. If they live in the residence hall freshman year, they often also have a few friends they meet in the residence hall. Those in sororities and fraternities make their friends and build their friendship network primarily with others in the Greek system. These students complain about other students who, they believe, are "too concerned about grades" and those who "ask a lot of irrelevant questions" related to the intellectual content of the class, which they believe interrupts the teacher from covering the basics they need to know for performing adequately on evaluations in the class and may encourage the teacher to raise the bar in performance expectations.

THE COLLEGIATE COLLEGE STUDENT CULTURAL ORIENTATION IDEAL TYPE

The collegiate, ideal-type college student cultural orientation emphasizes identity work and activities tied to the social aspects of college life embedded in the university institution in some way, such as through sororities and fraternities, clubs and other organizations, student government, and organized sports, but it is resistant to academic demands. This orientation is linked to the historic collegiate culture described by Horowitz (1987) and is closely aligned with the generalized college student culture described in chapter 3. Those who orient primarily toward participation in collegiate culture identify more strongly with the generalized culture and provide visibly enacted evidence of its centrality on campus and reinforce the perception that it is hegemonic. The institutionally framed activities that are central to the collegiates are those where they and their peers have relatively more autonomy and control over their status-seeking activities and are less subject to control and direction from adult authorities on the campus.

Relationships with faculty are generally limited to the classroom, interactions deemed necessary to pass classes, required by the fraternity or sorority to which they belong, and public functions of the university that focus on the nonacademic aspects of college life. Academic demands are viewed as something to be managed, and for some resisted, by those with this cultural orientation. Like careerists, some collegiates cultivate faculty relations for instrumental reasons, such as hoping to get good letters of recommendation, better grades, and other opportunities with which faculty may be able to assist them.

Collegiate culture engages participants in a type of codependent coming-of-age power struggle with adult authority of the university and the academic values and demands that are placed upon them. The desire to focus on peer social life is facilitated by the way that sorority and fraternity activities are organized and the relative autonomy they have from university administrative control, but they also are dependent upon the university for the college sports that are central in providing the events around which their peer organizing is centered. These students feel academic demands most directly from faculty. Collegiates complain about academic demands placed on them by faculty they view as being unreasonable and about faculty who do not understand that they are paying to be in college and deserve to have a good college experience.

Collegiate culture emphasizes college athletics, heterosexual dating (Holland and Eisenhart 1990), socializing with peers more generally (Robbins 2004), and being recognized by others with a similar orientation as being a part of the group. Of particular importance are parties where drinking is central and themed parties, where all who attend dress in accordance with the theme, signaling their insider status and offering a venue for demonstrating to others the college fun in which one is taking part. These events also offer an opportunity for participants to take photographs to put into their Facebook profile and to put on their refrigerator door.

Peer social networks, parties, organized activities, and visibility are central to this group. Their friends are made mostly through peer social networks associated with the sorority and fraternity system at Midwest or through high school connections. Women in this group often make a friend or two who are not in the Greek system while living in the residence halls, and they have a friend or two from home. The men often maintain friendships at Midwest with a friend or two from home. A few, in programs that enroll small numbers and move them through the program as a cohort, indicate that they do have friends from their program and have meaningful relationships with some faculty in the program, but most do not make close friends in their classes.

Those with this orientation who are in the Greek system sometimes complain about independent students they believe are critical of the Greek system without realizing the diversity that exists among Greeks. They believe they are not understood and are unfairly stereotyped by many students outside of the Greek system. Still, what is central to them are the identity and activities connected to the organization to which they have pledged, of which they were chosen by peers to be members.

THE ALTERNATIVE COLLEGE STUDENT
CULTURAL ORIENTATION IDEAL TYPE

Alternative students are those with lifestyle interests or concerns that are the center of their identity work and guide their use of time in college. They are interested in college primarily to support them in pursuit of their main interest, but they identify and prefer to interact with others who are detached from mainstream campus life. They seek courses that relate to their interests or specific educational goals, engage in activities and networks off campus that relate to their interests, and identify with those engaged in the arts, activism, church, or other compelling enthusiasms on which they focus their lives and center their identity in.

Examples include an artist who works in several different media and relates primarily to other artists, a sustainable agriculture supporter who, along with her father, got involved in policy work at the state level while in college, a person oriented toward a new-age religion and lifestyle, and a devoutly Christian woman whose life centers on church-related activities.

If they encounter faculty with similar interests, they say that they may build a relationship with them, but important connections to faculty are few and generally not central to them. Relationships with other students or people in the community with similar interests are characteristic for this group. They often describe the majority of other students as immature, of little interest, unquestioning, and lacking in values similar to their own. Those with an alternative student cultural orientation are critical of the generalized college student culture but do not focus on wanting it to be different as the academically oriented students do because their identity work centers on linkages to issues, concerns, and people off campus, and they are not as directly engaged in a struggle to define what college should be about as some other students are.

THE ACADEMIC COLLEGE STUDENT
CULTURAL ORIENTATION IDEAL TYPE

The academic college student cultural orientation ideal type represents those who emphasize academic achievement, say that they enjoy learning and gaining new knowledge for itself, read and seek learning beyond the classroom on their own, and are more likely to identify with faculty. They emphasize academics because they enjoy learning and are intellectually curious. They engage with the material they study and want to understand it. These students often build relationships with faculty that are based on their intellectual interests. They sometimes say that they get along better with faculty than they do with other students. Overall, they tend to describe their relationships with faculty in very positive terms. When they are critical of some faculty, it usually is couched in terms of disappointment that faculty do not demand more of students. A few also mention that they do not like faculty who brush them off when they want to get to know them and discuss intellectual interests with them.

Those oriented toward emphasizing academics usually report making their college friends in the residence hall primarily and then building a network of friends from these initial contacts, though some also become friends with people they meet in class. These students are often uncomfortable with or critical of the generalized college student culture. They complain that many students at Midwest do not really want to learn and create an atmosphere in the classroom that discourages serious intellectual discussions.

LITERATURE ON COLLEGE STUDENT
SUBCULTURES AND CULTURES

Clark and Trow (1966), Bank (2003), and Horowitz (1987) are important sources from which to draw when elaborating on the data from interviews and participant observation in order to arrive at the ideal-type model described earlier. Each includes a typology of college student culture that links in one way or another to the findings at Midwest.

Clark and Trow (1966) focus on the influence of class status and institutional structure in shaping the nature of the orientations and relationships of students in college. What is immediately relevant to this analysis, from their work, is the approach they take to understanding college student culture. They focus on the "normative content" and orientations toward a college education that they found represented on American campuses of the day. They hold that "these orientations are defining elements of student subculture(s), in which they appear as shared notions of what constitutes right attitude and action toward the range of issues and experiences confronted in college" (1966, 19). They created a model with four ideal types of college subcultures: vocational, collegiate, nonconformist, and academic.

Vocational culture is characterized by little attachment to the college "where" students "buy their education like groceries." These students "are also resistant to intellectual demands on them beyond what is required to pass the courses. To many of these hard-driven students, ideas and scholarship are as much a luxury and distraction as are sports and fraternities. If the symbol of the collegiate culture is the football and fraternity weekend, the symbol of this vocationally oriented culture is the student placement office" (Clark and Trow 1966, 21–22).

Some aspects of the vocational culture described by Clark and Trow as being prevalent on urban campuses that many commuter students attend overlap with the credentialist college student subculture orientation ideal type conceptualized in this book, and others link them to the careerist ideal-type orientation. These two orientations are quite distinct. For this reason the vocationalist subculture, as they define it, is not a very useful heuristic device for the purposes of this study. The credentialist orientation generally entails some level of resistance to intellectual demands beyond those required to pass courses, which Clark and Trow (1966) said characterized vocationalism. The strong orientation toward a professional career that they saw in the vocationalist orientation is often accompanied by a high degree of motivation to make good grades and master skills, not to resist study and learning. At Midwest a number of strongly careerist-oriented people are also academically engaged and interested. Clark and Trow (1966) also claim that the vocational type is mostly found among working- and lower-middle-class students, which may well have been the case at the time their research was conducted but is not the case with ten of the seventeen students who have primary orientations toward the credentialist college student cultural orientation at Midwest, and who are from middle- and mostly upper-middle-class family backgrounds, as are nineteen of the thirty-one students with primary orientations toward careerism. Midwest is a large state university with a relatively small, nontraditional student enrollment, and yet there is a strong presence of credentialism on the campus.

The careerist orientation also overlaps in some ways with the vocational ideal type of Clark and Trow, in that students with a careerist orientation are concerned about vocation, but unlike credentialists they are involved in learning and take their academics seriously, especially the courses and activities connected directly to skills they need to have in order to pursue their career of choice.

The collegiate college student orientation ideal type used in this book overlaps substantially with the "collegiate culture" definition by Clark and Trow (1966). They found this culture flourished on the resident campuses of big state universities, such as Midwest University, at the time of their study.

> The most widely held stereotype of college life pictures the "collegiate culture," a world of football, fraternities and sororities, dates, cars, drinking, and campus fun. A good deal of student life on many campuses revolves around this culture; it both provides substance for the stereotypes of movies and cartoons and models itself on those stereotypes. Teachers and courses and grades are in this picture but somewhat dimly and in the background. The fraternities have to make their gradepoint average, students have to hit the books periodically if they are to get their diplomas, some gestures have to be made to the adult world of courses and grades which provides the justification for the collegiate round. (1966, 20)

This study shows that the collegiate college student cultural orientation continues to flourish as a secondary orientation among students, as they claim to have an authentic college coming-of-age experience, but that it is not the primary orientation, consuming large amounts of time and energy, for the majority of Midwest students. The public visibility of the collegiate culture and its historic centrality and integration into the institutional structure continue to make it appear dominant in the generalized culture at Midwest, though most students are not devoting the majority of their time and energy to participation in collegiate cultural activities over the course of their college years. Still, when those with either a primary or secondary emphasis on the collegiate college student orientation are considered, over half in the sample are among them. About thirteen of the sixty students in the study focus their time, energy, and identification primarily with collegiate student culture, with an additional twenty-one students giving it secondary centrality.

Academic culture, as defined by Clark and Trow, has at its center "its identification with the intellectual concerns of the serious faculty members" (1966, 22). The academic cultural orientation found among students at Midwest is similar to the academic culture they describe in which the students involved work hard, get the best grades, talk about their coursework outside of class, and let the world of ideas and knowledge reach them. . . . For these students, the attachment to college is through the faculty and through campus friends of similar mind and temper. . . . The products of this culture are typically aiming at graduate and professional schools. . . . These students are often oriented toward vocations but not so directly or narrowly. (1966, 22)

The distinctive qualities of this group are, first, that they are seriously involved in their coursework beyond the minimum required for passing and graduation and second that they identify themselves with their college and its faculty. (1966, 23)

Another student subcultures identified by Clark and Trow is the nonconformist culture. According to Clark and Trow (1966), while the collegiate pursues fun, the vocationalist pursues a diploma, and the academic pursues knowledge, the nonconformist pursues an identity, "not as a by-product, but as the primary and often self-conscious aim of their education. And their symbol is often a distinctive style—of dress, speech, attitude—that itself represents the identity they seek" (24). The students who orient toward nonconformist culture

are often deeply involved with ideas, both the ideas they encounter in their classrooms and those that are current in the wider society of adult art, literature, and politics. To a much greater degree than their academically oriented classmates, these students use off-campus groups and currents of thought as points of reference, instead of the official college culture, in their strategy of independence and criticism. . . . The distinctive quality of this student style is a rather aggressive nonconformism, a critical detachment from the college they attend and from its faculty (though this often conceals a strong ambivalence), and a generalized hostility to the college administration. (1966, 23)

The alternative college student cultural orientation ideal type has some similarities to Clark and Trow's (1966) nonconformist culture but does not imply hostility to the university administration, as they suggest in their model. Alternatives at Midwest are engaged in activities largely unrelated to the university. Those who are nonconformist are not struggling with the university administration or faculty for change as the nonconformists described by Clark and Trow (1966) but are instead more likely to be critical of their collegiate peers and to look outside the university for peers with whom to identify and spend time.

Clark and Trow's (1966) model falls short when describing the contemporary college student culture at Midwest, in part due to the cultural and structural changes that have occurred since the time of their study, plus they derived their typology model of college student subcultures from the structural relations they wanted to link to the types rather than from ethnographic data. This led them to create ideal-type orientations derived from institutional structures and the populations they knew to be in attendance there. Then when they observed that many students fit into two of the types that had mutually exclusive characteristics, the academic and the vocationalist, they decided "it is not necessary to decide whether they (students) are concerned with their studies more for the sake of learning than because of their career ambitions" (1966, 22–23) and proceeded to lump those strongly oriented toward learning for its own sake in with academically interested vocationalists, though they defined vocationalists as being hostile to academics.

Developing careerist and credentialist ideal-type orientations and developing a model that incorporates primary and secondary orientations allow students with different orientations to have their various cultural orientations represented and understood. This approach shifts from a structurally determined model to one that synthesizes consideration of structure and agency in developing a model of primary and secondary college student cultural orientations allowing for a broader range of variations in patterns of orientations and representing the meaning making and behaviors described by and observed among students at Midwest.

Barbara J. Bank's (2003) research, conducted between 1991 and 1997 at a small women's college that she calls Central Women's College (CWC), which is located in the central United States, focuses partly on the extent to which women at CWC had academic and career orientations. She found that CWC students were more likely to be careerist in orientation than intellectual. Bank maintains that

> the orientations of entering CWC students reflect two tendencies among American college students. The first is the long-standing tendency among both college men and women to justify higher education not as an end in itself but rather as a

means to being a better person and to leading a better life. The second is the increasing tendency among college women, following the path of college men, to define that better self and better life in occupational terms. (Bank 2003, 70)

Horowitz (1987), a historian and cultural analyst, identified three primary college student subcultures. "College life," she notes, emerged out of violent revolts in the late eighteenth and early nineteenth centuries between the students, all of whom were men, and university personnel:

Pleasure-seeking young men who valued style and openly pursued ambition rioted against college presidents and faculty determined to put them in their place. In every case, the outbreaks were forcibly suppressed; but the conflict went underground. Collegians withdrew from open confrontation to turn to covert forms of expression. They forged a peer consciousness sharply at odds with that of the faculty and of serious students and gave it institutional expression in the fraternity and club system. (Horowitz 1987, 11)

Classes and books existed as the price one had to pay for college life, but no right-thinking college man ever expected to learn in the classroom, not at least the kind of knowledge that bore any relation to his future life in the world. No, college life taught the real lessons; and from it came the true rewards. (Horowitz 1987,12)

This early masculine "college life" culture that has its roots in the elite male-dominated student culture of the early college system in the United States, described by Horowitz, is the historically constructed culture from which the shared culture of Midwest emerges and within which contemporary collegiate culture described in this book is grounded.

Those who came to early colleges to study for the ministry and were joined in the mid-nineteenth century by others who were motivated by the promise of upward mobility through earning a college education that prepared them vocationally are dubbed the "outsiders" by Horowitz.

Beginning in the mid-nineteenth century other outsiders took the pastors' places: ambitious youth from all over rural America; the first college women, immigrants, especially Jews; blacks, veterans after World War II, commuters, and, beginning in the 1960s, women continuing their education. Such students have looked askance at their more playful classmates to wonder how they could waste their time with foolishness. . . . Whether vocationally or academically motivated, the outsiders avoided looking at other students and directed their gaze at the faculty. (1987, 14)

Those who called themselves college men created an alternative system that distributed status by their own standards, not those of professors, and denigrated the good student; the outsiders, however, who hoped to rise above their station, worked for high marks and professorial recommendations. (1987, 14–15)

The third major college student culture she identifies is that of the "college rebels" (1987, 15). College rebels initially came from "nurturant families of the middle class whose deviance—often the mere fact of being Jewish—barred them from college life" (15). Horowitz says college rebels were:

as excited by ideas as any outsider; college rebels could be as cavalier about grades or as hedonistic as a college man, for they did not see their four college years as instrumental to future success. College rebels fought the social distinctions that sorted out college students and reveled in difference, not uniformity. Not content with individual resolutions, they began to battle with college men for positions in student government and on undergraduate newspapers. (15)

The alternative cultural orientation ideal type has some similarities to Horowitz's rebels. They are from the middle class and often view themselves as different from the mainstream college students that surround them at Midwest, but those oriented this way at Midwest are not necessarily engaged in a radical power struggle with some other group, as are Horowitz's radicals, and none in the sample are engaged in struggle to change the university institutional arrangements or college student culture. These students may indeed reject the values of collegiate culture or be artistically or politically active as the radicals Horowitz describes, but they also may be disengaged from the politics of campus or nation and are not necessarily involved in the arts either. Some are absorbed with other activities. None of the students with this orientation in the Midwest University sample are particularly interested in engaging in conflict or competition with collegiates for control of the campus newspaper or student organizations, because they do not view them as being very important.

The 1960s, according to Horowitz, saw college rebels mobilize to protest the Vietnam War and participate in the civil rights movement and the women's movement of the era. "The cumulative events of the 1960s ended the hegemony of college life. At the end of the decade it remained as one option, but hardly the most important. Divisions persisted on campus, but they signified personal preferences unconnected with prestige" (1987, 19).

While the collegiate culture at Midwest is not truly hegemonic, making up only a little over 20 percent of the undergraduate population in terms of a primary orientation, and full participation in it is, as Horowitz suggests, a personal choice, it continues to be perceived by most students at Midwest as the dominant culture, and many aspects of the generalized culture that gloss over differences among students in their cultural orientations are drawn from it in part because of the strong historical institutional ties that make it highly visible, and in part because of the popular culture that depicts it as dominant. It continues to be the standard of college student culture against which students at Midwest judge their own experiences. In this way it continues to exert a powerful influence on the lives of students, regardless of whether they participate in it fully or partially or try to ignore or reject it.

From the period following the Vietnam War to the time when her book was written in the late 1980s, Horowitz maintains that most college students have focused their energies on becoming professionals motivated by the desire for financial well-being and security. The ranks of rebels and collegians were decimated, marking, according to Horowitz, the triumph of the new outsiders over the college men and women and the rebels. The new outsiders, like their early brethren, are oriented toward professional careers and seek good grades.

The new outsiders' culture is generally consistent with the careerist, ideal-type cultural orientation at Midwest, but the secondary orientations of students show that there is variation in the ways these students actually spend their time and energy. It is the orientation that attracts the highest percentage of students of any one orientation, but it is, even so, far from holding the sort of dominance that Horowitz suggests, plus the cultural boundaries between college student cultural orientations at Midwest are somewhat fluid rather than firm, and most students participate in more than one of them.

PRIMARY AND SECONDARY COLLEGE
STUDENT CULTURAL ORIENTATIONS

In describing the daily lives of students based on interviews and participant observation, primary orientations alone are an inadequate heuristic device for capturing the actual ideas and behaviors of students at Midwest. But when the secondary orientations are identified and included, the patterns students describe can be captured consistently and more completely. Secondary orientations span all five ideal-type cultural orientations, and the daily lives, values, and activities of students vary substantially based not only on the primary cultures they orient toward but are also shaped significantly by the secondary orientations they embrace.

The next section describes the daily lives of students, showing the variations in student experiences based on their privileging of particular college student cultural orientations. It focuses on the rich descriptions by the students of their goals, values, interests, friendships, social lives, dating, living arrangements, academics, relationships with faculty, organizational involvement, and work to show readers the patterned and varied ways that they use college to "come of age." The ways that class, race, and gender play roles in shaping their lives are also revealed as they tell the stories of their lives as college students. Detailed accounts of the most frequent primary and secondary orientation combinations are provided. Summaries of less frequent combinations follow.

CAREERIST

Those with a careerist orientation are much more interested in course work that relates to the professional careers they plan to pursue and the internships, organizational activities, and practical experiences that prepare them to succeed in getting jobs in their future professions. They often express frustration over the general education and humanities requirements they must meet in order to get to the good stuff that is really relevant to them. They relate to faculty, but from a more instrumental perspective than the academically oriented students. That is, they seek opportunities to collaborate in research, to work in labs, or to have other mentoring relationships with faculty in order to get good recommendations, to understand how things are done in their field, and to have these experiences to list on their resumes so they can have an edge in the job market. Students very directly say that these are the motivations behind seeking these experiences, along with doing volunteer work. Fourteen of the forty-three PGC students are involved in the careerist cultural orientation. Seven of the seventeen first-generation students participate intensely in careerist pursuits.

CAREERIST/ACADEMIC

Of the twenty-one people whose primary orientation is toward the careerist college student cultural orientation, the most frequent secondary orientation is academic. Eleven of those with a strong careerist college student cultural orientation have secondary orientations that are strongly academic. Of these five are PGC, six are FGC, seven are white, and four are racial and ethnic minority students. Talisha and Jim both focus on career goals primarily but also value the opportunity college is giving them to learn in their classes.

> Careerism with an Academic Twist: "I have a pretty open relationship with faculty. I think I actually get along better with them than the students, which is really weird to me." (Talisha, sophomore in journalism)

Spending Monday with Talisha, who is aiming for a career in magazine journalism and is interested in academics, brought back memories of my own undergraduate years at a large Midwestern university during the early '70s, but changes have occurred since my undergraduate days. Gone are the days of the large lecture hall filled to capacity with students watching television recordings of a professor giving a lecture or long, detailed, and unreadable outlines written on the blackboards of large lecture halls. Today Powerpoint slides and video clips prevail in the classroom. Many new buildings have been constructed at Midwest, and the grounds have been beautifully landscaped. It is a cool day in late winter.

Talisha's Monday morning starts with a breakfast of cereal and a shower. She lives in a basement apartment that is a short walk to campus. I park next to the house and walk down a short flight of stairs to the basement. I knock on the door, and Talisha calls to me to come in. The room holds a kitchen and living room area. An old coffee table and sofa sit in front of a television. The floor appears to be concrete and is covered with linoleum designed to look like wood. The kitchen looks like it is well used by Talisha and her roommate. Dishes are piled in the sink, but otherwise the room is tidy. Talisha later tells me that her roommate is a good cook and has prepared greens and chicken for them to eat that evening. She says she is trying to save money so she can study abroad in the summer and has to make herself eat at home more to save money. She is looking for a job again too. A few days later when I see her she tells me she has found a deal on dinner close to campus— she can get a burger and fries and a cookie for $3 and can avoid taking the time to walk home and back to campus, time that she needs to work on assignments. A friend in the journalism program told her about the deal at Howard's Restaurant, and she tells me it is a big relief.

Talisha's brother attended Midwest and gives her advice. Talisha gets no financial support from her family, but she gets $800 a month during the school year from the military as a dependent of her mother, who was in the army for a number of years. She came to Midwest because of the high-quality journalism program and the funding she was offered. She says she gets about $3,000 in scholarship money a year at Midwest and does not have to pay out-of-state tuition. She has worked off and on but had a couple of semesters where the journalism program requirements made it impossible for her to work and to do well in school, so she stopped working so much and focused on school. She has taken out some student loans, but based on her brother's advice, she says she is trying to keep them to a minimum. With in-state tuition, rent, food, and clothing costs, Talisha says she struggles to make ends meet, even with the scholarship she gets.

Talisha shows me around the apartment. Her bedroom holds a mattress on the floor and a table with a lamp. Her roommate is an anthropology student. They both have many of their classes on the west side of campus and found a place to live that is close. Unfortunately, according to Talisha, her first class of the day, in a subject that would normally be scheduled in a classroom on West campus, is held in a building on the other side of campus and requires a hike. She leaves the house early enough so she has plenty of time to get there, carrying all of her supplies in a backpack. Talisha wears jeans, a long-sleeved knit top, and a rust-colored velveteen jacket. Her brown hair is parted on the side and styled in a bob that falls just below chin length. She wears dangling earrings with salmon-colored beads that swing as she walks. Her eyes twinkle, and she has a ready smile and a ready laugh.

Talisha orients strongly toward careerism, and her secondary orientation is academic. She aims for a career in magazine writing. "I love magazines like *Rolling Stone*, and I want to write stories about music and art. I want a future where I have fun and enjoy my career!" Talisha says she does not want to get married. "I want to be able to come home and say 'Oh, I'm tired, I'm going to take a shower,' and not worry about having to do this and that." She says her most significant learning experiences at Midwest have taken place in the classroom and through her academic work. In describing one of her favorite classes, a writing class offered in the journalism school, she says the following:

> She [the teacher] really kicks my butt! And I love it! She pushes me to improve my writing. And I love it! I love, I have a pretty open relationship with faculty. I think I actually get along better with them than the students, which is really weird to me. I think I can have more in-depth conversations with them, and they seem nicer sometimes actually than students. Here it's like "hey let's get together for a cup of coffee." I'll come to your office hours, just randomly and it's just really cool. I never thought you could be friends with your professors. And that's just kind of interesting. I must admit some professors, like this semester, I'm not enjoying particularly. I think they are great people but their teaching styles affect your relationship with them. If you don't think they are a good teacher you don't usu- ally want to see them outside of class. You don't think you'll learn anything. But if you have a good teacher you want to have more of a connection with them.
>
> My favorite courses have been anthropology, English, and sociology, definitely. Anthropology because I just got to learn about different, a lot of different cultures and I enjoyed that. I can apply it, you know, be like "oh that's cool!" I can have interesting conversations about stuff. Sociology, I like to relate stuff that's happening around me in a theoretical perspective. And writing just because I like to write and it taught me to be a little bit of a better writer.

Talisha describes linking what she learns in the classroom to her every- day experiences and bringing academic learning into conversations with peers. She says she relates well to faculty and views some of her teachers as friends. Her descriptions of teachers acknowledge them as complex and fully human. She describes the potential for a number of different types of relationships with faculty, including getting to know them well. hooks (1984) describes the qualities in a teacher that are comparable to the qualities Talisha describes in her way of approaching relating to fac- ulty, one in which there is the possibility for an authentic human rela- tionship aimed at mutual recognition and her own self-actualization through the learning process linked to her relationships with others, including faculty.

Talisha and I are headed for class with Jared, a friend she met at a party given by John, one of her best college friends. She met John, who comes from an upper-middle-class family, in the residence hall freshman year. They found that they not only shared an interest in becoming journalists but that they care about similar social issues. When she and Jared were chatting at John's party, they discovered that they are both minoring in sociology. Once they got to know each other, they decided to take their sociology classes together. They often meet for lunch at the student union cafeteria before class, go to class together, share notes, and introduce each other to people they know in class. They study for exams together, and they continue to socialize with each other, often attending campus events together with other friends. A friend of that friend who works at a local restaurant is helping Talisha get a job there. Talisha sometimes asks new acquaintances to join her friend list on Facebook and then checks out the people in their friend lists to see if there is anyone in her classes or anyone who has a mutual interest listed on them.

Talisha spends a high percent of her time and energy on class work and going to cultural events and presentations on campus. This is in part because she believes that she benefits greatly from the classroom learning and events on campus. She points out that she has a friend whose family members read books together and discuss them, and that she wishes she had experienced a similar situation in her own family. She feels like she has to work harder than that friend to do well, because she is not as familiar with some of the things that come up in classes as her friend is. She senses that she is gaining exposure to cultural events, literature, and new ideas at a fast pace, and she is eager to acquire the knowledge. Talisha eagerly learned who the writers whose names were being bandied about in her classes were if she did not know, and then she read their work. She said that most of the students already knew all of the contemporary writers of note, and that she had to work hard to "catch up" on those writing for the New Yorker and Harper's. She also says that her classroom education has been lacking in some ways. She notes that no one discusses cutting-edge black and gay and lesbian magazines that are hitting the market (Talisha 2006), magazines such as Essence, Ebony, and Details, a magazine for gay males, which she reads and enjoys. This, she says, is a weakness in the very white, mainstream education she is getting at Midwest. Some of her peers, those in her inner circle, share her interest in experiencing a broader range of writing that is more representative of the diverse culture with which she identifies.

Talisha's friendship network reflects choices she has made and structural influences. The university offers students the option of being in a freshman interest group and provides the structure for that experience. Talisha though not formally a member chose to participate in one related to her career goals. This brought her into contact with a group of students with similar interests, including her freshman year residence-hall roommate, Anna, who is a middle-class white woman. They have remained close friends. Her roommate at the time of her first interview was Jana, a black woman majoring in anthropology, whom she had met prior to college. When Jana transferred to another university, Talisha found a new roommate. Her new roommate is from Africa and is also majoring in journalism, though in a different subfield than Talisha is studying. Talisha's friendship choices are made based on her values and interests and also on her comfort level and propinquity. Talisha lived in the least expensive residence hall, referred to by students as "the ghetto," as a freshman, and it was there that she made her core of new college friends, but over the course of college she made new friends, many of whom were in her major.

Talisha is concerned about social issues and racial and ethnic inequality, and she connects most closely with others who share these concerns. But she does not build close relationships with the black students who are conservative religiously and socially who, according to her, prefer not to mix with whites and to stigmatize other African Americans who do. She maintains ties with the Black Culture Center and views that as meaningful and important, but she chooses to be close friends with whites as well as blacks. Most of her close friends share similar career or academic interests. She sees the college education she is getting as being important for her to achieve her career goals and upward mobility. She chooses friends, at least in part, who help her achieve her goals, because they are taking similar courses. She also chooses friends based on similar values, concerns, or career goals, which often lead them to be interested in their similar course work.

Talisha has a network of friends, what Nathan (2005) calls "ego-centered networks," that has supported her in developing her authentic self and in carrying it into the public sphere where she has protested the lack of diversity in the student population of Midwest and has written newspaper stories about folk art and eclectic artists that her editors tell her are "great stories." Her friends, some of whom are also interested in writing, help feed her creative energies and encourage her to follow her instincts about what she finds interesting to write about. Talisha's "private pleasures" activities are intertwined with and carried into the public sphere. Her obvious desire to improve her skills and her eagerness for feedback from teachers and peers have produced rapid development in her writing skills, knowledge base, confidence level, and relational skills. She says that the change in her since she was a freshman is significant. Her interpersonal skills have become more sophisticated, and she interacts with ease with faculty and people with whom she works in her role as a student journalist. She now engages people in intellectual discussions on social issues, music, and art. She says, "I like smart people," and she has friends who care about understanding things.

Talisha has a limited budget and has to work some to pay for basics. Her ability to go out frequently is restricted by money and time. She wants to make good grades and really learn her craft; just getting a diploma is not her goal. Events on campus are usually free or less expensive than a night at the bars would be. They link with her interests, and her friends like going to the same kinds of events she does. In part she has chosen these friends because they have similar interests, but the institution also has supported her in building a network of peer support by organizing and offering students the choice of participating in freshman learning communities and a wide range of campus events.

Talisha is disappointed in the dating opportunities for her at Midwest. Though she is not interested in a serious relationship and has reservations about ever getting married, she says that men at Midwest are "totally not interested in me!" She is seeing a white interdisciplinary studies and business major whom she met at a party at John's house. Dennis is politically liberal and concerned about social inequality. He has traveled abroad and done volunteer work in Latin America. These experiences intrigue Talisha, who plans to study abroad in Italy over the summer and make trips to other parts of Europe. She says he is one of the few men at Midwest who has been interested in her at all, and that his interest developed after John's party when she ended up staying at his house due to really bad weather and not having a ride home, and Dennis ended up staying too. They talked for hours and then fell asleep. Talisha says she honestly does not see the relationship going anywhere because they each plan on careers that will take them in different directions. She sees herself moving to the big city, with a high-paced career in magazine journalism, and she sees him locating in Latin America to work in business and economic development. At the end of the semester Talisha told me that they had agreed to end the relationship. "It just makes sense," she said. "I'm going to Italy and he's going to Mexico, where he'll be spending time with his girlfriend down there." She said that even though he agreed to end the relationship, he then got upset with her for not being upset at the parting. "I don't get it! I just don't get it!," she said, shaking her head, a perplexed tone in her voice.

Careerism with a Critical Edge: "The thing that bothers me the most is the self-promotion and empty ceremony that seems to be a continuous background noise in what I consider mainstream midwest culture." (Jim, senior in a five-year professional program)

Jim came to college after working a number of years in a small factory. Largely raised by his mother, who was a custodian, he says he was not encouraged by her or his father to aspire to a university education, and that neither parent helps with college costs. Jim lives with Annie, his partner of five years. He has a few close friends in Midwest City and enjoys spending the little leisure time he has enjoying the out-of-doors. He says his goal is to become a physical therapist, and he is well on his way to achieving it. He has short red hair, is of medium height, and is wearing jeans and a T-shirt. He says he enjoys working out with weights regularly and playing his guitar to relax. I first met Jim as a freshman he was taking mostly general education courses. Typical of those with a strong careerist orientation, Jim found much of the general education curriculum frustrating. Jim's eyes are intense as he describes his frustration with "jumping through the hoops" of general education requirements.

Jim's other main complaint about his courses is that some of them are just too easy. He likes to be challenged and is frustrated by the numbers of students he feels are not serious about academics and try to get the teachers to dummy down the content. Walking from his first class of the day to the second, he explains to me that the class we just sat through is just too easy. He is concerned that he may not be getting the type of background he needs to really be successful at his job. He says he never has to study for exams in the class but just goes over the review sheet and skims notes. He also mentions that he is irritated that the people teaching physical therapy do not question deeply the things that are wrong with the way the profession is developing and being shaped. He mentions how they will not push for legislation or policies that will make insurance companies cover best-practice treatment, instead teaching it and saying, "Most insurance won't cover this. So we opt for this other treatment that is not as good but costs less and will be covered."

Later, when I ask him to tell me more about his thoughts on this, he sends me an e-mail that says the following:

The thing that bothers me the most is the self-promotion and empty ceremony that seems to be a continuous background noise in what I consider mainstream Midwest culture (it just happens to be distilled down in the PT/OT programs I have come into contact with so far). It's usually jabbering about fund raisers or promoting "awareness" about something or other. It just so happens that the fund-raisers are for our program or someone's fraternity/sorority. The "awareness" events do nothing to help people who actually need it. It's all for PR for Midwest and the PT program. BUT they push it like some noble and necessary task, and nothing ever really happens to change things or make the world a better place. They just carry on without asking why they do these projects and fund-raisers or who it really benefits. Maybe they are fine with giving more money to Midwest, maybe they don't actually want to help people outside of their comfort zone, I don't know. All I know is that I am getting very tired of the rhetoric and just want to get my degree and get away from these people. My outlook has changed a lot since I got into the PT program and I am having a hard time playing along with these people. I should have gone into physiology/sociology like I want to do, job outlook be damned. I just hope my off-campus clinical experience goes as well as I hope. It will be a grim two more years if not. OK enough ranting for now.

Jim is frustrated with the strong pressure to become a professional person, to participate in the collective identity constructed by mandatory attendance at professional student organization meetings and fundraisers, and to conform to the norms of the profession that steer students away from questioning the political economy within which the profession operates. Jim's choice of a strong careerist path is one he now, at times, questions. He was frustrated with general education early in his student years but recognizes that some courses he took early in college played a role in his development of a more sophisticated critical perspective during his years in school.

He says he is not friends with any of the students in the program he is in outside of class work and academic assignments. Jim and Annie moved to Midwest City together to attend college. On the upcoming weekend they are participating in a fund-raising bike ride organized by students to raise money to help South African children attend school. Jim says he has a good friend at Midwest, one he met through a friend from home, with whom they hang out. Jim plays guitar with another friend to relax. He likes fishing and camping with Annie and enjoys playing Frisbee, even in cold weather, something Annie laughingly says she is not as fond of.

Jim has little tolerance for the collegiates he encounters in his classes. He points out that he expects to be $50,000 in debt when he completes his studies. He has worked ten to twenty hours a week much of the time he has been in college as a grader and at a local grocery store. At times the program requires him to do "clinicals" that may require him to be in another city or state for a time, so he cannot always work. He says he was not eligible for academic scholarships beyond the $1,000 Pell Grant that he received early during his college years. Watching others, those, he believes, who do not even really want the education, have their expenses paid for by their parents irritates him.

CAREERIST/COLLEGIATE

Careerists with a collegiate secondary orientation include eight people, seven of whom have at least one parent who is college educated. Four women with primary careerist orientations have secondary orientations that are collegiate and have college-educated parent(s). One is multiethnic, and three are white. One Asian American woman, who is FGC, is careerist/collegiate in orientation. She was in a sorority early in her college career but dropped out due to financial constraints, the need to work more to help pay for college, and a desire to focus more on academics in order to get the grades needed to get into medical school. The multiethnic PGC woman pledged a sorority and has since become quite involved in Greek life but continues to primarily emphasize her career goals, as she is in a very demanding professional program. Three men careerists have secondary orientations that are collegiate. One is white, one is Hispanic, and one is black and a college athlete. All have college-educated parent(s).

CAREERIST/ALTERNATIVE

Julie and Paula, two white women, whose parents graduated from college, with primary careerist orientations have secondary orientations that are alternative. Paula aspires to medical school with hopes of working with underprivileged people, and Julie is deeply involved in creative arts and only enrolled in the university initially because of a particular photography course she heard was good. One thing led to another, and she ended up working in multiple media in the art department, mounting her own shows in a large city in the state, teaching art off campus in several venues, and eventually going overseas to study art for a summer. She organized several events to highlight women's issues on campus. She also was concerned with making Midwest a campus friendly to students, regardless of their sexual orientation. Her focus was on creating and showing her work whenever and wherever she could throughout the time she was in college.

CREDENTIALIST

More men than women orient toward the credentialist cultural beliefs and behaviors. Sixteen students overall have a primarily credentialist orientation. Of these, ten are men and six are women. Four of the women and nine of the men are white. Three racial and ethnic minority students are in this group. One Asian American man and one black woman have parent(s) who earned college degrees. The black woman was raised by her single father with a bachelor's degree. One American Indian woman who is a first-generation student is also in this group. The parents of seven of the white men and three of the white women have college degrees. Two white men in this group are first-generation college students. One white woman in this group is a first-generation college student. Four of the seventeen first-generation students included in the study are credentialist/careerist in orientation. Twelve of the forty-three students whose parent(s) have college educations are credentialist in orientation.

Students who are credentialist in orientation do not say academics do not matter at all, since they have to keep a grade-point average that allows them to stay in school and graduate, but for them just earning the degree itself is enough. They emphasize the idea of having the diploma in hand. The balance between academics and social learning is one that privileges several different types of social learning while in college and devalues the academic side. The secondary orientation that most often accompanies the primary credentialist college student cultural orientation is collegiate. Thirteen of the sixteen students with credentialist primary orientations have collegiate and three have careerist secondary orientations.

CREDENTIALIST/COLLEGIATE

Nine men and four women describe themselves in terms that link them to the credentialist/collegiate orientations. All of the women and eight of the men have college-educated parent(s). Among those whose parents are college educated are one black woman, one Asian American man, three white women, and seven white men. These students are focused on earning a degree and having college fun. The women say they feel strong pressure from their parents to earn the degree, and that they are focused on that, but they really enjoy college fun more than they do their studies. The men believe it is important to have a degree in order to get a decent job but say they also want to have fun going out to bars and parties and attending sporting events during their time in college. A number of these students said that college would be great if only they did not have to go to class or study. For most of them the important part of college is getting the degree in the end and the fun they have along the way, the friends they make, and the things they learn about themselves in peer relationships.

Earning the degree comes first for these students, but they are highly social in orientation and enjoy spending time with their friends, going out on Thursday, Friday, and Saturday nights, and dating. One of these women discussed in some detail how difficult it was for her not to get involved with men frequently because there were so many good-looking ones available at college. Several of the men also made comments about there being many attractive women at Midwest, and said that they enjoy meeting women socially, but none complained about struggling to resist becoming involved with them.

> Credentialist/Collegiate: "I hate classes with a lot of reading that is tested on. Any class where a teacher is just gonna give us notes and a worksheet or something like that is better. Something that I can study and just learn from in five (minutes) I'll usually do pretty good in." (Bob, senior business major)

Bob[1] has brown hair and eyes. He appears relaxed as he leans back and pulls his arms up and back, interlacing his hands behind his head. He is wearing jeans and T-shirt. He sighs and says:

> Well, I don't really like school that much . . . [the worst thing about school] is going to class, but I enjoy the other aspects of being at college. I meet new people and just going out and having fun and being free, having my own house [is nice]. I own a house and rent to friends. I live with two roommates. It's fun to go to bars, fun to party, but actually I enjoy playing basketball, enjoy doing other sports and stuff. Oh, I watch television, clean around the house, mow the yard.

When asked about his goals, he said he was not sure which career he would pursue but indicated that he would really like to work on a ski and rescue team, because

> those guys just basically ski the mountains every day and they get to help people, obviously, you know, probably save a lot of lives, probably see a lot of really sad stuff too. Those groups, those are usually like the best groups of skiers, you know, that I've seen and I've actually skied with some of them before in Colorado. They've told me about their job. It seems like they've got a pretty cool lifestyle. Spend the whole day on the mountains, and then they're all kind of, you know, they go out at night and they still have fun! They don't just go home and watch TV 'til they go to bed. They definitely say they keep themselves entertained on and off the job. So, that'd be cool.

Academics are not a central focus for Bob, whose focus is on peer fun. He describes his approach to academics in the following way:

> I rarely do assigned readings and stuff like that. Basically anything that's never gonna be turned in. I hate to say it, but I don't usually do stuff that's not going to be turned in. I'd like to change that 'cause I was just actually thinkin' recently about how, this whole college experience might just be a waste of time if I don't take anything from it, you know I can get out of here with a 3.5 but it doesn't really matter if I don't remember anything you know. It's one thing to get the grade in a class and it's another to actually take something from it, you know?
>
> I hate classes with a lot of reading that is tested on. Any class where a teacher is just gonna give us notes and a worksheet or something like that is better. Something that I can study and just learn from in five [minutes] I'll usually do pretty good in. Whereas, if I'm expected to read, you know, a hundred-and-fifty page book and then write a three-page essay on it, you know, on a test let's say, I'll probably do worse on that test because I probably wouldn't have read the book. Maybe ask the kids, what's in this book? And I can draw my own conclusion, but I rarely actually do reading assignments or stuff like that, which is a mistake I'm sure, but it saves me a lot of time.

One thing that really annoys me is the unrealistic standards they [faculty] have. They think that you have the only class, and the only class is theirs, and that they can assign tons of group work and expect you to spend like three hours a day in a group or something. They don't realize that we have other stuff going on! Relationships with faculty? I have none at all! I've never, I've talked to maybe one or two of my professors down here. You know, short conversations in their office hours. Other than that I really have not talked to professors at all.

I live with three roommates in a duplex off campus. My roommates are friends of mine. Everyone of them gets on my nerves in a certain way, and I'm sure I do theirs, but besides that I really like living with them and it's fun there. It's kind of like back at home, you know, 'cause you've got your friends that are close to you and you can still hang out and do whatever you want.

I had a girlfriend all year last year. I'm not with her, but I still end up seeing her every Friday or Saturday night. I don't get the chance to really talk to any other girls. She's always around. I'm trying to change that though. There's a lot of beautiful girls here at Midwest. I like, I'm going to sound like an alcoholic here, but going to bars and drinking and I like to exercise but basically I like going out with my friends, going to bars and meeting people. I would say just hanging out [too]. I mean watching TV. I'm a laid-back person, but I also like to go out and have fun. Partying, having fun, meeting a variety of people. You can go out every single night and drink! Monday through Thursday I'll maybe go out once or twice a week to a bar or a friend's house or something, just to hang out and drink a couple of beers. That's pretty much as much as I ever do on weekdays. And then on weekends I'll either go back (home to the city) or stay down here. There's usually a party to go to on Friday and Saturday night and I do that, just a lot of going out, social parties or whatever you want to call them. I play a lot of sports. I play basketball, hit golf off my driveway. Just hang out with my roommates, we play video games every once in awhile. Go to some football games and watch basketball on television. If I'm tired I'll sleep. If it's the middle of the afternoon or something like that I'll usually work out with one of my roommates or play basketball, nothing really productive.

I'm a bit of a procrastinator and a huge slacker, I guess. So it always comes down to getting stuff done at the last minute.

I've probably got too much free time. I've got a bunch of good friends down here. Not many people I see in my classes strangely enough. All three of my roommates are actually people that I knew before I came down here. They all went to my high school. Actually since I've been in college I think I've been sleep deprived, and I probably drink too much. I'm pretty disappointed in the university. If I could start over, I'd probably have preferred to go to Boulder, Colorado, but out-of-state tuition was too expensive, so I'd probably be still at a community college after two years.

Bob is not working presently but says he is looking for a job to bring in some extra spending money. He is not involved in any clubs on campus or in student government or the Greek system, but he enjoys the athletic facilities on campus and the college sports scene, along with the off-campus college student bars.

CREDENTIALIST/CAREERIST

Two women who are first-generation college students have credentialist primary cultural orientations with secondary characteristics consistent with careerism. One woman is American Indian, and the other is white. One white man, also a first-generation college student, has this combination of orientations. These students want careers but due to other constraints, such as needing to work to pay for college, involvement in ROTC, which they find very challenging, maintaining long-distance romantic relationships, being married, and commuting to college from another town, they find that their primary goal is earning the degree rather than immersing themselves in collegiate fun or the professionalization process in a career-directed program of study.

COLLEGIATE

The collegiate college student cultural orientation ideal type was the primary orientation for thirteen students. Seven men and six women in the sample gravitated primarily toward the collegiate student-culture ideal type. All thirteen are white and have parent(s) who went to college. The men are in fraternities, the women in sororities. Interestingly, not all of the people in the Greek system gravitate primarily toward the collegiate culture. This is particularly true when their career aspirations lead them to enter demanding professional programs that force them to spend a high percentage of their time and energy on academics and a great deal of time working in groups with other students in the same program who are not involved in the Greek system. For some, the involvement with students who are primarily career oriented encourages them to shift, over the course of their college years, to a stronger identification with careerism. Collegiates in the sample are about equally divided in their secondary orientations, with a total of six emphasizing careerism and seven focusing secondarily on credentialism.

COLLEGIATE/CAREERIST

Five women and one man with a primary orientation that is collegiate have secondary orientations that are careerist. Todd, the man whose secondary orientation was careerist, spent a great deal of time on homecoming and other fraternity-related activities early in his college years and failed to get into the professional program for which he came to Midwest. Todd's parents and sister all graduated from Midwest. Todd pledged a fraternity and felt that his most significant learning centered on the experiences related to fraternity life. He noted:

> I've grown a lot since pledgeship. I hang out there [at the fraternity house] or the annex, that's where you'll find me. I go to the basketball games, football games. . . . The pledgeship really, I think, it's a really good experience. I think just for you [to] actually care about something, [makes] you work. That's where you want to be included, so you work to become what everybody else has gone through and learn and grow.

Todd took his responsibilities in his fraternity very seriously. He said that he was not used to "taking care of himself" and that he had to learn to pick up after himself and do his own laundry, and do the things that his fraternity brothers required of him. Todd was the youngest child in his family and said that growing up he had not been required to do things for himself. He merged pledging his fraternity and the demands his fraternity brothers placed on him to work on homecoming, to do volunteer work, and to drive them to and from classes with learning to be responsible for his own laundry. He connected doing what he was required to do to succeed as a pledge with "becoming a man," and he centered his energies on that activity. Todd wanted to follow the path that he believed his fraternity brothers had followed to become fully one of the group. He embraced this goal as his most important and meaningful activity while in college. Todd emphasized his willingness to endure the demands placed on him in his fraternity in order to achieve his goal.

He left Midwest with plans to attend a school in the city where his family lives. The last time we talked he bemoaned the fact that he had really been looking forward to the payoff of being able to live in the fraternity house rather than the annex, and now he would not get the chance. He voiced more regrets about not being able to live in the fraternity house than he did about not making it into the professional program for which he came to college.

> Collegiate/Careerist: "I did not realize the hours spent studying. I thought that it would be more fun and games." (Jane, junior biology major)

I first met Jane when she was a freshman living in the residence hall. Now Jane is a senior nearing graduation. It is 8 a.m. when I arrive at her apartment, located just a few miles from campus. Her roommate opens the door when I ring the bell. She calls upstairs to Jane to let her know I have arrived. The downstairs of the apartment is nicely furnished with a neutral-toned sofa and loveseat with blond wood side tables and a coffee table. A candle, surrounded by a sachet made up of pine cones and leaves, sits on the coffee table. A large potted plant is near the window, and a print of a photograph of the Eiffel tower taken through a window hangs on the wall across from the sofa. A mirror framed with a silver-toned frame hangs over the sofa. A chrome lamp with a paper shade sits on the side table. Sunshine streams into the orderly room, casting a warm glow. A television set rests on a blond wood-tone hutch. Everything is tidy. Between the living room area and the kitchen are a round dining table and chairs. The table is adorned with a candle in the center and red placemats. The kitchen counter holds a small football. In the kitchen are a coffee pot, a blender, two George Foreman grills, breakfast dishes, and SKY, Rum, Smirnoff, and Southern Comfort bottles and on the refrigerator are pictures of Jane and her friends and a sign that says "Go Midwest!" Jane leads me upstairs to her room. She is wearing slacks and an orange-and-tan striped Izod top with sandals. Her room features a large, framed photograph of the football team, signed by all the players, the year she was the student coordinator for homecoming. Also framed is a large, illustrated map of the homecoming route. A well-worn Bible sits beside the bed. The television is on, and her computer sits next to it. The room is spacious and bright. Everything hanging on her walls is Midwest related. Clearly Jane identifies with Midwest, particularly with sports and homecoming.

Jane was most enthusiastic in talking about her collegiate-related activities and said she learned the most from her college experiences that involved planning homecoming and social learning connected to her social life in college. Her secondary orientation was strongly toward her career and becoming a professional early in her college years, but over time she has become less enthusiastic. Parental involvement in her college education, in particular her father's insistence that she prepare for a professional career, clearly played a role in her secondary careerist emphasis. Jane, a biology major who started out with plans to become a doctor, now plans to move home after graduation and spend a year out of school, take the GRE, and then attend a two-year physician's assistant program at the local university in her hometown.

For her, sorority life was the most important part of her college years, particularly the friends she made, the role she played in planning homecoming one year, and the volunteer work with which she was involved. She believes planning that event, which involved her working with people in the community, students, and university officials, was a profoundly important learning experience for her. Her eyes brighten, and she looks excited as she says the following:

> Oh my gosh! I've done a lot of stuff with my sorority, I was vice president of my class, well, I am vice president of my pledge class. I was serenade chair, which you have to put all the serenades together. And go do that. Um Homecoming of course, homecoming, it's huge. (laughs) I mean, I wanted to change my major to a, to um, event planning after that. Like that's all I wanted to do. My parents were like "you've gotta think about this one." I mean, I feel Midwest! I feel like I'm true [to] Midwest, you know, it's just wow! I never knew I could put a show on for twenty thousand people. I mean, my entire heart went out to that. And to balance school. I missed two days of school, like just two classes, even during the week. I told myself, "If I take on a job, I do not let my grades fall." Like, in any way possible. They told us our GPAs would go down tremendously, and I did not allow it. I do a lot of volunteering. I love to volunteer. In fact, I switched my major to be a social worker for one semester because I just got so involved in it. I used to work at Fun City out at the Midwest Center and those kids, and seeing just how they view life and how I'm able

to view life and how we came together and how every time I walked in the room every kid would just grab a hold of me, we'd play. It's just, oh it's a blast. I just, I see things a little bit differently now. And even though they might not get the same education as me, I feel like they've got the social skills to do anything they want, honestly.

I live with two sorority sisters now. I go out to bars now, I mean, I see that side of things and I, I never experienced that and I see my friends drink a lot. I mean, you know, I'm usually the sober driver (laughs). But seeing how boys act towards girls and girls act towards boys, and they, they just almost soak it up and they almost just crave the attention. (laughs) I mean, ugh, I've never been experienced to that. I mean, now I've got a boyfriend of nine months and it's just, wow, it's just, alcohol has so much effect on people and my friends are like "oh I was drunk, I don't remember." No, you really do remember, because you cannot blame all that, I still believe you know what you are doing when you are drunk. I've only skipped ten classes in my entire career. Some of them were due to getting my friends help and getting them out of trouble. First semester I was gung ho study, everything, but then second semester I was like, "Hey!" You know? It happens. Now I love to see my friends all the time, just watching TV or coming home. I like "Blind Date." I think it's hilarious. I love it. I think it's so funny. Oh, we go to the movies. When's the last time I've seen a movie? I mean, honestly, I think I actually got to see one over Thanksgiving break. It's just, and I want it so bad, but everything's going back to my dad. You can tell I'm a daddy's girl. And he's like "Jane, put in the time now. Just put it in [Put in the time studying]. Four years, put it in, and you will reap sixty years." And I'm like, "Dad, you're right."

Jane's relationships with faculty are varied. She says she gets along well with some faculty but expresses frustration about some of her classes:

[I got along with some faculty] extremely well, others I just didn't care to get to know, honestly. Some teachers I just don't care for, you know? Some I call home and I cry about. "I can't believe you didn't put things on the final that you taught us, instead of this! I mean it wasn't even in the book, you didn't teach it! Why?" Another day we had a lecture, like a ten-minute lecture, on how you are not allowed to come into economics class, with her, I can't remember her name, um late. "Don't come!" And I just wanted to raise my hand and go "I'm paying for this class. I should be allowed, if I don't slam the door, to come in whenever I want to come in." I did not realize the hours spent studying. I thought that it would be more fun and games. I'm trying my best to pass, and like I have to do really good and I have no teacher-student communication and that gets really frustrating. I get really frustrated when I'm in a class of five hundred people. I came in with good study habits. I made myself have them.

Jane attended a good high school and took college-level classes at a local community college while she was still in high school but says that the academic demands at Midwest are harder and more frustrating. She believes that she really benefits more from social learning and fun than being a grind. During college she has felt secure in her social status and has had plenty of money for clothes and leisure activities. The sorority she is in provides a ready-made social network that also serves her in classes where there is almost always another person from her sorority or a fraternity where she knows people. Jane wishes she did not have to study so hard to maintain her grades but is overall pretty comfortable with her college experience. The last semester of her senior year she says she is a little stressed about the future and wishes her parents would not put so much pressure on her.

When Jane thinks back over her college years she says her volunteer work stands out as being very important in her development. She started doing volunteer work in connection to her sorority early in her college career but continued to volunteer throughout her college years because she came to find it so fulfilling. Now a senior, she says she gets a strong sense of satisfaction from the work she does as a volunteer. Her authentic self is clearly engaged in the public sphere of the local hospital where she volunteers and in her work with disadvantaged children in a community center in town. Jane says her roommate graduated last semester but has not yet been able to find a job. Jane says "she's dating a guy who doesn't have a job either, and I always wonder who takes who out when they go to dinner. Neither of them has any money. I don't think the job market is that good right now."

At the end of a day spent together, she excitedly shares with me that we are not going to be going to the recreation center for her workout as planned because she got a call from a friend who is a former football player, and recent graduate of Midwest, who is visiting town while he waits to hear from the NFL if he is going to be picked up, and he is coming over to her place in the late afternoon. She says once she found out he was visiting, she asked him to sign a small football she has gotten to give a patient at the hospital where she works. She says the woman, who has cancer, is a big Midwest football fan, and she wants to give her the football to cheer her up. Jane's volunteer work makes her feel good about herself, and she says "I think I make a difference" through volunteering.

Summing up her college years, Jane says she still feels like the friends and organizational involvement she has had in college have taught her the most. Academics, she says, are something she had to do, but they did not produce the meaningful learning she had in getting along with her peers, assuming responsibility in her sorority and in the university administration during the homecoming planning when she was a student representative and coordinator for the event, and doing her volunteer work.

COLLEGIATE/CREDENTIALIST

One of the women and six of the men have secondary orientations that are credentialist. They are focused on a social life that involves parties, sports events, planned activities centered in Greek life, and doing what they have to academically to earn a degree. All are white and have college-educated parent(s).

> Collegiate/Credentialist: "We usually have tailgates for every home game. I go to bars maybe every other week depending on like studies. I generally like to go over to friends' houses like hanging and not doing anything productive (or) having parties at our house. I'll admit it, I'm just, I love going out to a nice restaurant, like sitting down and having a good dinner. My favorite restaurant is Josephine's. I love to go to that place because the food is amazing. They have a really good wine selection and everything." (B. J., junior, business major)

Bradley James, whose nickname is B. J., is a business major. His parents attended college, but he explains that they went to a smaller regional college, not Midwest. He has been very active in a fraternity. B. J. plans to get a job in sports marketing or sports administration after graduation and then eventually to get an MBA, a master's in sports administration, or a master's in higher education administration so that he can eventually work in the college setting. The undergraduate degree is, in B. J.'s view, just the first step. He says that he needs the degree to get started, but that the real purpose of college at the undergraduate level is as a space between high school and the "real world."

> The best thing about college is that it provides a kind of a time in between high school and the real world to kind of get to know more about yourself and get to know other people and to kind of transition from home to work in a positive environment.

B. J. says he is a brownnoser when it comes to relating to faculty, explaining that he believes having faculty know who you are and be favorably disposed toward you cannot hurt.

> My mom always makes fun of me because I try to brownnose as much as [possible]. As people say, like it helps if the faculty, like the person, knows you and knows who you are. They're more likely to help you out than not. I don't go like every week to talk to professors, but the first week I usually introduce myself. I visit office hours if I feel like I need to. Try to sit in front of the classes and interact, get noticed. That way when I need a recommendation they'll remember me. I suck up a lot.

B. J. says so far the best course he has had at Midwest is business etiquette.

> Actually my favorite class in college was golf class. All we did was go out and play golf every week. Yeah, it was a two-hour class, all we did was go play golf. It was for people who come from rural agricultural areas that don't know anything about it, but like that's where a lot of business is done. And I grew up playing golf, I would say like 60 to 70 percent of business is done on the golf course. You go out, you have four hours to go over stuff with people, and you know, it's a really relaxed atmosphere. They taught a lot of skills, like, it was actually really funny, we learned a lot of things about a bunch of new gambling games and how to gamble playing golf, like betting games that I didn't know before. They did teach us a few new things, like I learned how to slice the ball and hook, which is like curving to the left or right. It was actually a pass/fail course.

B. J. doesn't spend most of his time thinking about course work, however, his focus is on spending time with peers and having fun.

> I think it's a really good dating scene [at Midwest]. It's sort of funny, one of my mom's friends put it like this, cuz she went, they were alums, like her and her husband are both alums and they're like "you better get a girlfriend before you get out of there," cause you get out in the real world and it's hard to date people. Like when you just know them from school it works. I don't know. I never had any trouble meeting girls here, like dating. I'm very open-minded and relaxed with a person, and I don't have any problems with whatever girls do, unless they're really aggressive. Girls "calm down! I don't need in your pants that bad!"

B. J. says "right now" he's single and goes out with the fiancé of one of his best friends with whom he has become close friends and then to bars with his buddies. His best friend has graduated and gotten his first job, and his fiancé is still in college. He says they go out to eat at nice restaurants together and talk about everything that is going on in their lives.

> All my best friends from high school came to school here too. Like there's a really, really close-knit group of us, like six of us, and all but one started out here. I'm from the suburbs of [the city]. I am totally single. I've enjoyed everything. I love collegiate athletics, especially here at Midwest, basketball, cuz my Dad was a huge basketball fan! I love athletics, I love having all my best friends here. Like two of them just graduated, but there's still like me and two other ones that are doing the five-year plan. (laughs) [One of my roommates] this year is a friend of my best friend's former high school girlfriend. Their girlfriends were roommates, so we got to be really good friends with him too. We're a really good match, like we have a lot in common, and we like to do a lot of the same things. And we're always trouble when we are together. We're all like just really good friends. We get along, there's no friction between us, like if something comes up we throw it right in each other's face and call each other homos. It's comforting to have that, because I've had living arrangements in the past where I really didn't get along with my roommates.

We usually have tailgates for every home game. I go to bars maybe every other week depending on like studies. I generally like to go over to friends' houses like hanging and not doing anything productive (or) having parties at our house. I'll admit it, I'm just, I love going out to a nice restaurant like sitting down and having a good dinner. My favorite restaurant is Josephine's.[2] I love to go to that place because the food is amazing. They have a really good wine selection and everything. I've gotten to be really, really close with his girlfriend who is now his fiancé since he graduated, like, they just got engaged two weeks ago. And we love to go there, just the two of us, and talk about our week. Go out to dinner, whatnot. I play video games. Like Seals versus terrorists online with my Play Station. It's scary, I think I spent, I don't have class on Tuesday (or) Thursday. I think I spent from the time I woke up until the time I went to sleep last night, I probably spent a total of two hours not playing it.

B. J. works about fifteen hours a week at a local store to supplement the funds his parents provide him. He works summers too. But most of his college education is financed by his parents. Being an in-state student makes it more affordable, but he says sometimes his parents bring up the fact that they have had to tighten their belts to afford to send him to Midwest. He has assured them that it is well worth the cost, because the school has a pretty good reputation and is the best in the state.

He says he is active in his fraternity but does not spend much time describing those activities. He says he spent a lot of time on fraternity-related work during the first years of college, serenading, volunteering, building floats for homecoming, helping to organize events, and attending parties. He still participates but is less immersed in those activities now that he no longer lives in the fraternity house.

Randy also is in a fraternity and enjoys the organized events and activities associated with it, but he says he moved out of the fraternity house to live with his closest college friends who share his religious values.

I lived in a fraternity house. Now I live with two other guys in an apartment, a three-bedroom apartment. And the reason for getting away was kind of to live with guys who I guess, who kind of came from a Christian background, who shared my beliefs and values and things like that. Recently four of my five closest friends have become engaged, which is kind of scary. I feel like I guess it depends on the circle you run around with, because there's obviously guys who I'm friends with in the fraternity that have no intentions of getting married anytime soon and would like to date as many girls as possible but I feel like, in my subculture of friends, there is a strong emphasis, like, on being committed early and lifelong. Like getting very serious very fast and not necessarily like the dating around type of thing.

I'm active in my fraternity, playing sports with the fraternity, and I'm active in Campus Crusade for Christ, which is a Christian outreach program. I've been involved in Homecoming Steering Committee. I love watching sports, sporting events here are a great time, and just being with friends is a good time. We spend a lot of time just around the TV talking about, watching sports and talking about sports. Just going to church and Crusade is like a big part of our lives as well. Talking about our faith, maybe praying and sharing experiences, that sort of thing.

Randy enjoys and participates enthusiastically in some aspects of the culture he perceives being dominant at Midwest, particularly sports. He enjoys his fraternity brothers and fraternity activities, but he talks about his fraternity affiliation in a way that shows he wants to distance himself from the easygoing, hedonistic aspects he has observed among students. He notes that his close friends are interested in finding marriage partners, while some of the people he knows in his fraternity are interested in living the single life. Randy does not say he is eager to settle down to marriage himself, but he identifies most strongly with the group of men he says do, his Christian friends with whom he goes to church and with whom he lives. Randy's indirect critique of collegiate culture is similar to some found more forcefully among the students who embrace an alternative college student cultural orientation.

ALTERNATIVE

Six students in the sample, three men and three women, described themselves in ways that are consistent with a primary orientation that is alternative. Two of the women and one of the men are FGC, and one of the women and two of the men are PGC. All are white. Some of these students express a variety of criticisms and levels of discomfort with the values and behaviors they observe in the dominant college student culture based on religion, political orientations, and social values and concerns they claim, indicating that their detachment from campus culture more generally is based on a sense of alienation from the values they believe are being expressed in the behaviors of other students and/or in classrooms. The idea that the campus is too liberal or too conservative, Greek, and party centered was expressed by several in this group. Some of the alternative students said that most students do not have values similar to their own. Most of the alternative students felt separated from the majority of students on the campus. The idea that other students are generally "immature," "stuck up," "superficial,"and "rude" came up in some of the interviews. What was not a central concern among these students was any indication that they want to do anything to change the generalized college student culture or the institutional arrangements of the university. They want to use the university for their own purposes and to be detached as much as possible from participation in aspects of the generalized culture that they find distasteful. The reasons these students are uncomfortable with the generalized culture vary, but they are consistently focused on identity work and activities that are more detached from the campus culture.

> Alternative/Careerist: "My first semester here I hated it because I didn't know hardly anybody. I knew the guy I was dating and that was about it. Then I met Caroline at church. I had met her a couple of years earlier at church camp, but we had lost contact. But then, once I started hanging out with more people at church it got better." (Mary, sophomore, education major)

Mary, an education major, says her plan is to get married and to approach her career as being secondary to the needs of her family. Her experience in college has been shaped significantly by her participation in a church in Midwest City. Many students report that their participation in religious student organizations, which number over forty at Midwest University, and in church is central for them. But in Mary's case, and in the case of two of the other students, the centrality of the church was such that it was the center of their lives while in college, and it gave them the support they needed to stay in school. She says she was raised in a sheltered Christian environment, and that her early experiences in the residence hall were shocking for her because so many students were experimenting with sex, drugs, and alcohol. Still, she believes this exposure to the real world was beneficial for her. But she did not build close friendships with students who did not share her values, instead learning to get along with everyone but building close friendships with those who held similar beliefs and values. Though Mary lived in the same residence hall Bob lived in during freshman year, the experiences she is having as a student are very different from his. She says she never goes to bars and socializes primarily with people she met at church.

> I plan to get married. I want to teach kindergarten. I'd like to take time off when I have kids and maybe, I know there's a lady at the day care that I work at back home who taught kindergarten for six years and then she had her kids and now she works at the day care part time and she's like the specialist, so she'll do music time and art and whatever like during their special times. So she's only there half a day, and her kids can go there for free while she's there. So I thought that was a neat idea, 'cause I don't know if I'd actually want to open up my center.

Mary focuses on relating to faculty in the classroom setting. She says the following:

> Most of my teachers in the field where I am now in the program, they're more of your guide than a strict teacher. Several of my professors want you to call them by their first name, so it's really a relaxed setting. I don't know if some of them realize that we have other stuff going on, though, it's hard to get done everything that they want us to do. Right now I'm in an art class for elementary teachers and that's a lot of fun. She's [the teacher is] really nice and wants us to just focus on the process rather than the product. I haven't really decided how she's going to grade us on any of this, but I mean, it's a really laid-back class.
> Infants and toddlers, last semester, the teacher was off the wall! It was her first year of teaching, which I can understand all of that. The first day she brought in our syllabus and she called it a syllabook. It was like twenty-five pages long. And just some of the things she expected us to do I think were a little out there, and she just lacked organization. Like on the syllabus it said she'd be talking about one thing and she'd be talking about a completely different thing. She'd talk about the same thing that she talked about last week, so none of us liked that class. And sometimes I'm kind of shy, I don't always speak up unless more so in my education classes, because I know

those people, there's like twenty-four of us, and we're all in the same classes, so that makes it easier. But like in my education class right now it's like people I don't know as well and it's a little bit bigger so I don't usually speak up as much.

Mary, like many students, values predictability and good organization of a class and is critical of faculty perceived to be disorganized. Smaller classes made up of peers they know also are preferred by most students who have the opportunity to experience them. For Mary, like many of her peers, the peer relationships within the class are very important to students' comfort in class and willingness to participate as active learners. But even in small classes Mary has not made close friends. Her close friends in college are made at church.

Most of my friends I met at church here, that I usually hang out with, and they're mostly from Midwest state, but they are from different parts, like southern Midwest, so there's a little difference. My first semester here I hated it because I didn't know hardly anybody. I knew the guy I was dating, and that was about it. Then I met Caroline at church. I had met her a couple of years earlier at church camp, but we had lost contact. But then, once I started hanging out with more people at church, it got better. I have dated a few boys in my church. I'm very involved in the church activities. I don't work. I live with Caroline. We usually have people over every weekend, and we'll either play games, watch movies, or we'll go out to a movie, go out to eat, go ice skating, go shopping. We've been in here (an apartment off campus) for two years. I hated living in the dorm, so living off campus makes a lot of sense. I've dated some, but most of them have been people from my church, because there's not a whole lot of males in my field. We had one guy in our classes last semester, and he was like boring. So I know a lot of people, I guess meet people at clubs, but I don't really go to those.

Mary says now that she has friends who share her values and beliefs and is progressing in her degree program, she is happier at Midwest University. She is not involved in collegiate activities, instead centering her social life off campus with like-minded people from her church.

Mary's parents are paying for most of her college education. She works summers, but during the school semesters her "work" is school. Mary is a first-generation college student and says she did not really know what to expect at Midwest. Part of her difficulty in adjustment was the shock she says she experienced upon entering the college student culture in the residence halls. Her retreat from that culture into a network of friends from church is what saved her from deciding to leave Midwest. Yet she notes with pride that she did survive the exposure to the real world and managed to get along with people whose values she questions deeply. Mary is not critical of the institutional structure of Midwest or of the faculty. She focuses her criticism on other students and the generalized college student culture.

Rodney was critical of other students and faculty. He described the culture of the campus as distasteful and said that he preferred not to socialize with other students or faculty on the campus. He is in the marines and spent most of his time with his wife and a few close friends in the region whom he knows through other activities. He described his dislike for the liberals, those who, he believes, dominate the campus, and their behavior irritates him. He says he is a redneck and a conservative and only goes to campus when he has to because he does not like the atmosphere. He also voiced a strong dislike for the group work he was required to do in some of his classes that brought him into contact with other students whose views he did not like. He said that they lacked focus and a work ethic. He said that he went to college because it was paid for by the marines. He earned a degree in education and plans to return near his home to teach after he leaves the marines.

ALTERNATIVE/CREDENTIALIST

Sarah and Ed are concerned about the impacts of industrialized agriculture. Ed's concerns are centered on the environmental and health consequences, while Sarah is focused on the impact on small farmers. Sarah's parents are European immigrants who have a small farm and are struggling, as are many relatively small farmers in the Midwest. She says she would have liked to return to the family farm but that it cannot support her along with her parents. While in college, Ed, who is from a suburb of a large city in the state, was concerned about the environmental and health issues related to the food system. He worked on a local organic vegetable farm and for a small goat-cheese producer. He designed for himself an individualized study abroad program to Japan in order to learn about how organic farming is practiced there. Ed wants to be an organic farmer. Both he and Sarah managed to craft programs of study through an interdisciplinary major option to focus on their interests and concerns. Ed felt the campus was a fairly conservative environment, and that he had little in common with most of the undergraduates he encountered. Sarah enjoyed college sports and hanging out with college friends but spent much of her time in college working with the National Farmer's Union and lobbying for legislation and practices in the state aimed at helping small farmers. After graduation, Sarah went to work for a nongovernment organization dealing with the issues of small farmers. After graduation, Ed continued working on organic farms. The last time I heard from him he was working on an organic farm in the northwestern United States.

ACADEMIC

Only two women and two men expressed ideas and behaviors most consistent with the academic culture ideal-type orientation. The women have parent(s) who went to college, are white, and have alternative secondary orientations. Karla is a nontraditional student who worked full time to put herself through college, graduating in 2004. She lived off campus with her grandmother while in college. She said that she made no close friends there. She said she loved learning but was disappointed in the lack of rigor or challenge the classes at Midwest provided.

Genevieve, the second woman with a strong academic orientation, came from the suburbs of one of the large cities in the state but decided to major in animal science. She was fascinated by a wide range of disciplines and enthusiastically explored diverse topics. She said she relates better to faculty than to other students she finds immature. She maintained a strong relationship with her single mother and brother and had a strong sense of herself as "different" from the average student on campus. Her plans were not focused on a career but on adventure and a lifetime of exploring, learning, and trying new things. She said her high school years had been boring, and that college is exciting because, "College is different! I can explore all kinds of different things that interest me." She wore long, flowing skirts amid a throng of blue jeans and T-shirts.

The two men who gravitated toward the academic ideal type, Kevin and Jared, were both first-generation college students raised by single mothers. Both wanted to go on to graduate school and become college professors, gravitating secondarily toward careers. They came to college uncertain about exactly what they wanted to do and discovered their career of choice through what they found intellectually compelling. Jared majored in history, while Kevin majored in interdisciplinary studies, with a particular focus on sociology and religious studies. He wanted to study the sociology of religion in graduate school. These two men identified with faculty and tried to build relationships with them with varying degrees of success. They expected lives that engaged them in research and teaching and wanted to interact with faculty both intellectually and as mentors.

The two women with strong academic cultural orientations are PGC and bring relatively high levels of cultural and economic capital to college. These women do not identify as strongly with faculty as role models as do the FGC men, nor do they envision themselves becoming academics. Interestingly, the women who orient academically either as a primary or secondary orientation are each in some way free of the types of parental pressures that other middle- and upper-middle-class white women described in which economic dependence and patriarchal family expectations intersect to pressure them toward other cultural orientations. For instance, Karla is older than the typical college student, has not been economically dependent on her parents for a number of years, and was home schooled. She is supporting herself through college and has a secure job already, so she is not motivated by a desire to get a degree aimed at being able to get a job. As a lesbian who has come out, despite her parents' initial discomfort, she also freed herself in some ways from pressures of the dominant collegiate student culture for women to spend a large amount of time on their appearance and dating and romance central to some college women (Holland and Eisenhart 1990).

Genevieve, the other woman with a primary academic cultural orientation, is of college age but has other characteristics that play a role in orienting her this way. She, like the two men, came from a single-parent home. She reported none of the pressure from her mother that women from two-parent households tended to describe. She and her mother are very close. Her mother and brother encouraged her intellectual and experiential exploration, and her alternative orientation and the friends she had from high school and cultivated in college were like-minded people. She had a boyfriend from high school but she said that she does not envision herself having a traditional career future or marrying, emphasizing her freedom to pursue her intellectual interests.

The academically oriented men, on the other hand, are both from working-class backgrounds. Like the women, they are white. Jared was an older student, and one was of the traditional college age. The thirty-three-year-old man had worked as a manager of a restaurant at a large hotel in San Francisco prior to coming to college. He had quit school at an early age to help his single mother raise his siblings and then to work. More recently he had experienced a painful divorce following the tragic death of one of his children. He had come out as nonheterosexual around the same time and moved to Midwest State, where he had family. His sister, who had recently divorced, moved to Midwest City, with her two children to live with him. He moved out of the residence hall after freshman year to live in subsidized housing with them to help out with child care and finances. While living in the residence hall he made friends, and because he was older than most of the students, he assumed the role of confidant and advisor. He continued to be close to several of the students from his residence floor during the time he remained in college. He felt he had to downplay his intellectual interest and reduce his engagement in class content just to get along with the other students who insisted on setting a lower standard for learning the material than he wanted. His interactions with an instructor in the required English composition course freshman year almost made him drop out. He described being devastated by the instructor telling him he had to leave the class, because the instructor felt he could not teach him how to write.

He interpreted this as a commentary on the hopelessness of his ability to perform as a college student. In fact, his description of his questions and strong insistence that the teacher explain things clearly suggested that he simply made the instructor feel threatened. With the support of his much-younger peers in the residence halls, he persisted and took the English composition class with someone else the next semester and received a good grade in the course and in the many other writing assignments he completed during his brief college career.

Kevin, the other academically oriented, traditional, college-age man, is the son of a single mother who had moved to Midwest City in order to make going to Midwest University doable for him. She was very supportive of him and encouraged his intellectual interests. He had a girlfriend throughout college whom he met freshman year but was critical of other students in general, maintaining that they had no interest in learning and were wasting their time in college. He spent most of his time outside of class reading widely. Though he had been able to develop good relationships with some faculty, he said one faculty member he wanted to talk with about intellectual matters beyond the course material told him not to return to his office unless he wanted to discuss class-related material. This made him angry, and he expressed frustration that some faculty did not want to take the time to talk with him about his interests.

The strong academic orientations of Karla and Genevieve are supported by factors that offset the influences of parental interference associated with helicopter parenting and acceptance of the values of the shared college student culture, combined with relatively high levels of cultural capital and economic means. The strongly academic orientations of Kevin and Jared, who are from relatively less privileged circumstances in terms of cultural capital and economic means, are encouraged by strong parental support, especially from their mothers, and by the opportunities in academia of which attending college has made them aware. Of the six men with primary or secondary orientations that are academic, four were first-generation college students and three came from single-parent, female-headed households.

The men in this group have secondary orientations of careerism, that is, their academic orientation leads them to plan for careers as faculty or professions that depend upon scholarly knowledge as a base. Neither of the women at this point is strongly committed to careers related to their academic interests.

The job market reward structure, parental desires for children to choose undergraduate majors that give them a secure professional career path, and the fact that academically oriented students may go to places other than Midwest are factors that may contribute to the low numbers of college students in the sample that gravitate toward the academic culture as the primary energy focus.

CONCLUSIONS

Tracing the patterned variations in the ideas and behaviors that students in the sample emphasize and creating a typology of college student cultural orientations drawn from what students highlight in their daily lives in college reveal a much more complex and varied college student culture than is observed when focusing on the generalized culture. While the cultural orientation, identified by Moffatt (1989) as all pervasive in the Rutgers dorms of the 1980s, is recognized and described by most students as part of the dominant shared culture at Midwest, especially when focused on describing the freshman experience and life in the residence halls, it is far from all pervasive in the daily lives of most students at Midwest. Actually the fun-focused college student-centered culture of partying, drinking, and sex appears to be one most strongly invested in by males (thirteen of the twenty-nine interviewed) and a few females (five of the thirty-one interviewed) who gravitate to the collegiate/credentialist and credentialist/collegiate cultural orientations at Midwest University. The culture in which they participate is recognized as central in the generalized college student culture by most students, but most do not really say that, for themselves, college is primarily about having fun, partying, attending football and basketball games, or casual sex, nor do they spend most of their time and energy on those activities.

Moffatt notes a value for college fun linked to sexuality, drinking, entertainment, and being away from parental control (Moffatt 1989, 30). While this is not completely inconsistent with the somewhat fluid shared college student culture described by students, it gives salience to themes that are strongly slanted to the male dorm culture and fraternity and sorority life carried mostly by those who gravitate to the collegiate culture, with the strongest linkage being for those with a secondary orientation that is credentialist. Credentialist/collegiates also carry this culture, though less strongly than those steeped in the collegiate culture. Two of the men who are collegiate/credentialist did not gravitate strongly to the hedonistic aspects of the collegiate tradition, instead emphasizing sports and student government involvement that they associated with it. Of the four women who are credentialist/collegiate, only one embraces the hedonistic aspects of collegiate fun. The three who choose not to participate in hedonistic fun all say that they enjoy college sports tremendously—two are involved in college athletics but say they do not like heavy drinking and have no interest in casual hookups, and the third woman is engaged and shares her fiancé's enthusiasm for college sports and enjoys going out with him and their friends but frowns on heavy drinking, drug use, and casual sex. The one woman who is collegiate/credentialist enjoys sorority activities and the hedonistic side of college life. Fifteen students, thirteen men and two women, identify strongly with the hedonistic, fun-loving collegiate culture. They are all collegiate/credentialist or credentialist/collegiate culture participants. Of the thirteen men, three are deeply involved in video gaming and leisure activities that use up as much or more time than their traditional hedonistic college fun.

Careerist/collegiates and collegiate/careerists carry a weaker, less hedonistically oriented form of collegiate culture tempered by their strong emphasis on career goals that leads them to focus on aspects of collegiate culture that are beneficial to their career aspirations, such as working in student government, taking on big responsibilities in the Greek system, and doing substantial amounts of volunteer work. These students identified strongly with college life through the Greek system and the connections it has to the university institutionally, and to college sports. The four women and one man who are collegiate/careerist in orientation are all in professional programs that are demanding, and each emphasizes that the responsibilities each has assumed as a collegiate will look good on resumes, which are fulfilling and important to personal development rather than hedonistic fun. The five women and three men who are careerist/collegiates emphasize career goals as being very central and having college fun going to parties, football games, and bars as a part of college life they value but do not spend nearly as much time on as they do their studies and other career development opportunities. If the strong participants in hedonistic collegiate culture, the two collegiate/credentialist men who are focused on the institutionally framed collegiate activities, and the three women who enjoy sports but are not actively involved in the party scene, are added to the fourteen who identify weakly with the hedonistic aspects of the culture, the careerist/collegiates or collegiate/careerists, then thirty-four students, over half of the sample, hold collegiate cultural orientations to varying degrees. This helps to explain why most students think collegiate culture is the dominant one at Midwest, when the actual heavy and consistent involvement in the hedonistic aspects of collegiate culture involves about 25 percent of the undergraduate population in the sample.

Though all of the sorority women in the sample had some degree of collegiate orientation, most of the women in sororities were involved in careerist/collegiate or collegiate/careerist college student culture paths and used the collegiate cultural orientation as a support structure that provided them with a network of friends, nice living facilities, study rooms, computers, parking, prepared meals, and opportunities to assume responsibilities assigned by peers, and to prove themselves as competent organizers and planners. They participated in parties and went to bars, but this was not the central focus of their collegiate cultural orientation, as was the case for many of the men. One sorority woman even remarked, "I go out and date when it's required, but I'd never have a serious relationship with any of the men I meet through those activities, because the basis for dating them is superficial. As soon as I can leave [the organized events] I go home and wash my hair and study."

Most women and racial and ethnic minorities as well as nonheterosexuals in the sample prefer to spend their time in other cultural spaces where the culture does not subordinate and marginalize them. Women and racial and ethnic minority students, once admitted to the university, are treated with relatively high levels of respect and given equal opportunity to achieve within the formal institutional framework at Midwest, in comparison to the subordinated, ascribed statuses they are given within popular-culture depictions of college student life that students link with the generalized college student culture, described in chapter 3.

This is not to say that racial and ethnic minorities and women, as well as first-generation students, would not benefit from more and better institutional support at Midwest, but that their opportunity to achieve is better within the bureaucratically structured, fairly egalitarian academic and professional programs of the university than in the dominant college student culture as depicted in contemporary movies and described by students. With this in mind, it is not surprising that most women and minorities in the sample do not gravitate to collegiate/credentialist or credentialist/collegiate cultural paths, but instead primarily to careerism, where they quickly learn that their use of time and energy allows them to compete successfully with others in their classes for an achieved status as capable students with good professional careers ahead of them. This arena also links significantly to their friendship network development, providing the opportunity to link being a good friend to being a competent, dependable peer in classes. This preference in cultural orientation is not surprising in light of parental pressures, as described in chapter 2, combined with career goals and an equally significantly sense of relative ascribed subordination just beneath the surface of the generalized college student culture, drawing on historic collegiate student-culture and popular-culture images for its content. Women, minorities, and the few men in the sample who have careerist/ collegiate orientations and are in sororities and fraternities use the collegiate student culture in quite a different way than do the students who are collegiate/credentialist, drawing from it for structure, recognition, and experiences in organizing, planning, and volunteering that are fulfilling, allowing them to increase their skills, and looking good on their resumes.

It also becomes apparent why collegiate and credentialist orientations attract more white males in the sample, especially those from middle- and upper-middle-class families. In the settings where careerist and academically orientated students focus their energies they have to compete as equals to gain status as promising professionals and academic achievers. They often prefer to spend their time in settings where their ascribed characteristics provide them with a comfortable sense of social worth that requires less of them academically and allows them to work on finding their place in the social pecking order of their similarly located peers, with whom they choose to network in college in anticipation that they will be significant to them in later life. Young men doing masculine identity work also look to male peers to help them become "men," as Todd said his fraternity brothers had done for him. Sports, parties, bar hopping, romantic involvements, and hanging out with buddies are the venues for doing the identity work in which these men are most centrally engaged. The statuses they bring with them into college, and the relative privileges they associate with it, are ones they feel fairly secure in taking with them when they leave.

White (PGC) men and FGC men from relatively affluent families were more likely to choose collegiate and credentialist cultural paths in college and to emphasize the importance of having fun by partying, going out, and attending sports events than other groups. These men, as a group, are likely to be less invested in and engaged in academics. The emphasis in identity work is on becoming men through peer interactions in the settings that their orientation toward collegiate fun privileges.

PGC women in the sample are more likely to emphasize their struggle to gain autonomy from family relations that are felt as oppressive particularly when they are combined with financial dependency and to try to use preparing for professional careers in college and seeking marriage partners as methods for gaining autonomy.

Racial and ethnic minority students in the sample tend to take college seriously, and to seek careerist paths, especially when they have financial need. Racial and ethnic minorities tend to strive to enter professions and build lifestyles that are upwardly mobile while holding onto family ties that are important to them.

First-generation college student women and men in the sample tend either to be strongly careerist and academic in orientation or to opt for a credentialist approach. Male first-generation students with low parental financial investment tend to be the most academically and career motivated, while men with higher levels of parental financial investment, whose parents more frequently graduated from college, are drawn toward a credentialist approach while emphasizing college fun rather than career future.

Shifts in the relative levels of difference in cultural capital and skills gained by students in college, derived from their college student cultural orientations toward the ways they choose to spend their time, and the friends they make, do occur, and it was the white, upper-middle-class and middle-class men who opted for collegiate/credentialist and credentialist/collegiate paths who fared the worst overall in making gains in their sense of what they want to do in life and more concretely in the job market (Côté 2002).

In one way the college student cultural orientations of students can be viewed as responses to the pressures of late modernity, risk, the radical destabilization of modern economic and social relations, and the individualistic ideology and consumer, choice-based framing of their lives as college students in late modernity (Giddens 1991; Bauman

2001; Beck and Beck-Gernsheim [2001] 2002). Responses vary in somewhat patterned ways based on their relative positions at the intersections of class, race and ethnicity, and gender stratification but are also shaped by how they make meaning of individualism and the blueprints of individualism that they employ in mapping a life trajectory project while in college. Choices that they make about how to spend their time and use their energy while in college are very important, and they are influenced by the blueprints of individualism that students embrace.

Chapter 5 outlines a typology of blueprints of individualism that students gravitate to, integrating them into a framework for understanding what the generalized college student culture and the different patterns of college student cultural orientations at Midwest tell us more generally about our culture.

5

BLUEPRINTS OF INDIVIDUALISM AND LIFE TRAJECTORIES IN LATE MODERNITY

"A twenty-two-year-old kid does not need to know what they're going to do. That's later!" (Beth, senior)

Students at Midwest State University talk about being in college to prepare for professional careers, earn college degrees, and have college fun with peers. They continue the developmental path laid out for them as people whose parents attended college, or break new ground as first-generation college students in twenty-first-century America. They seek to escape their parents' homes, or find that they must move beyond them, learn how to stand on their own two feet and take care of themselves, build relationships on their own, and balance work and play as independent adults. How students approach this project is based on the blueprints of individualism that guide them, and the blueprints they adopt are connected to their life experiences.

This chapter describes the three primary blueprints of individualism found among Midwest students and integrates them into a framework for understanding what college student culture at Midwest tells us about the culture of the contemporary United States. The ideal types are best viewed as existing on a continuum rather than being rigid, ideological models that students neatly adopt. In one way the experiences of contemporary students at Midwest can be viewed as part of an "individualization" (Côté 2002) process in late modernity. The ways students respond to the challenges of college life are "strategic" (117) responses to the culture and economy of later modernity that "make it necessary for people to undertake the process of individualization in the transition to, and through, adulthood" (117). In describing American culture Bellah and colleagues (1985) note that in a culture that emphasizes the autonomy and self-reliance of the individual, the primary problems of childhood are what some psychoanalysts call separation and individuation—indeed, childhood is chiefly preparation for the all-important event of leaving home. Though the issues of separation, individuation, and leaving home come to a head in late adolescence, they are recurrent themes in the lives of Americans, and few if any of us ever leave them entirely behind. . . . While it sometimes appears to be a pitched battle only the heroic or rebellious wage against the parental order, more often the drive to get out in the world on your own is part of the self-conception Americans teach their children. (56–57)

They conclude, "However painful the process of leaving home, for parents and for children, the really frightening thing for both would be the prospect of the child never leaving home" (58).

The problems of life on which college students are most focused are those associated with becoming successful individuals. For most of the students at Midwest, the process of individualization involves at least starting to find their way in life beyond their parental home. As we have seen, this involves changing relationships with parents, learning the college student culture of Midwest, and engaging in practices aimed at developing and presenting a self that appears to be independent and competent to deal with the demands of college life. This entails engaging in preparing in one way or another for the future beyond college. Many students speak of this future as "real life." Students entering the culture of Midwest learn to focus on making the choices from the available options such as choosing which courses to take, which student housing to live in, which organizations to join, which friends to make, what to major in, and how to spend their time. Over the course of college, even for those who are ambivalent about these choices, an adult life trajectory begins.

Three ideal-type primary blueprints of individualism emerged as central in guiding students on this path: (1) an independent individualist blueprint that relies on images of the autonomous self as the central locus of fulfillment and meaning in which institutional and interpersonal connections are viewed primarily as serving the individual's needs and goals with identity centered in the desires and tastes of the individual who chooses affiliations of all sorts to fulfill those desires and tastes. These are viewed as changing over time, with the individual changing affiliations to meet the needs of the self; (2) a traditional individualist blueprint that relies on traditional role fulfillment in the institutions of family, marriage, work, church, and community as the basis for adult identity and meaning. These connections are viewed as somewhat fixed and unchanging; and (3) an interdependent individualist blueprint that relies on relational self-development for fulfillment and constructs identity self-consciously in interaction with others in all different types of settings with a sense of ongoing change, negotiation, and communication expected. The self is viewed as being responsible for working to maintain interdependent relationships over time and to change and adapt to new circumstances in concert with others. Fulfillment and meaning come from being able to sustain a stable identity and ongoing sets of relations in multiple contexts and to relate to others so all needs are met as circumstances change. Appendix 5 includes two tables and descriptions of them. The first, Table 5.1, shows ideal-type blueprint orientations of students by college student cultural orientation, gender, and race and ethnicity. Table 5.2 details blueprint orientations by gender and parental levels of education.

FULFILLMENT THROUGH AN INDEPENDENT INDIVIDUALIST LIFE TRAJECTORY PROJECT

It's [College is] how I get thrown out into the real world in a sense, you know. You don't have a job and your parents are still kind of supporting you or at least mine are but you're on your own and you definitely learn. . . . I tell them [my parents] that I'm having a good time down here, and I'm glad that they sent me, but if I was completely honest with them, I don't think that their however many thousand of dollars a year worth that they're paying to send me here [is worth it]. I could easily be paying a tenth of that price going to a community college learning the exact same amount of material. I almost feel bad continuing to go here, because of the fact that it's so expensive, and I guess I've been a little disappointed in the university as far as education programs and the professors.

[What do I want to do?] I wish I knew. I'm completely unsure of what I'm going to do career wise or, you know, what my future is going to be. I really don't know. I think if I could pick my little dream job I'd want to work on a ski and rescue team, maybe in Winter Park or out in Yosemite. . . . But I'm getting a degree in business from down here with [an] emphasis on finance and real estate, so maybe I'll be working for some investment company. Hopefully not some big company where

I'm never really going to make a lot of progress. I'm going to get into the world of business, which I find incredibly dull. I'm going to do it for the money. That sounds bad, but there's a lot of things that I want to do in my future, a lot of traveling that I want to do. I want to have my nice pair of skis. I want to have whatever, a ten thousand dollar boat so I can play on the lake, stuff like that. Money isn't everything to me as far as my future goes, but I am going to need a lot of money to live the life that I want to live and [to afford] all the toys that I want and stuff like that. So yeah, I don't know what the future holds. (Bob, senior business major)

Many Midwest students, both women and men, emphasize the private sphere as the location and source of real satisfaction in life, embracing self-responsibility to find fulfillment through intimate relationships and activities that the individual finds fulfilling. Over half (53.3 percent) of the students in the sample (fifteen women and seventeen men) (two FGC females, two FGC males, thirteen PGC females, and fifteen PGC males) gravitate to independent individualist conceptions of identity work and life trajectory. The seventeen men in this group represent 58.6 percent of the men in the sample, and the sixteen women represent 51.6 percent of the women. Most come from two-parent, college-educated, middle- and upper-middle-class families. Four of the racial and ethnic minority students (one multiethnic woman, one Asian American woman, one black woman, and one Hispanic man) and twenty-eight white students (twelve women and sixteen men) expressed ideas and described behaviors consistent with independent individualism.

Students adopting this approach to identity work and life trajectory often viewed private life as central and focused on leisure activities and consumption for fulfillment. Some also mentioned hoping that work will provide more than just income, but most did not imagine that work would be a major source of fulfillment in life. The ideas that Bob expresses are consistent with this approach. He chose to go into accounting, even though he found it boring, because he believed it would afford him a good income so he can enjoy his private life and the travel, skiing, and other consumerism to which he looks forward. His activities and goals are aimed almost exclusively at self-fulfillment in the private sphere, with no expectation of finding meaning beyond income in the public sphere. Bob suggests that he wishes it were different. He wishes he could combine helping others by being on the ski rescue team with the self-fulfillment he believes he would gain from skiing all day and going out at night with the guys as a ski rescue team member. He does emphasize the pleasure he would get from doing this over the satisfaction he would get from saving people, but he mentions it.

Bob, who described in rich detail the consumer lifestyle he plans on having, the boat, the vacation home, the travel, skiing, and golf, his strong connection to his parents, his desire to locate near them in the long term, and his desire to have the same sort of lifestyle they have, but not to work as hard as they have, is typical of the students whose views of self and fulfillment are strongly centered in the private sphere. Many in this group describe relationships and activities in terms of what they stand to gain from them. His ambivalence about work and career and the fact that he has chosen a career path in a field he says is "boring," but that he believes will be lucrative, are indicative that his identity work as a college student and his visions of the self he is developing are linked more closely to consumption than production. His involvement in a fraternity where he made friends and connections provided a network of similar others where he found his sense of belonging while in college. Bob's identity work privileges his private life, a connection to family as a support for the fulfillment of his needs, and the status associated with it, and consumerism and leisure pursuits for fulfillment, and it is largely detached from paid employment except as a means to gaining income to enable the pursuit of meaning and fulfillment in private pleasures.

FULFILLMENT THROUGH A TRADITIONALIST LIFE TRAJECTORY PROJECT

[Campus culture] is about as far away from religious, right-wing conservative good people as it can possibly be . . . it's very different from what I grew up in, I would have to call it very secular and self-centered. I wouldn't say that everybody's bad. But like, just the climate and the goals that people have are just, gosh, I mean they're just totally, "it's all about me," type of thing, if that makes any sense. I mean really it just seems like monkeys climbing up a tree trying to push down other monkeys and get to the top. It really is. I mean, students, all they want is the grades so they're going to, like, try to beat down everybody else. Faculty, all they want is the next thing up, you know, the next big research grant, so they're trying to bash everybody else down and get themselves up. It's very competitive. . . . I avoid campus as much as humanly possible. . . .

I mean most kids my age I realize have no clue what's going on in the world, but we're going to have to pay for that, you know. And I mean it shouldn't be. Like, for instance, my grandparents get sick, we don't ship them to a nursing home. You take care of them. If they couldn't afford their medicines, it's the family's job to make sure they're taken care of and get what they need. I mean Daryl's grandmother is really sick and has been for years, for years she's been sick, and so they've done all they can to keep her out of the nursing home. One daughter makes sure they get to all their doctor's appointments, drives them there. [Another daughter] takes care of getting a lot of their medicine. One daughter-in-law is a nurse, takes care of that. One daughter comes every weekend, cleans their house, takes care of her. I mean, that's how it's supposed to be, but that's not how it works anymore and that's sad and it's going to be a problem. . . .

The majority of people today don't go to church. They aren't Christians. I personally think it's a problem. And it's not getting better. I think the lack of religious upbringing and morals is contributing to drugs in teenagers, alcoholism. I'm not saying it never happens within a child that's been brought up in church, but it's less likely.

I'm going to go to medical school in the fall. Four years there and then I'm going to take a family practice residency and that's three years. And then after that I might do a one-year fellowship in OB-GYN and get board certified in that also. And then after that I want my own little practice where I am boss and I do not have to listen to anybody else. So that's what I want to do with that. I want to have a farm, small farm with cattle to piddle with and eat. And let's see here, I'm getting married in sixteen months. And so then I'll have Daryl all to myself and we are not having any children until I am out of medical school and residency because that's so not happening and, then we're hoping to have kids. I think we've settled on four. So [we will] probably [have] four [children]. He says four boys; I say half and half. (Kathy, senior biology major, graduated in 2004 and is now nearing completion of medical school)

Thirty percent (eight women and ten men) (four FGC male, five FGC female, six PGC male, three PGC female) of the sample of the students at Midwest draw their coming-of-age identity work primarily from a set of traditional ways of defining their belonging and community that may include fulfilling traditional gender roles, the religion and church affiliation in which they were raised, and career aspirations and educational preparation aimed at professional careers linked to traditional conceptions of occupational status and upward mobility. Five of the racial and ethnic minority students (two black men, one Asian American man, one black woman, and one black African woman) and fourteen white students (six women and seven men) adopt a traditionalist blueprint of individualism. These students describe the roles they will assume as a set of responsibilities and obligations that will bring satisfaction and belonging. This blueprint aims at constructing a predictable and stable life trajectory based on traditional historical patterns linked to family, church, community, and work that to one degree or another rely on ascribed identity characteristics, boundary setting with outsiders, and scripted expectations for the life course. While most students say they want to marry and have children, it is the traditionalist in orientation who highlights the responsibilities of family life, while the independent individualist highlights the pleasures and emotional support family will provide. A little over half of the FGC students orient toward identity work that aligns primarily with traditional roles for achieving adult identity.

Kathy adopts a traditional blueprint of individualism in constructing her life trajectory plan. Her identity and life trajectory plan are embedded in traditional institutional forms. Family ties and church membership in the small-town community in which she grew up and the relationships she has and roles she fulfills in these institutions were central for her throughout college, and she anticipates they will continue to be throughout her life. She plans to live and work in her hometown after completing her education and to make a good living and a meaningful contribution to her community through her work as a much-needed doctor.

Her relationships are, in part, tied to clearly defined role expectations linked to the patriarchal nuclear family form, traditional gender roles, and a worldview in keeping with the *"Gemeinschaft"* community (Tönnies [1887] 2002). But she leverages her relative advantage in strong support from her family for her to be a doctor and the anticipated labor market and status advantage her profession will provide making clear that she will not be pressured to have children earlier than she wants or to value having sons over daughters. She adopts an assertive stance to her life trajectory, saying that she wants to be her "own boss" and to fulfill a much-needed role in her home community which, like many rural communities in the United States, is underserved in medical care. Similar patterns of meaning making are noted by Edgell in *Religion and Family in a Changing Society* (2006). Work, as in the case of Kathy, is often viewed as both a way to provide for family and as a calling (Weber [1904] 1958) that will serve the collective. Most students are not as explicit as Kathy is about their intention of helping their community through the education they get and the work they will do, but many mention hoping their work will not only be fulfilling but will "make a difference" or "help others."

Some women who choose a gender-traditional life trajectory view college as an enhancement to their ability to be good wives and mothers, mentioning that a college education will make them better able to help their children with homework, or that having a college education will enable them to get a better job to help support their family. Men who choose a gender-traditional life trajectory do not describe themselves as planning to be primary breadwinners, instead focusing on wanting to have a happy family and on being able to give their children the same benefits their parents gave them.

The accounts of those aligned with the independent blueprint are consistent with Bellah and colleagues (1985) thesis that modern Americans view themselves as autonomous individuals who are able to choose the roles they embrace and the commitments they make based on their "life effectiveness as the individual judges it" (47). Turner (1976) maintained that in modernity people's conception of their real self is increasingly coming to be embedded in satisfying, noninstitutional impulses rather than in institutional roles. He noted that younger people in the United States were increasingly defining themselves through noninstitutional impulses, while those of previous times established a sense of self through acting out institutional roles. The traditional blueprint followed by Kathy is fairly consistent with Turner's description of the "institutional self" in terms of the way identity is grounded. And Bob's emphasis on satisfaction to come from consumption and leisure time activity can be linked to the "impulsive self" identified by Turner. But the third blueprint of individualism found among students is quite different from either of these two models of self-definition.

FULFILLMENT THROUGH AN INTERDEPENDENT INDIVIDUALIST LIFE TRAJECTORY PROJECT

Q: Why did you join the Peace Corps?
A: I don't know.

Before I left the States my reasoning included such profound statements as "because I'm done with school," or "because I like to travel," and "why not?" If I felt like getting into a deeper conversation on the matter I maybe added "because I've wanted to go to Africa for a long time to work with AIDS." My vague responses to others were a result of a lack of assuredness myself.

Internally I dreamed of living abroad. I was excited for another chance to practice French and the opportunity to learn a local language practiced by a culture thousands of years in the making. I wanted to give my knowledge and experiences to people whom I already knew had more to offer me than the other way around. But still, I wanted to help.

In all honesty, the first month was hard. I cried on a fairly regular basis. I became a devout journal writer, and I went through Internet/phone/contact with loved ones withdrawal. And while family and friends assure me I can come home at any time and have nothing to prove, I feel this urge to push my own boundaries and stretch my own limit. I have something to prove to myself.

And Togo grows on you quite literally sometimes. Mail every 12–16 days is the most action I get now. I'm pretty sure I've found the right combination of foods to stay "solid," and communication barriers are dropping like flies (although the saying doesn't really mean much in Africa, where flies seem to multiply by the second). My friend and fellow PCT Amy said it best when she said, "I have no clue what I'm doing here most of the time, but I wake up every day and find a reason just for that day." And that's how life is here and for the next 25 and a half months I'm okay with that. . . for today anyway (:. (Whitney, journalism major, graduated 2004—blog entry while in Peace Corps in Togo)

[Moving to the city in the Northwest] was a complete turn-around for me. One, I went from all-black surroundings with family in Mississippi to a predominately white suburb with no family around except my mom, who worked every day. I was scared. But the fact that I was the only black girl in my class (except one other girl who hung out with only the gothic crowd. I tried to be friends with her, but she wasn't feeling it.) I was deemed as the cool, in, exotic girl in the land of "Leave it to Beaver." The fact I was from someplace so remote from the Northwest liberal hills was another reason I think I made friends so easily. Portland and my friends showed me a side of life that was so foreign to me in the South. They emphasized health food, competition in school (you weren't cool unless you had pretty good grades), and the music from hip-hop to hard-rock alternative. Running into hippies came frequently, and I actually learned some things from the random discussions in the streets. Portland was also a place where it was common to go to the mountains and ski, well that could be because I was also in the richer area. In Natchez I lived on MLK street, I think that should say something. As I love Portland, I did have conflicts with the naïveness of the people there. Some of my friends were interested in my adventures in Natchez, but many people there stereotyped the South to the point where I would get offended. They made it out to be only evil, slavery, conservative. What they missed was the Sunday dinners and the wise women who could argue her way with any Northwest intellectual and their philosophy of life. The South has a different taste about them. People in the Northwest were too quick and busy to look at other's point of view before arguing their points. There were also few black people in Portland. I missed those inside jokes that some blacks are too scared (to be honest) to say to their black friend. (Talisha, journalism major, via e-mail, while she was studying abroad in Italy in 2006)

Jared lived for almost seven years in San Francisco, where he was the manager of the banquet department of a hotel. He came to Midwest with plans to become a veterinarian but quickly realized that he loved history and decided he wanted to become a history professor. His face saddens as he says:

I had a daughter who passed away. She was ten years old. That event in my life really made me sit back and take a look at myself. I decided then that wasn't what I wanted to do for a career for the rest of my life. All of my family's back in [Midwest State] so I decided to move back here to go to school.

Jared's face brightens, and he smiles as he says:

My parents and siblings, we're such a close family. They all live in [the same town]. Everybody is right in this little tight circle. My experience last year was so incredible! I've always been a very shy person and I didn't go to high school, but when I was in school I sat in the back of the classroom and nobody knew I was there and the teacher didn't call on me to ask questions because I wouldn't have answered them anyway. I ended up dropping out of school at the end of the eighth-grade year. My mom had just gotten divorced, and I had two younger brothers and a younger sister, and there was no way she could afford to work and pay for a babysitter and maintain the household, so I dropped out of school to take care of my siblings and got my GED and scored high enough on the GED to get accept[ed] in here. But I had no preparation for college at all. I completely and totally changed myself last year. I joined RHA (Residence Halls Association). I was in the prevet club. I was in the prevet FIG, and I was definitely papa hen on the floor last year. The girls when they had to go somewhere in the evenings, they came down to my room and got me and I walked them to wherever they went and then I walked back to pick them up so nobody would be walking alone in the dark. I was definitely papa hen last year. . . . I'm involved in the gay and lesbian group. That has been another big social change for me. The majority of the time I lived in San Francisco I was married and very insecure in myself. I've made some major life changes. Family has been really, really, really great! When I told my mom, she was like, "Um, yeah, I've known that since you were like twelve." I was like "hey" a little input would have been [helpful].

Coming out in college was very important in Jared's identity work and linked to his belief that he was changing himself by taking on new challenges, exploring new aspects of himself, new interests, and tapping into his authentic self and true capabilities. His view of himself was that he is a work in progress.

I go to the theater productions as much as I can. I'm in stage makeup class for next semester. So hopefully I can actually get involved in a production or something. That would be great. I'm more a theater, opera, kind of person and there's not really that much going on around here.

Though he viewed himself as playing the role of "father hen" in the residence hall and as taking an active part in student organizations, he did not identify with the collegiate student culture. His critique of the generalized college student culture centered on the waste of opportunity he believed it represented. He described it and the relational dynamics he believed the behavior was anchored in as follows.

I think the whole town is very party oriented, and that's kind of disappointing. As far as the residence halls, I think there's way too much emphasis on partying among the students than on studying and going [to] beneficial activities. From my personal observations . . . the more sheltered they were at home the more rules they had at home, the wilder they got once they got down here. I think it's really "my parents aren't around attitude." As far as our floor, it really, really slowed down after about the middle of first semester, because I think people actually saw what it was doing to their grades and decided "OK, I've really got to crack down." I'm going to make myself sound bad, but I think the female students here on campus are probably the rudest people I have ever come across. I mean they will flat walk right into you and be staring at you the whole time. They seem to be even ruder than the guys students [who are] loud, obnoxious, looking for the next party.

As far as professors, everybody has been so supportive and glad to see me here. I envision a pretty good future for myself. I'm extremely comfortable with the experiences that I've had in college so far. . . . I wish that I had that opportunity years back. [I've learned] that I can accomplish, [I've learned] my own abilities. That's been my biggest learning experience. Up until I came here last year I didn't know exactly what I was capable of. (Jared, history major)

A small number, eight women and two men (two FGC females, raised by single mothers/grandmothers; six PGC females, two of whom were raised by single mother's; and two FGC males, both from single-mother families), comprising just under 17 percent of students in the sample, emphasize interdependent, self-directed construction of relationships to provide them with a sense of belonging through connections they describe as their "community." They describe relationships that are fluid and differentiated in terms of their participation in them and the composition of the group that makes them up. The three people, Karla, Julie, and Jared, two women and one man, who indicated that they are nonheterosexual hold interdependent blueprints of individualism.

The responsibility for this form of community falls very heavily on the self-reflexive, autonomous individual and often requires, as Talisha pointed out, "a lot of work" to maintain. Rather than centering on consumerist leisure activities as the center for fulfillment, these students focus on interpersonal relations based primarily on intangible identity capital, particularly the capacity for self-expression and self-reflexivity. Those who orient toward high levels of interdependence with others as the basis for their self-fulfillment and self-development project describe relationships with others that resemble Cancian's ([1987] 1990) concepts of the "flexible self" and an "interdependent blueprint" for building relationships that are based on intimacy, support, trust, communication, and commitment within an assumed context of change and negotiation. Women, whose psychosocial development and socialization in contemporary America shape them to have a more interdependent relational style (Cancian [1987] 1990), adopt this approach in their individualization process in larger numbers than men.

Life trajectory plans for these students rely more heavily on images of ongoing self-development and development and maintenance of multiple types of relationships and connections, many of which are not organized through formal institutions but through individual choice. Commitments for these people are linked to self-fulfillment but are viewed as changing and open rather than fixed and dictated by traditional roles or institutions. Lines between self-interest and the common good and between public and private spheres are more open and blurred for these students.

> The self has become more and more self reflexive in the sense that the identity of the individual is constituted in increased "self-monitoring" and "self-control." It is a view of the individual as one who can shape his or her own life project. Ulrich Beck also advocates this view of individualism as "individualization" (Beck 1997, 1998; Beck and Beck-Gernsheim [2001] 2002). This does not mean simply freedom as an individual fate but as a social fate. It may also mean more anxiety and insecurities (Pahl 1995). Individuation is a product of the breakup of traditional roles and the organization of society around the individual who is becoming increasingly cut off from collective ties. . . . In this kind of society there is more and more choice and the individual is constantly having to make choices of all kinds. (Delanty 2003, 128)

Whitney, Talisha, and Jared engage in identity work consistent with interdependent individualism. Whitney, a white woman from an upper-middle-class family, came to Midwest State University from an adjoining state to study magazine journalism and pledged a sorority through which she made many of her closest friends. Talisha, who is black, also came to Midwest from out of state, but from farther away, from the

Deep South, with some time spent living in Portland, Oregon. She has struggled to make ends meet while in college. She too came to Midwest to study magazine journalism. Jared came to Midwest with a career interest in veterinary medicine but quickly decided he loved history and wanted to become a history professor.

They have embraced a project of self-development and reflexivity that is distinct from Kathy's traditionalism and Bob's strong focus on leisure consumerism and private life as the source for his anticipated self-fulfillment in life. And while those with a traditionalist blueprint look to assuming roles for fulfillment, and those with an independent individualist blueprint look to fulfillment by selecting commitments and roles that will fulfill their desires for an enjoyable leisure-, consumption-, and private-life-centered lifestyle, those embracing an interdependent individualist lifestyle look to their ability to negotiate relationships and institutional affiliations over time in a world they perceive as rapidly changing.

Whitney's description of her public meaning making about why she joined the Peace Corps after college and her private revelations about her self-reflexive process of identity construction focus on self-fulfillment, demonstrate sophisticated humor and self-deprecation, and construct a persona that displays personal autonomy, is engaged in ongoing self-development, and is proving to herself that she is capable of finding belonging and meaning as an individual.

Her identity project and life trajectory are consistent with the individualization theorized by Bauman (2001), Beck (1992), Beck and Beck-Gernsheim ([2001] 2002), and Giddens (1991) as one that is open and full of choices and insecurities. Whitney links what is good for her own self-development to her desire to engage in doing work in the public sphere that involves commitment and a sense of responsibility to the collective well-being of people globally. The project of self is central, but it is linked to a complex set of belongings in different forms.

She has a boyfriend she met while in college, but he attended a different university. She went to Togo knowing that their relationship might change as a result of that choice. She said that she was committed to him and to having a relationship with him, but she also was committed to her own self-development and growth and to making a difference through her work. They maintained their relationship during the years she was in the Peace Corps and became engaged during a vacation in Europe while she was still working in Togo. After completing her work in Togo, she traveled with a friend to Singapore where her father and brother live and work for a farm equipment manufacturing company. They traveled in Southeast Asia, and then she came back to the United States.

Whitney recently started a job working as a customer service representative for a company that needs service representatives who speak French. She commented that it is a good job for the time being because it will help her keep up her French language skills, and it is a "laid-back" work environment. She and her fiancée will wed in the fall. She is considering graduate school as well as other options. She is very close to her mother, father, and brother and often talks about how much she values and enjoys them. Her negotiation of autonomy was complicated during her college years by her parents' divorce, but she approached the process of change with the certainty that she would continue to have good relationships with her parents and a commitment to helping her younger brother adjust to the change too.

Whitney developed a circle of friends in college and maintains relationships with them as well as faculty with whom she built relationships. On a recent trip back to Midwest City with her fiancée, she stayed with a friend from college who lives in a nearby town. At the same time she is open to new relationships and has built relationships with other Peace Corps volunteers. Whitney's description of her thoughts about why she joined the Peace Corps includes a focus on self-fulfillment centered on an ongoing, reflexive life project and process of self-development. It links personal self-fulfillment to a complex web of interconnections to others in a way that suggests she does not experience the private/public dichotomy in the same way traditionalists such as Kathy or independent individualists such as Bob do. Relationships are viewed as more flexible and fluid and self and others as mutable, changing, and becoming. Commitment is not based strictly on self-fulfillment or traditional role fulfillment but on recognition of interdependence and the need to allow for change in others as well as self. The project of self involves developing the ability to adapt and change in relation to the changes in others. Set roles linked to traditionalism are less central to these students, though most continue to recognize that the generalized culture rests on them. Rather than a rejection of institutional structures such as marriage outright, most of these students shift the relationship styles they adopt within those structures.

Talisha participates in different communities and moves across fluid boundaries between them. The meaningful connections she has developed are defined primarily based on activities and practices that provide her with a sense of belonging rather than boundaries. She reflexively joins in creating a community upon entering groups where she experiences connection and finds support and others who are concerned with similar issues and trying to achieve similar goals as she is. She helps her friends and is supported by them as well. Her goals include traveling abroad to learn how people in other cultures live, and being creative in her career. She wants autonomy in her life and to link her work with helping others to have the same opportunity.

Talisha's connection to her family is central as a part of her identity, and her grandmother and brother are people she admires and selectively wants to model herself after. Her brother's high energy and creativity and her grandmother's work ethic, wisdom, and ability to endure are admired by Talisha, and she modestly claims some level of these qualities. But she does not look to them for the model of lifestyle or career she plans on having. She lived part of her youth in Mississippi, close to her extended family. Then she moved to Portland, Oregon, where she experienced being one of the only blacks in her high school and living in an affluent neighborhood. Talisha identifies with both her economically disadvantaged extended family in Mississippi and the "Northwest liberals" who became her friends in Portland. Her experiences developed skills in finding her way in different cultures and carrying them with her to draw from in her life trajectory project and as resources in her identity work.

For career and lifestyle models Talisha looks to writers for the *New Yorker* and *Rolling Stone* and to faculty and peers who also write. Her concerns about social justice link her to those who have similar concerns, those who take the same courses she takes, or those who teach them, some of whom overlap with the writing community she moves in. Those in her friendship circle who write tend to be aiming for careers that depend on writing and editing skills, so they are as focused as she is on practices that privilege developing their writing skills, with the aim of having a writing-related career, and they often are as concerned with academics, since the journalism program in which most are enrolled is very competitive. They read each other's work, they edit for each other, they discuss the ideas they write about or are going to write about, they attend lectures, art exhibits, and poetry readings, and they discuss and write about them. They also have parties and meet for lunch at the student union.

Talisha assumes responsibility for creating and maintaining any enduring ties she wants to have from her Midwest experience. Though still in school, she is already establishing a set of relationships that she plans to maintain and is beginning the process of staying connected. Facebook, e-mail, her blog while in Italy when studying abroad, and her drop-in visits to faculty with whom she has studied in past semesters are all part of this pattern. She says she is not interested in getting married and is not sure she wants to have children. Instead, she looks forward to having a good job and the time and money to enjoy her interests in literature, music, and the arts and spending time with people who have similar interests. She does not see herself as a "do-gooder" but wants to be involved in addressing inequalities, particularly those linked to race and sexuality.

Talisha's identity is much more complex than the structural factors that have influenced her opportunities prior to or during college. She views her identity as being based on her experiences, interests, concerns, tastes, talents, and goals that are linked to her self-development project and are changing and emerging as she has new experiences and meets new people. She does not define herself primarily through the career she wants, though that is part of her identity. In her Facebook profile she says she is "smart" and likes "smart" people. She builds a profile that shows she knows how to have fun too and that she can be a little edgy. Her identity is complex and multifaceted and includes a diversity of relationships with peers, family, and faculty.

Talisha's community in college was built based on propinquity with other prejournalism students in the residence hall during her freshman year, people she met through her early friend network at parties and socially, and sometimes in classes frequented by people striving to be good writers as she was striving to be, or where people shared her desire to understand the structures supporting inequalities and work for a more socially just society. Her concerns about racism and heterosexism influenced the courses outside of her major that she chose to take and brought her into contact with some people in her classes who were of like mind. The community of which she is part also was mediated by technology and travel that linked her to extended family in Mississippi and friends in Oregon, Mississippi, and all over the country, as high school friends went to colleges and some of them, already, on to jobs. After graduation, Talisha got a job with an advertising agency in Mississippi. She says that she is enjoying the work and the people she meets there. She has begun the process of applying to graduate programs and plans to go to graduate school in the near future.

Talisha's identity work contrasts with Kathy's. Kathy defines herself in terms of the roles she has or plans to have in life—those roles of daughter, wife, mother, church member, and doctor are central to her. In contrast to both Kathy and Talisha is Bob's focus on the consumer goods he wants and the leisure activities he enjoys as the sources for his fulfillment in life and the center of his life trajectory project goals. His relationships with his parents and peers also are important to him, and both are embedded in institutions, the family and fraternity, which provide a patterned path for the form the relationships take. But Bob makes meaning of his participation in institutional arrangements and relationships largely through the lens of satisfying his noninstitutionally anchored individual desires.

Moffatt (1989) suggests that the importance of friendship to the students he studied are based on an assumption that "the true self desires or ought to desire autonomy, choice, and equal "natural" relationships with other selves" (41). This perspective of the self in relationship to others is described by Bellah and colleagues (1985) as being linked to a general shift in American society that turns to private-sphere pleasures for satisfaction and meaning in life rather than to the public sphere. This kind of individualism, what Bellah and colleagues referred to as "expressive individualism," with its strong emphasis on self-fulfillment, has been critiqued (Lasch 1978; Bellah et al. 1985; Putnam 2000) as one in which people focus on private pleasures at the expense of public engagement or investment of the authentic self in the collective good.

Nathan (2005) also found this to be the case with students at AnyU. Most students, she found, linked volunteer and other community-oriented activities directly to their own self-promotion in the job market or as things they did to fulfill sorority or fraternity obligations rather than focusing on the beneficial social outcomes their involvement produces or the importance of those social outcomes for their own well-being and quality of life.

The patterns in the identity work of Midwest students in the sample, their meaning making about their lives, and the practices in which they engage present a complex and varied understanding of the relationship between community and individualism. If we focus "on what communities can do for individuals and more on what members do to maintain a community" (Lichterman 1996, 10) instead of adopting a "'see saw' image of self-expression and private life pulling down public virtue, civic engagement and morality" (Delanty 2003, 121), then the way students live shows that many students do not choose between self-expression and private pleasures versus civic engagement and concern about collective well-being.

At Midwest, the orientations of students in the sample toward public service, volunteer work, and concern with making a contribution to society are better viewed as complex pictures. A few students, mostly those involved in a social movement or church, express a strong concern with making a contribution to society as primary for them, and a large number of students express a desire to help others through their work and in volunteer activities. A larger number of students focus, as the students at AnyU, on the personal benefits of volunteer work and group activities. This is not to say that most students did not state that they enjoyed helping others and felt good about it. They did, but even in those instances the emphasis, for the majority, was on the self and not the collective benefits of these activities.

The faces of individualism that present themselves through the interviews and observations upon which this book is based are varied and nuanced. A few students adopt a blueprint of individualism that relies on an individuated politics that is based on interdependent autonomy and reflexivity, and they undertake the lifelong project of integrating them. A somewhat higher percentage adopts a traditional blueprint with their identity anchored in many ways by the sense of community, the loss of which Bellah and colleagues (1985) bemoan. Students guided by the traditionalist blueprint of individualism rarely experience the generalized college student culture or the academic side of university life as locations where they find meaningful community. Instead, these students look to their families, communities of origin, and church for meaning and fulfillment. Some also describe the goal of work as a calling. Over half of students express ideas consistent with expressive individualism, looking to leisure activities and consumption for fulfillment in life.

The occupational status or graduate programs entered, satisfaction with college, and confidence and comfort with their current life trajectory link to the blueprints of individualism that guide them and are influenced by the choices they have made in college about how to spend their time and energy (reflected in the college student cultures to which they gravitated), and are also shaped by class background, gender, and race/ethnicity.

The college student cultural orientations of students and the practices and ideas associated with them represent a set of cultural tools from which they draw when solving the problems of life as students, and the choices they make are important in shaping their trajectory for the future. Students most satisfied with college, and their view of their own future, are those who have adopted an interdependent blueprint of individualism and had primary college student orientations that were academic or careerist overall, but again those with careerist primary orientations are more satisfied with college and confident about the future. Traditionalists are generally fairly satisfied with the life trajectory path they are on but are less enthusiastic about the college experience, although traditionalists with careerist primary college student culture orientations are generally satisfied with college outcomes. Students guided by an independent individualist blueprint are less satisfied with college, and less confident about their future fulfillment. Men in this group generally are more ambivalent about the future than are the women. The highest career rewards in terms of occupational prestige and entering graduate programs and the highest levels of satisfaction with college and initial jobs or graduate school go to those with careerist/academic college student cultural orientations/practices, with careerist/collegiates following close behind. A high percentage of the women and minorities in the sample gravitated to the careerist/academic and careerist/collegiate cultures.

The choices and practices of students while at Midwest, in concert with the fact that they have made it into a tier-one public university, play a role in the narrowing of structurally derived inequalities of cultural capital (Bourdieu 1986) during the college years. A high percentage of women and racial and ethnic minorities invest their time and energy into academics and careerism, broadening their knowledge and skills, building "identity capital" (Côté 2002), and preparing for professional careers. College does appear to move the students who persist at Midwest and gravitate to the careerist/academic college student subcultures into graduate programs and competitive professional careers fairly successfully. These students are those who are successful in moving along a career path in college, and the professionalizing process they experience encourages them to view the work they will do as central in having a fulfilling life. In one way these students express views consistent with being satisfied consumers, often saying that they made the right choice in coming to Midwest.

Most, though not all, students also anticipate love, marriage, having children, and a fulfilling family life.[1] But marriage as a goal is most significant in the identity work and the construction of an individualization project of those adopting a traditionalist blueprint and is less central for those students guided by interdependent or independent blueprints. This is consistent with Arnett's findings, that the majority of college students do not view marriage as significant in establishing adult identity (Arnett 2000). Of course, choices regarding marriage, having children, divorce, and the job market are some of the factors that will come into play in shaping how the success of women and racial and ethnic minorities will play out for them in the long run (Spain and Bianchi 1996).

A central problem of late modernity (Côté 2002; Giddens 1991; Bauman 2001) is how to develop skills in ongoing self-development and negotiation in order to create and sustain an identity and life trajectory in the context of almost constant economic change and instability with its accompanying shifting cultural sands. "Given the compulsory nature of this task, people will differ in terms of how enthusiastically and actively they approach it" (Côté 2002, 119). Not surprisingly, in the case of college students, those who perceive that they have little to gain from embracing the demands of adulthood and who have access to parental resources that enable them to resist and delay the effects with relatively manageable parent control are the most reluctant to embrace the challenges of ongoing self-development and negotiation demanded of them by a rapidly changing culture and global economy.

Arnettt (2000) and others have found that the period of youth is increasingly extended in industrialized societies. This research has shown that among the Midwest college students studied this is particularly evident among students whose parents are college educated and who are making significant financial investments. Relatively affluent males whose parents have high levels of financial investment in their college lives and are college educated themselves are more ambivalent about entering real life than any other group in the student population.

Arnett indicates that "in a variety of studies with young people in their teens and twenties, demographic transitions such as finishing education, settling into a career, marriage, and parenthood rank at the bottom in importance among possible criteria" (Arnett 2000, 472) deemed central for achieving adult status (Arnett 1997, 1998; Greene, Wheatley, and Aldava 1992). But this is clearly not the case with men or women with traditional individualist orientations for whom these criteria are key in their coming-of-age life trajectory plans.

The three things Arnett finds at the top of the list for achieving adulthood for the contemporary college-age student are "accepting responsibility for one's self and making independent decisions" and, to a lesser extent, "becoming financially independent" (Arnett 2000, 472–73). This seems to be the case with many of the students at Midwest, but the meanings of responsibility and independent decision making vary considerably for the differently oriented students. Financial independence is defined most similarly across students. The few men who do experience their parents as controlling helicopter parents express discomfort and frustration with their parents, especially their mothers, in keeping with the women who describe these parental behaviors. Like their female peers, they say that they are highly motivated to use college as a means to get a good job in order to reduce parental pressures and control.

Côté (2002) links the extension of the period of youth in industrialized societies to broad social and economic changes chronicled in later modernity. He notes that the problems and issues that were once managed with collective solutions are increasingly becoming the responsibility of the individual (Côté 2000, 2002; Beck 1992).

One result of these changes is that expectations have risen in late-modern societies regarding what the life course has to offer people in terms of their own personal development and life-project achievements. . . . At the same time, people are expected to "individualize" their life projects, by embarking on self-styled career/lifestyle trajectories based on their own personal preferences and choices. At the aggregate level, reflecting how the transition to adulthood is being restructured, we are witnessing increasingly prolonged, decoupled transitions between education and work, dating and mating, and childhood and adulthood. . . . As institutional supports have become more tenuous, leaving disjunctures among institutional networks (like the university-work and youth-adulthood transitions), the life course has become somewhat destabilized for many people with less predictable trajectories. (Côté 2002, 117–18)

One common complaint by students is that their college academic preparation is not tightly enough connected to the job market or real life. This complaint can, in one way, be understood to be a complaint about the lack of a tightly coupled, institutionally mediated path for their life trajectory progression, especially since these same students often are the ones who express ambivalence about entering real life.

In a ten-year longitudinal study of a sample of Canadian university students, most of whom are middle class, Côté (2002) employs an "identity capital model" to explore "(1) how their various individualized trajectories to adulthood work out; (2) what effects factors like gender and differing parental financial support for their trajectory choices have on later occupational attainments and personal fulfillment; and (3) how they deal with the middle-class competition for career advantage" (Côté 2002, 118–19).

Côté identifies several distinct "stances toward developing an individualized life project" that loosely link to patterns found among students a Midwest. These include "'default individualization'—or the passive acceptance of mass-marketed and mass-educated prepackaged identities, which can lead to a deferred membership in an adult community—through degrees of 'developmental individualization,' or at the other end of the continuum, the active, strategic approaches to personal growth and life-projects in an adult community(ies) (cf. Evans and Heinz 1994) and their concepts of 'passive' and 'active' individualization)" (Côté 2002, 119). Côté links this way of conceiving of individualization to conceptualizing a range of "agentic" behavior and potential. According to Côté, the identity capital model proposes that people can take advantage of or compensate for the institutional holes and deficits of late modernity (like making the university-work transition) by making "identity investments" as they individualize. This can involve a strategic development of "who one is" on the basis of exchangeable resources like abilities, appearance, and interactional skills. The resources can be both *tangible* (e.g., parents' social class and their investment in offspring, gender [2], and key group memberships like sororities and fraternities) and *intangible* (e.g., an agentic personality, prior identity capital acquisitions, or advanced forms of psychosocial and intellectual development). Together, these can be used to establish and accumulate certain identity gains, like securing memberships in adult communities, and being recognized as a fully responsible adult who is accorded certain forms of respect and privilege. (Côté 2002, 119–20, emphasis in original)

In footnote [2] in the passage above, Côté points out the following:

Gender varies as an identity capital resource depending on the context. Historically, "gender" favored males in the university setting, but this is no longer the case, especially in programmes that have become female dominated (see Allahar and Côté 1998) for a discussion of "gender convergence" in Canada). Further study of variations in the contextual benefits and liabilities of gender is clearly needed in light of recent societal and institutional changes. (Côté 2002, 132)

Overall, Côté finds that "low parental transfer of capital (PTC) males seem to take advantage of college to accelerate their development by acquiring more identity capital in the short run" (Côté 2002, 127). During the course of college, high PTC females initially slow their development and then "catch up to the overall sample in the timing of their transition to adulthood . . . while the low PTC males maintain their accelerated development" (127).

While the patterns identified on the adult identity measure and the community identity measure are found to be quite similar, the "community identity resolution scale" (125) revealed a "contrast between low and high PTC females in moratorium effect: low PTC accelerated a lagged development when in school and continued accelerating afterward, while high PTC delayed and then accelerated" (127). Côté notes that on this measure the high "parental transfer of capital" (PTC) males "become distinctive with the lowest scores in terms of this form of identity capital acquisition" (127).

Côté concludes that "with respect to financial support, females who received high levels of financial support and males who received low levels of support (from parents) appear to benefit the most and agency seems to play a role in long-term outcomes regardless of structural factors" (Côté 2002, 131). He finds that neither structural or "pure choice" (131) logics explain the variations in the transition to adulthood found among college students, but that "there seem to be weak structural influences (parental financial support and gender (PTC and SEX)), potentially over-ridden by agency in the long run" (131).

Overall, these findings are consistent with the patterns found among Midwest students, with one nuanced exception. The middle- and upper middle-class women at Midwest (the group that would be comparable to the women Côté focused on in his study) did not appear to be delaying development as a group. Instead, the women who had already adopted a lifestyle trajectory plan linked to identity work and a sense of individualism consistent with independent individualism delayed early in college and then resumed development consistent with Côté's findings, but those with traditional and interdependent primary orientations in identity work and individualization did not delay, because their blueprints of individualism linked to visions of how their adult life fulfillment could be enhanced by embracing the development opportunities available.

The intersections of patriarchal family relations and capitalist class relations in contemporary America encourage a greater number of men from relatively privileged backgrounds to delay or feel ambivalent about entering real life where they will, to some extent at least, presumably have to achieve their social and economic status through entering the job market. These men also are less likely to express high levels of satisfaction with college despite the relative advantages with which they enter college in terms of parental cultural capital and financial investment.

Men from relatively affluent families, a higher percentage of whom at Midwest are white, have to compete with women and racial and ethnic minority students on a more level playing field in the academic arena at Midwest, and presumably more in the entry-level job market (Spain and Bianchi 1996) than in the collegiate social arena of college sports and partying, where more traditional gender roles are scripted into the institutionally sanctioned normative behaviors and are supported by popular-culture images that give salience to college fun. In these settings they feel comfortable and engage in establishing status relative to similar peers. Often their experiences in high school (Foley 1994) encourage them to think that they can maintain their relatively privileged social status through collegiate subculture social ties more readily than through academics or career pursuits. This, along with parental acceptance of their boundary setting and an emphasis on living their own lives, linked to gendered parenting styles, encourages them to opt, in fairly high numbers, for "default individualization" connected to "mass-marketed and mass-educated prepackaged identities" (Côté 2002, 119) and reliance on tangible identity capital. Financial resources also are an advantage for them, since they can often use money to enhance their status in the settings where this form of individualization exists, for instance, by consistently paying for the first round of drinks.

They are likely to have demands for relationality, clear communication, and cooperative behavior placed on them in the workplace that are consistent with the cultural changes that have taken place in interaction with economic and global processes of change. But cultivating these relational styles would not necessarily support them in masculine identity work linked to broadly diffused cultural notions that define masculinity in terms of dominance, silent strength, and autonomy.

Among women and ethnic and racial minority students in the sample, greater numbers are strongly oriented toward professional careers. These students engage in building more diverse relationships and are interested in academics to varying degrees. Men in the sample whose parents give them no financial support, mostly first-generation college students, are either strongly oriented academically toward professional careers or take a credentialist route through college. For women whose parents graduated from college and who are relatively affluent, the careerist focus derives, at least in part, from a strong desire to establish autonomy from their helicopter parents by becoming financially independent. Additionally, their efforts to do well academically and the time they spend on professional development activities in preparation for careers often result in recognition from peers, faculty, and family and in a sense of accomplishment that affirms their movement toward adulthood.

In January 2007, *The Chronicle of Higher Education* reported that college women outperform college men in a number of ways. "College women earn better grades, hold more leadership posts, spend more time studying, and earn more honors and awards. They report being more involved than young men in student clubs and volunteer work" (Wilson 2007, A37). College men "spend more time than their female counterparts exercising, watching television, playing video games, and partying" (Wilson 2007, A37). Education sector findings show that boys continue to improve their performance in education, but girls have improved their performance even faster (Wilson 2007, A37). To try to blame schools and universities for the disengagement of boys and young men misses the core of the problem, which rests on a cultural struggle about defining masculinity in late modernity (Connell 1987).

The popular culture continues to rely on impoverished representations of masculinity that depend on dichotomies of masculine rationality over feminine emotionality; masculine strength and invulnerability over female weakness and vulnerability; and masculine assertiveness over female malleability. Young men influenced by the popular culture image of hegemonic masculinity (Cornell 1987), who are focused on their own masculine identity work while in college, do not necessarily find settings structured for merit based achievement opportunities in which women and men are expected to compete and relate as equals that compelling.

In the case of the daily lives of college students, gender identity issues and shifts in the structure of patriarchy in intersection with capitalism clearly contribute to the differences in the ways students focus their energies while in college. Not surprisingly, some young men who are very focused on gender identity work turn to their college peers with whom they live and spend much of their time in their struggle to construct healthy masculine identities, with varying degrees of success. The impoverished version of masculinity that persists in the generalized college student culture and popular-culture images of college life is not a very workable basis for a well-rounded, secure sense of adult masculine identity. The lack of desire to be deeply challenged intellectually and academically seems a secondary feature of this situation rather than the root of it.

This research shows that gendered patterns of separation and individuation and parenting styles in contemporary American culture (Chodorow 1978; Dinnerstein 1976) and the different relational styles they encourage for men and women (Cancian [1987] 1990) intersect with class-based concerns and racial and ethnic relations in shaping the everyday lives of students.

College-educated parents who are investing financially in the college educations of their children are often very involved in their lives and expect to be able to influence the choices their children make about where to go to college, what to study, and how to spend their time. Their desire to have their investment result in careers for their children is shaped by the financial costs of a college education and the beliefs students say their parents have about an increasingly competitive job market.

As federal and state support for institutions and student needs-based and merit grants declines and student loans are given primacy as the means for making college affordable, parents or students themselves have to pay more for the education at institutions such as Midwest (St. John and Parsons 2005). At the same time political struggles over defining the purpose of higher education and the funding of it emerged, universities also began a process of strategic planning, which involved taking more market-oriented approaches aimed at competing for students.

The students whose parents are not financing their college and who are attending college supported substantially on grants, scholarships, loans, and through their own work, a higher percentage of whom are first-generation college students and/or racial and ethnic minority students, link finishing education and settling into a career with coming of age. They often are already accepting responsibility for themselves, making independent decisions, and managing their own finances. Completing college and getting a job are central to them.

McPherson and Shapiro (1997) documented that cuts in needs-based aid associated with new federal student aid policy caused losses in access. The loss of support for equity-based student aid has resulted in a widening of the gap in opportunity between high-income and low-income students (Advisory Committee on Student Financial Assistance 2002; St. John and Parsons 2005). In light of perceptions of an increasingly competitive job market and narrowing access to good universities for the less privileged, it is understandable why parents of modest means are adamant about their children taking advantage of the educational opportunity and demand that they focus on academics in order to achieve upward economic and social mobility.

Since the 1980s, shifts in higher education policy at the state and national levels, strategic planning by university administrations, and a globalizing job market have played a role in shaping parental politics and college student culture. Increasingly, even upper-middle-class families are taking out loans to finance their children's college educations. First-generation college students with financial need and racial and ethnic minority students, many of whom are likely to fill high-skill professional jobs essential for a competitive economy and healthy society, if they are able to acquire a good college education, are the most likely to be harmed by the shift of public funding away from needs-based grants to student loans as the way to fund public education. And parents who are paying back loans may well feel that helicopter parenting well beyond the college years is legitimate and even necessary. The extended period of "emerging adulthood" (Arnett 2000) of some college students, while often appearing to be a personal choice, is constructed in interaction with their parents and peers within the context of higher education policy and the current global economy. Both social and economic development goals linked to higher education are likely to be undermined by this trend (St. John and Parsons 2005; Selingo and Brainard 2006).

PATHS TO FULFILLMENT

The generalized college student culture at Midwest is a highly individualistic one that privileges the ideals of self-fulfillment and self-development. The ways students approach the problems of college life vary, but the common thread in the shared college student culture involves a cluster of practices involving identity work aimed at becoming a competent individual who assumes responsibility for one's own life project and demonstrates the ability to meet the demands of adult life. The generalized college student culture leaves space for a wide range of individual responses.

The majority of students at Midwest say they want to learn academically and socially. They want to take part in the authentic college experience. Most students say they value social learning that takes place outside of the classroom more than classroom learning. Most students claim they are enjoying a successful college experience, in which they are developing as competent and independent individuals. Beneath the surface of similar discursive patterns employed by students about the importance of social learning, which includes "taking care of your self," "getting along with people," "making new friends," "knowing how to have fun," and "balancing work and fun," is the cultural ideology of individualism framed by increasingly rationalized institutional structures.

Over the years I worked on this research it was heartening to witness the many students who gained academic, interpersonal, and self-knowledge and confidence during their years in school and to follow their achievements as they entered graduate school, got jobs, joined the Peace Corps, established themselves in careers, entered partnerships, married, started families, and became involved in their community. At the same time I noted that some students at Midwest (25 percent of students in the sample) were primarily engaged in status and gender identity work among peers and had little investment in other aspects of college life beyond wanting to get a diploma at the end of four or five years. These students focused, almost desperately at times, on becoming men or women through peer culture involvement at the expense of their broad intellectual and social development. Milner (2004) found a similar pattern among high school students, those he found develop complex peer status systems as a response to the lack of power and choice they have economically and politically in the institutional setting of the high school. For those students at Midwest who are engaged primarily in peer identity work, a pattern established in high school may simply continue in college.

The *National Survey of Student Engagement Annual Report 2005* noted that among first-year students "close to one-third (30 percent) did just enough work to get by" (NSSE 2005, 16). Just under 30 percent of students in this study, including not just freshmen, but sophomores, juniors, and seniors, described attitudes and behaviors consistent with these findings. The report also found that 46 percent of seniors said they did more than was expected of them in academics. Seniors at Midwest said they focused more on academics early in their senior year, before they came down with "senioritis," because they were taking courses directly related to their career futures and had started thinking about life beyond college. Those students at Midwest who lacked academic motivation earlier in college as seniors generally continued to do what they felt they had to do to graduate and did not become highly motivated beyond earning the diploma and showing a level of interest they felt would help obtain letters of recommendation. More highly motivated students complain about these students, believing they pressure faculty to "dummy down" course content and requirements and are not serious about academics. This is particularly irritating to students when they feel it is happening in courses they perceive as being important for the skills they need to have to perform well in their careers.

Can we reasonably expect higher education institutions such as Midwest to engage students who arrive at college with little motivation or interest in being challenged academically or of moving outside of their relational comfort zone? The simple answer is that engaging disinterested students authentically in academics and other activities that broaden their interpersonal skills and worldview is a daunting challenge for faculty and staff in higher education institutions such as Midwest, particularly within the context of competitive recruiting based on rhetoric that is consumer-choice centered and within a popular-culture environment that highlights peer-centered hedonistic fun and denigrates intellectual and academically oriented college students.

Universities need to be competitive in providing quality education, but universities such as Midwest also need to be sheltered by public funding from the worst excesses of the service industry model, or they will become institutions catering to the consumer desires of emerging adults and their parents. If our workforce is to remain competitive in the face of increasing global competition, then it is imperative that higher education institutions address this issue head on.

Midwest's college student culture supports a plurality of ongoing discourses about fulfillment and belonging that presupposes individualism, resilience, and the reflexivity required to make choices and chart a course while in college. The generalized shared college student culture supports posttraditional forms of identity work and participation in community. Though there is a generalized culture linked to traditional culture and conceptions of community present at Midwest and sanctified by some of the institutionalized cultural practices,[2] this thread in the generalized culture must not be mistaken for being the primary basis for college student culture. Traditional and posttraditional forms of community are both present, but the majority of students studied have chosen to privilege posttraditional forms as the focus of their energy by adopting either an independent or interdependent blueprint of individualism. Instead of internalizing the values and beliefs of the generalized college student culture at Midwest, many students borrow selectively from it.

They are not at Midwest to meet the needs for order and integration of the institution, to comply with academic demands they often view as irrelevant to their future, or to develop long-term tight bonds and loyalties with formal institutional actors. Most students view themselves as being at Midwest to meet their own individual needs, which include cultivating social ties that support them in the individuation process they are engaged in while in college and identity work aimed at establishing themselves as competent individuals able to meet the demands of life while earning a degree. Meaningful bonds, they are sure, are those they choose based on sharing similar interests and concerns. Students with this view turn mostly to other students who are in the same situation.

The highly individualistic ethos prevalent among American college students is linked to an economy and a culture that are increasingly consumerist and market driven, and as higher education institutions such as Midwest become more deeply drawn into the market economy in order to survive as public financial support dwindles, the characteristics of consumer culture and the consumer expectations in service delivery, comfort, and exchange are taking root in college student culture. Customers do not expect to have to struggle to acquire the product or service they are buying, nor do they expect to experience discomfort, to be negatively evaluated by service providers, or to be chastised for disrespect to those who serve. As one student said: "I don't think the teacher should be able to require that we get to class on time, after all, we are paying for the class!"

College student culture and community are fundamentally based on an individualistic cultural ideology and are at heart based in choice and transience. One finds oneself in a new situation and seeks bonds with others in the same situation. Individual responsibility for generating and maintaining meaningful connections with others, selecting a major, a course of study, developing skills, embracing activities, and having fun while in college is the expectation. The approach Midwest uses in recruitment, after all, highlights the choices and services available there, encouraging students to view choosing a university as a consumer choice to be made based on how best to meet their individual needs and desires. It is framed by structural constraints and supports that touch differently situated students in different ways. Students learn that to survive and succeed in this culture they must establish identities as independent and competent individuals by proving that they can take care of themselves, make new friends, and establish belonging in the cultural order they have entered, all things they will need to be able to do throughout their adult lives. Students interpret and respond to this culture based on their locations at the intersections of class, race/ethnicity, and gender relations and the relative levels of autonomy or insecurity they experience as college students.

Shared practices associated with coming of age constitute communities of belonging for most college students. What is central to them is a shared process of becoming in a contextual framework that encourages, even demands, that they act as individual choice makers. The individual becomes the locus for the creation of a sense of belonging to collectives rather than preexisting collectives encompassing the individual and defining them (Delanty 2003). "Consequently, more and more young people around the world are finding that they must organize their own paths through life, and they are increasingly left to their own resources to do so. This can be tremendously liberating—or terrifically burdensome—depending on the resources at the person's disposal (Wallace and Kovatcheva 1996, 1998)" (Côté 2002, 118). And, as this research reveals, economic and cultural resources available and the relationships, networks, and everyday interactions of students, many of which are shaped by their agency, shape the experiences of college students, their identities as maturing people, and their life trajectory plans as they prepare for "real life" after college.

Rather than going through developmental stages, college students appear to experience college as a set of relationships, networks, and interactions shaped by their choices and actions. The blueprints of individualism that they bring to college with them shape, in a dialectical fashion, the relationships, networks, and ways they focus their activities and draw from the cultural tool kit available to them while in college, and these in turn shape their identities and life trajectories in an ongoing process. This dialectic of relationships and interactions occurs within the context of how they are situated at the intersections of class, gender, and race/ethnicity, by the institutional structure and resources of Midwest, and by the political economy of the United States within the global capitalist economy. The stories that college students tell about the generalized college student culture, the college student cultural orientations that they embrace, and their everyday experiences are in a significant sense stories of the challenges they face and the choices available to them as college students coming of age in twenty-first-century America.

Appendix 1.1

Thirty-one women (52 percent of the sample) and twenty-nine men (48 percent of the sample) were interviewed and observed for this research, providing a quota sample that closely approximates the gender composition of undergraduates enrolled at Midwest University in 2003, when the research began. Table 1.1 shows the gender and racial/ethnic composition of the sample.

TABLE 1.1
GENDER AND RACIAL/ETHNIC COMPOSITION OF STUDENTS IN THE SAMPLE

	Racial and Ethnic Minorities	White	Totals
Female	7	24	31
Male	4	25	29
Totals	11	49	60

Ten of the sixty students included in the sample are classified as U.S. racial and ethnic minority members by Midwest, with one in this group indicating that she did not report her ethnic origins to the university. One student in the sample is African and immigrated to the United States with her family. The nine racial and ethnic minority students who reported their race/ethnicity to the university, and who are from the United States, comprise 15 percent of the sample.

The minority students include three African American women and two African American men (in 2003, 63 percent of African American graduates were female, while 36 percent were male); an African woman whose parents immigrated to the United States; an Asian American woman and man; a "multiethnic" woman who describes herself as being of Hispanic, European American, and American Indian heritage; a Hispanic man; and a Native American woman.

Table 1.2 shows the social class composition of the sample. As mentioned previously, class background of students was established using parental educational levels, occupations, family structure, and the descriptions students gave of their lifestyles prior to coming to college.

TABLE 1.2
SOCIAL CLASS BACKGROUND OF STUDENTS IN THE SAMPLE BY GENDER

Class Background	Female	Male	Total Number
Working Poor	3	3	6 (10%)
Lower Middle	5	5	10 (16.6%)
Middle Middle	11	11	22 (36.6%)
Upper Middle	7	7	14 (23%)
Lower Upper	5	3	8 (13.3%)
Total	31	29	60 (100%)

Overall, the educational levels of parents and the social class status of the families of college students at Midwest, in keeping with the population in general, are linked. Sixteen of the students in the sample come from lower-middle-class or working-poor backgrounds. Of the students who are from lower-middle-class or working-poor backgrounds, thirteen (81 percent) are first-generation college students. Three come from households in which one or both parents have college educations. Eight come from single-mother households and three from reconstituted families. Four are African American, and one is American Indian, representing close to 27 percent of minority students. Eight are female, and eight are male.

Twenty-two are middle-middle class and twenty-two come from upper-middle- or lower-upper-class backgrounds based on educational levels and occupations of their parents and the lifestyles they describe having. Of the middle-middle-class students, eighteen (nearly 82 percent) come from families where one or both parents graduated from college. Three are first-generation college students. Four (18 percent) lived in single families, and one lived in a reconstituted family. Two are single-father and two are single-mother households. Five students in this group are racial- or ethnic-minority students, making up 25 percent of this group. One is an African immigrant, one is African American, one is Hispanic, and two are Asian Americans. Eleven women and eleven men are in this group.

Of the students who are located in the upper-middle- or lower-upper classes, twenty-one (95 percent) have parent(s) who graduated from college. One is a first-generation college student. Twelve women and ten men are in this group. Two come from single-mother-headed households. One ethnic minority woman and twenty-one white students are in this group.

Though reliable data on the class background composition of the undergraduate student population at Midwest was not readily available, I was able to synthesize data provided on the university Web pages and gain assistance from staff in institutional research to allow for a rough sketch of the population based on financial aid distribution and the numbers of students who establish financial need through FAFSA (Free Application for Federal Student Aid).

Table 1.3 next shows the number of students who received financial aid without establishing financial need, with financial need, and those who received no aid. In 2003, some 24 percent of on-campus Midwest undergraduates paid the entire cost of attendance out of pocket. Slightly less than 42 percent of students at Midwest established financial need through filing FAFSA and received aid.

TABLE 1.3
FINANCIAL AID STATUS FOR FULL-TIME, DEGREE-SEEKING
UNDERGRADUATES AT MIDWEST STATE UNIVERSITY 2003

	Number Total Population	Total	Percentage Total Population*
Aid received no need			
Completed FAFSA no need	3,153		17
Grant aid no FAFSA	3,107		17
Total aid no need		6,260	
Aid received with need	7,553		42
Full pay/ no aid	4,381		24
Total		18,194	

*Percentage totals were rounded up at .5 and down at .4

Just over 58 percent of students at Midwest in 2003 either did not establish that they had financial need under FAFSA, or when they filed FAFSA they were found not to have financial need based on FAFSA criteria. Seventeen percent of the roughly 58 percent of students who did not establish financial need under FAFSA did not file FAFSA but received grant aid. A little over 17 percent who filed FAFSA but were found not to have financial need also received aid. Thus those who received aid without being defined as having financial need totaled a little over 34 percent of the undergraduate population. In 2003, 76 percent of Midwest students received some form of financial assistance, though only 41.5 percent established financial need through filing FAFSA.

According to the financial aid summary report that explains how financial aid is determined for students who complete FAFSA, when a student files for FAFSA a budgeted Cost of Attendance (COA) is determined based on factors such as residency status, full- or part-time course load status, and living arrangements. Then the expected financial contribution of the student's family is determined based on several factors, including the family's adjusted gross income. If the calculated value of financial need exceeds the determined COA after the expected family financial contribution, then the student is eligible for need-based assistance such as Pell grants, college work study, and need-based loans.

In 2003, annual tuition and fees for in-state students were $5,208 and out-of-state costs were $13,752. Annual total costs estimates were $13,952 for in-state and $22,496 for out-of-state students. By 2006, costs at Midwest University for in-state students were estimated at just over $17,000 annually, with tuition being about $7,000 of that amount. Out-of-state students paid about $26,000 a year, once the out-of-state fees of approximately $9,000 were added into the total cost. The majority of Midwest students had some assistance in the form of loans, grants, scholarships, or work study. A review of grant aid at Midwest between 2001 and 2005 showed that the budgeted cost of attendance increased 36.1 percent, but that during the same period grant aid increased only 20.5 percent, producing a widening gap between costs and grants (Office of Institutional Research, Midwest University Undergraduate Financial Aid Summary Report FY2001–FY2005 of Midwest Resident Undergraduate Students). A notable trend is that parent loans for undergraduate students (PLUS loans) increased substantially from 2001 to 2005 for both students with and without financial need. Though lower-income students who have the highest financial need on average do receive much more grant aid than higher-income students, they continue to have the greatest amount of unmet financial need (Office of Institutional Research, Midwest University Undergraduate Financial Aid Summary Report FY2001–FY2005 of Midwest Resident Undergraduate Students). Unmet financial need is that remaining after all financial assistance has been provided.

TABLE 1.4

FIRST-GENERATION COLLEGE STUDENTS (FGC) AND STUDENTS
WHOSE PARENT(S) GRADUATED COLLEGE (PGC) BY GENDER AND
RACIAL/ETHNIC MINORITY AND WHITE STATUS

	White		Racial/Ethnic Minority		Totals	
	Female	Male	Female	Male	Female	Male
First-Generation College (FGC)	5	7	4	1	9	8
Parent(s) Graduated College (PGC)	19	18	3	3	22	21
Totals	24	25	7	4	31	29

Seventeen students in the sample are first-generation college students (FGC) whose parents did not graduate from college, and forty-three have parent(s) who graduated from college (PGC). The FGC students make up 28.3 percent of the sample for this research.

Twelve people, representing 20 percent of the sample are from out of state. Twenty percent of the students included in the sample upon which this research is based are participants in the Greek system at Midwest. Seven sorority women and five fraternity men are in the sample. Two of the women and one of the men left the Greek system during college.

As mentioned previously, the sample upon which this research is based includes students from all of the undergraduate colleges and schools at Midwest. In general, the sampling procedures tried to take into account the proportion of all Midwest students receiving bachelor's degrees from each college and school. For example, arts and science awarded 39 percent and 36 percent of all bachelor's degrees granted by Midwest in 2002–03 and 2004–05 academic years, respectively, and the proportion of sampled students participating in the first interview and with majors in arts and science was 35 percent (N = 21). During the same years, the school of social work gave fewer than 1 percent of all bachelor's degrees awarded by Midwest, and only 1.6 percent (N = 1) of sampled students majored in social work. The total sample of sixty students included the twenty-one arts and science majors and the one social work major, mentioned above, and nine business majors; nine majors in agriculture, forestry, and natural resources; six majors in journalism; four majors in the college of education; four from the school of health professions; three engineering majors; one major from the college of human environmental sciences; one from the school of nursing; and one non-divisional student who eventually became a business major but dropped out of Midwest prior to graduation.

Ten freshmen, fifteen sophomores, eighteen juniors, and seventeen seniors were interviewed with participant observation and/or follow-up interviews conducted with a subset of twenty of them. At the time of this writing, only three students in the sample dropped out of Midwest—all were white males, two of whom were first-generation nontraditional students, and one who did not get accepted into the professional program of his choice and moved back to his home city to attend a local university.

In 2003, a report on six-year graduate rates among the student population at Midwest showed women's graduation rates to be consistently higher than those of men, with women being 4 to 5 percent more likely to graduate. Higher college attendance rates and higher graduation rates of women are well documented in the literature on higher education generally (Buchmann and DiPrete 2006; DiPrete and Buchmann 2006). What was not consistent with the graduation rate data on the overall population rate at Midwest was the fact that all of the men in the sample who dropped out were white. Overall population data show that racial and ethnic minority students have lower graduation rates, with African Americans having the lowest. In this sample, none of the racial and ethnic minority students failed to graduate.

Data provided on Web pages of Midwest University indicated that the six-year student graduation rates by race and ethnicity in 2005 for the 1999 cohort were American Indian/Alaskan Native 70.8 percent, Asian/Pacific Islander 63.2 percent, African American 56.9 percent, Hispanic 62.7 percent, and white 66.8 percent. International students had a 52.6 percent graduation rate. Notable shifts in graduation rates by race and ethnicity that occurred between 2003 and 2005 were that five-year graduation rates improved for American Indians and Alaska Natives, Asian Americans and Pacific Islanders, Hispanics, and whites, while they declined for international students and African Americans. Graduation rates provided online on the registrar's Web pages show the trend was toward an overall higher five-year graduation rate.

Table 1.5 provides a comparison of key demographic characteristics of Midwest, discussed in chapter 1, and the sample characteristics.

TABLE 1.5

COMPARISON OF MIDWEST AND SAMPLE POPULATION PERCENTAGES BY GENDER; RACIAL AND ETHNIC MINORITY STATUS; FIRST-GENERATION COLLEGE STUDENT; OUT-OF-STATE; AND FRATERNITY AND SORORITY MEMBERSHIP AT THE TIME THE RESEARCH BEGAN IN 2003.

	Female	Male	Racial and Ethnic Minorities	Race/ Ethnicity Unreported	Nonresident Alien	White	First Generation	Out-of-State	Fraternity & Sorority
Midwest	52	48	11	3	1.6	85	24	13	21
Sample	52	48	15	*	*	82	28	17	20

*One person in the sample.

Appendix 1.2

RELATED LITERATURE

Ethnographies of College Student Life

Two ethnographic studies of student life at large universities in the United States have provided important insights and comparisons in writing this book. The first is Moffatt's (1989) book *Coming of Age in New Jersey: College and American Culture*. This anthropological study of college life between 1977 and 1987 is based on participant observation living in a residence hall at Rutgers College. One strength of Moffatt's book is the insight it gives into the young male view and experience of college life, with an emphasis on sexuality.

The second ethnographic study of college students that has been useful as a source of comparison and elaboration of the analysis in this book is Nathan's 2005 book, *My Freshman Year: What a Professor Learned by Becoming a Student*. Nathan, a pseudonym used by Cathy A. Small, a professor of anthropology, did participant observation of college students by enrolling as a freshman in college again and going to school. She conducted her research of undergraduate students in 2002–2003 at AnyU, the pseudonym she gave to Northern Arizona University.

The entrance Moffatt (1989) gained into the male peer college world, which gave him access to the world of college men centered in male sexuality and hedonistic fun, may have reduced the likelihood that his informants would share certain types of information with him, such as the details of their struggles with separation and individuation in relationships with their parents. After all, college student peer culture encourages identity work that distances from parental authority and dependence and establishes an identity that is rooted in being independent and adult. For whatever reason, Moffatt (1989) gives little consistent attention to student-parent relationships in his analysis. Nathan (2005) also chose not to focus on parent-student relations in any significant way. Student-parent relationships are explored in this book in more detail because early in the data-gathering process it was noted that parents and family more generally were very central and important in the descriptions students gave of their lives as college students, revealing that it is an important area to explore.

Both Moffatt (1989) and Nathan (2005) center their analyses of college student culture on the experiences of students living in residence halls. The college student culture they describe is in most ways similar to the generalized college student culture at Midwest State University (MSU), described in chapter 3, and "learned" by students interactively early in their college experience. Nathan (2005) and Moffatt (1989) both find that college student culture is highly individualistic and antithetic to supporting a sense of integrated community. Moffatt turns to Bellah and colleagues (1985) and Nathan to Putnam (2000) to support their findings about the individualistic and highly self-centered college student culture they observe, culture that is viewed as lacking in the characteristics necessary to produce individuals who are committed to participation in civic life, instead adopting a strong orientation toward private-sphere pleasure seeking and self-fulfillment instead of sacrifice for the benefit of the social collective.

Late in her book Nathan (2005) acknowledges that there are college student subcultures and adopts the typology developed by Horowitz (1987) in her discussion of them, but she does not explore these in any depth, instead focusing on the generalized culture as the central focus of her work. For the purposes of this analysis, understanding the generalized college student culture is useful, because this understanding forms the backdrop or the broad cultural "field" (Bourdieu 1993) upon which students engage in learning culture, select cultural tools from the "tool kit" (Swidler 1986) available in that culture, and do identity work aimed at "individualization" (Côté 2002), thus beginning an adult life trajectory either by choice or through default. Rather than a monolithic culture of students who view themselves as individualists seeking fulfillment almost exclusively from the private-sphere pleasures that college has to offer, this research suggests a more nuanced and varied set of orientations toward identity, individualism, and relationships, and how students find meaning and fulfillment.

COLLEGE STUDENTS AND ADULTHOOD

Considerable media coverage has occurred regarding the delayed adult-hood of American young people college age and beyond. Scholarly work points to this trend as well. Arnett (2000) maintains that this period (ages eighteen to twenty-five) is one of "emerging adulthood" (469) and is a distinct period demographically and subjectively and in terms of identity explorations, existing only in cultures that afford the young this extended period of independent role exploration. Arnett maintains that this prolonged period of quasi-independence encourages people in this age range to shift the way they define the attainment of adulthood, linking the achievement of adulthood to subjective, individ-ualistic qualities of character (Arnett 1998) rather than to "demo-graphic transitions" (Arnett 2000, 472) such as finishing education and settling into a career, marriage, and parenthood. But he also finds that financial independence ranks at the top of the criteria for achieving adulthood, along with the qualities of character such as "accepting responsibility for one's self and making independent decisions" (Arnett 2000, 473).

Sociologist James E. Côté (2002) deals with some of the same research interests as Arnett but contextualizes observed changes in the transition to adulthood by synthesizing the individualization thesis found in theories of the life course with a social change perspective that includes social structural factors. He maintains that the prolonged period of emerging adulthood identified by Arnett and others is shaped by market-oriented policies and consumption-based lifestyles that char-acterize late modernity, the same patterns that a number of sociologists have theorized are changing the identity construction process and nature of human relationships more generally in late modernity (Bauman 2001; Giddens 1991).

Côté begins his examination of the influence of structural factors versus individual agency with the assumption that the Canadian univer-sity students he is studying have already been "roughly but not absolutely" sorted by social class, with "the secondary educational level constituting a structural barrier separating the (lower-income) working and (higher-income) middle classes (Andres, Anisef, Krahn, et al. 1999)" (Côté 2002, 118). Within the population of university students, Côté tries to learn the effects that gender and parental financial support have on their occupational attainments and personal fulfillment.

Quantitative research dealing with the factors contributing to the increasing college completion rates of women provides an important backdrop for some of the findings of this analysis. "From 1982 onward, the percentage of bachelor's degrees awarded to women continued to climb such that by 2004 women received 58 percent of all bachelor's degrees. (U.S. Department of Education 2004; Buchmann and DiPrete 2006, 515–16). The trend of higher college completion rates for women exists across all racial and ethnic groups in the United States. Of course it is important to remember that gender segregation of majors (Charles and Bradley 2002; Jacobs 1995; Turner and Bowen 1999) and under-representation of women at top-tier institutions continue even as more women than men earn college educations.

Sociological literature dealing with the reasons underlying the rise in college completion by women relative to men has focused on a wide range of factors such as higher returns to college education for women in the labor and marriage markets and protection against deprivation (Becker 1964; Goldin 1992, 1995; Jacobs 1996; DiPrete and Buchmann 2006); parental education and other family background characteristics (Blau and Duncan 1967; Jencks 1972; Sewell, Haller, and Portes 1969; Behrman, Pollak, and Taubman 1986; Hauser and Kuo 1997; Jacobs 1996; Powell and Downey 1997; Sommers 2000); the role of gender differences in academic performance and behaviors in explaining the growing female advantage in college completion (Jacob 2002; Downey and Vogt Yuan 2005; Bae, Choy, Geddes et al. 2000; Buchmann and DiPrete 2006); changes in higher education, including the growth of the community college system during the second half of the twentieth century and the expansion of the four-year college system (Buchmann and DiPrete 2006), and the influence of gender-segregated majors and possible higher rates of grade inflation in female-dominated majors (Charles and Bradley 2002; Jacobs 1999).

Buchmann and DiPrete (2006) integrate consideration of these varied explanations and find "no strong evidence that the female-favorable trend in college is being driven by compositional changes in the family situation that would give women a specific advantage over men in the educational attainment process" (526). They use data from General Social Surveys (GSS) from 1972 through 2002 and also from the National Educational Longitudinal Survey (NELS) from 1988 to 2000 and find no gender-specific effects for family background on academic performance in college. Gender-specific effects instead involved educational transitions. Fathers' education is more important for sons than for daughters in college enrollments. In the analysis of college completion, given enrollment, they found that for those enrolling in four-year colleges, coming from a household with an absent father reduces the likelihood of college completion for males but not for females. They show that "the gender-specific effects of father's status have their primary impact on the likelihood of the transition into a four-year college and college completion rather on academic performance" (Buchmann and DiPrete 2006, 534).

They conclude that for white students "it is now clear that the proximate cause of the female overtaking is found in gender differences in behavior during four-year college" (534). Superior academic performance in college rather than gender segregation by college type or major is the primary cause of the female advantage in college completion. While they recognize that the roots of the female advantage in academic performance lie earlier in the educational experiences of students, they caution that it is important to understand that the female performance advantages are relatively minor for high school completion or the transfer to college (534), and only "after enrollment in four-year college is the female advantage in academic performance converted into a solid female advantage in educational attainment" (534). Regarding racial and ethnic minorities, they conclude that further research is needed to better assess the source of the female advantage in college completion.

Noting that the total value of college has risen faster for women than it has for men Buchmann and DiPrete (2006) theorize that "the change stems from a combination of declining gender discrimination and women's growing interest in possessing autonomous resources by which they can pursue opportunities in both the labor and marriage markets while protecting themselves against adversity in both realms" (535). Still, they acknowledge that this rationalist explanation cannot account for gender trends in test scores that arise at an age when children are relatively ignorant about labor or marriage markets (535). They also note that the value of education has risen for men as well as women, and that it is puzzling that women are responding more forcefully than men to the advantage that a college education provides. They conclude that there must be a socialization-based disadvantage for males that is relatively stronger in families with fathers who have high school educations or less, or absent fathers, but they are uncertain whether this disadvantage stems from a lack of knowledge about the value of postsecondary education or a lower priority placed on education relative to other goals (536).

They find that two-year colleges play a role in the overall proportion of people who complete a four-year college, but that they are not a major source in producing the female "advantage" in college completion. They conclude that "the simple story" for white women in the later cohorts covered by their data is that they "graduate in higher numbers because they do better in college" (532). At the time of this writing, women outnumber men in four-year colleges, earn more bachelor's degrees, and enroll in graduate school in higher numbers than do men (U.S. Department of Education 2004).

This literature is important for this book, because the findings about the cohorts closest to the cohort of students in this book are in keeping with patterns among Midwest students in that there are more women than men enrolled at Midwest, and the students in the sample who dropped out were all males. Two were first-generation college students from single-parent, female-headed households.

An even more important role this literature plays for the work at hand is that the trend of higher female college completion and the conclusion by Buchmann and DiPrete (2006), that the different behaviors of female and male students in four-year colleges are central in this trend, are confirmed in the experiences and orientations reported by Midwest students that are patterned and vary along gender lines. The qualitative data discussed in this book reveal that there are some very basic influences at work in the daily lives of college students that are impacting the behaviors and orientations of students and encouraging them to adopt a different set of priorities relative to balancing academics with social life and having fun at Midwest.

The relationships that students report having with their parents are shaped by a constellation of factors, including parental educational level and other aspects of class background, race, ethnicity, and gender, and to some extent family structure. The type of relationship that students report having with parents plays a significant role in shaping their experiences as college students. The dominant culture of Midwest is also a central feature of the environment that students enter, and it impacts females and males differently. Not surprisingly, women and men respond to and participate in the dominant culture of Midwest in somewhat patterned and different ways. The subculture orientations of students also reflect the influence of the different ways men and women orient to the college experience and choose to focus their energies.

While rational decision making associated with higher returns on college educations for women in the labor and marriage markets may indeed play a role in the behaviors of students, much more immediate pressures and desires, described in this book, also play a role in the stronger orientation among women overall toward careerism and academics and the overall stronger orientation toward college fun and credentialist approaches to college among males.

COLLEGE STUDENT SUBCULTURES
AND CULTURAL ORIENTATIONS

Three studies of college subcultures turned out to be central in elaborating the findings that emerged from the data upon which this book is based. Clark and Trow (1966), Bank (2003), and Horowitz (1987) include a typology of college student culture in their works that links in one way or another to the findings at Midwest.

Clark and Trow (1966) focus on "normative content" and orientations toward a college education, which they found represented on American campuses of the day. They hold that "these orientations are defining elements of student subculture(s), in which they appear as shared notions of what constitutes right attitude and action toward the range of issues and experiences confronted in college" (1966, 19). They created a model with four ideal types of college subcultures—vocational, collegiate, nonconformist, and academic, and they linked these to the variations in student populations they knew to be in attendance in the varied institutions of higher education under consideration. They gave particular attention to the influences of class status and institutional structure in shaping the nature of the orientations and relationships of students in college.

Bank (2003) focuses her research on the "contradictions surrounding women's education" and the fact that the college experience for women is different from that of men, "despite the fact that many women will experience more gender equality in college than in the workplace or home" (1). Central Women's College (CWC), as Bank refers to the college, is located in the Midwest. Bank's research, conducted between 1991 and 1997, explores the student culture during the last years the college served women exclusively.

Bank deals with the tensions involving gender traditionalism, careerism, and community that she demonstrates have characterized women's higher education. She explores the extent to which college student culture supports gender traditionalism that encourages women to emphasize sociability, concerns about appearance, and male orientation. She evaluates the importance of careerism for women at CWC with attention to the extent to which careerist aspirations are viewed as emancipatory and/or are channeled into careers defined by the dominant culture as appropriate for women. She also explores the nature of community at CWC and points to the importance of friendship networks and participation in clubs, sports teams, and other extracurricular activities and the ties students have outside the campus community with family and others as being central to the type of college culture that prevails. Bank's study of the experiences and orientations of college women provides a basis for comparison with the orientations and experiences of women at Midwest.

Horowitz (1987), a historian and cultural analyst, identified three primary college student subcultures: college men and women, outsiders, and rebels. Her analysis also includes an analysis of a more recent version of outsider subculture that she calls the "subculture of the new outsiders." The subculture of college men, and later women, emerged, she notes, out of violent revolts in the late eighteenth and early nineteenth centuries between the students, all of whom were men, and university personnel, including faculty. The subculture of "college men," characterized by high spirits, insubordination, sexuality, and strong ties to peers, was the bedrock of college student culture and included an ongoing hostility to the intrusion of adult authority or control. College sororities and fraternities have their roots in the historic subculture of college men.

Outsiders who viewed college as a means for entering a profession or who strived for a career that would move them up the social class structure, and who were therefore interested in doing well in their studies and in the approval of faculty, were viewed as "grinds" by college men and women. In turn, outsiders generally viewed college men and women who focused on peer fun as immature and frivolous. Rebels entered the college scene as children of middle-class families who were excluded from the dominant college man culture, initially often because they were Jewish or lacked the family background and status prerequisite to entering the college man fraternity world. The rebels engaged in conflict with the values and domination of the college men subculture on campuses and struggled for positions in campus politics and journalism. They also often had intellectual interests beyond the curriculum in the arts and politics.

New outsiders, she maintains, now dominate the college scene and are focused on maintaining or gaining social status through occupations that require them to earn specialized college degrees. This group, she maintains, unlike earlier outsiders who embraced mastering the skills and gaining the knowledge they needed to move ahead socially and who used college as a time to gain cultural skills and knowledge through interaction with faculty, is primarily focused on making good grades almost exclusively. From the period following the Vietnam War to the time when her book was written in the late 1980s, Horowitz maintains that most college students focused their energies on becoming professionals motivated by the desire for financial well-being and security. The new outsider orientation, according to Horowitz, has triumphed over the college men and women and the rebels in numbers on contemporary college campuses.

Horowitz (1987) places the subcultures she finds on contemporary college campuses in historical perspective, tracing their roots to earlier eras when the subculture orientations emerged in colleges in the United States. Her work became particularly important as a source of comparison with the college student subcultures at Midwest. The contextualization of the college student subcultures she found present in the 1980s, within broad social patterns of change and the shift of U.S. society from an agrarian to an industrial society, provided an important basis for thinking about the patterns of social change since the 1980s that are shaping college student subcultures and experience today.

CHANGING FORMS OF INTIMATE RELATIONSHIPS IN CONTEMPORARY SOCIETIES

Lasch's (1978) *The Culture of Narcissism: American Life in an Age of Diminishing Expectations*, Bellah and colleagues' (1985) *Habits of the Heart: Individualism and Commitment in American Life*, and Cancian's ([1987] 1990) *Love in America: Gender and Self-Development* make significant and distinct contributions to our understanding of the interconnections between social and cultural change and changes in identity construction, intimate relationships, and the changing nature of community in contemporary industrialized societies. While theory, methodology, conceptual tools, and conclusions diverge, these sociologists share core concerns that are relevant to the analysis at hand. First, each work puts forward an argument that theorizes connections between childhood psychological development, identity, and broader patterns of social change. Second, each attempts to capture the nature of contemporary intimate relationships (friendship and family, sexual relationships, marriage). And third, each outlines how changes in the private and public spheres are interconnected and suggests or implies how the relationship between public and private spheres can be altered to improve people's lives.

Lasch argues that there is a crisis in U.S. society rooted in the basic features of modernity, such as changes in the division of labor and the development of bureaucracy, but he focuses on the problems emerging from the more recent transition from competitive capitalism to monopolistic bureaucratic capitalism, a process that has undoubtedly become more intense since the writing of his book. It is characterized by the invasion of the family, intimate relationships, and virtually all aspects of the private and public spheres by bureaucratic apparatus and expert knowledge, resulting in the increasing predominance of narcissistic personalities. Narcissists are being produced, according to Lasch, in ever-increasing numbers by the institutions of advanced capitalism, especially in the nuclear family in which the father is absent. Sustaining relationships and commitments to others and the community are key concerns for Lasch, and he holds that narcissistic culture discourages commitment to others and the community and is a critical feature of the (moral) crisis in the United States (Lasch 1978, 32).

Lasch's analysis assumes that social life involves an essential tension between the individual and culture, and that limitations and, to some degree, the subordination of the self to the social order are essential for a viable society. He advocates a moral culture drawn from historical experience, not a therapeutic culture in which the goal is to free the individual from repressions of the past found in the family and in society. He employs historical critical analysis of structural, cultural, and psychological changes in the family, intimate relationships, the workplace, education, politics, and sports, and he concludes that America is becoming a society of isolated individuals, increasingly oppressed by the ruling class, corporate managers, experts, and the government, in which individuals are manipulated by the mass media and a cultural apparatus of consumer society. The root of the social crisis is based in a social structure in which the welfare state has invaded the family and transformed citizens into clients and producers into consumers and has produced personalities with malformed superegos who have no "individuality." Lasch believes that "new social forms require new forms of personality" (1978, 51), and that social patterns reproduce themselves in personality through the intermediary of the family. There is an unresolved and unacknowledged tension between his Marxist and Durkheimian orientations, which results in a lack of clarity regarding the social change he envisions as possible or desirable. For the purposes of this analysis, what is important in Lasch's analysis, primarily as a sounding board for the findings of this study, is the critique he makes of therapeutic culture and his contention that increasing numbers of narcissists are being produced in contemporary culture, and the sources he posits for this development. Twenge (2006) offers a perspective that is consistent with Lasch's (1978). Taking a social psychological approach in her analysis of contemporary youth, or the Gen Y generation, which she dubs "generation me," she maintains that they are far more narcissistic than previous generations. She looks to parents, education, and media as influences shaping this trend.

Bellah and colleagues (1985) emphasize the role of radical individualism in weakening social integration and strong community commitments among Americans. While Lasch (1978) focused on social structural influences in shaping the psychological development and

behavior of Americans, Bellah and colleagues (1985) focused on therapeutic culture and the values associated with radical individualist ideology as the sources of social malaise. Bellah offers a quasicommunitarian
critique and approach to restore a sense of civic commitment and
engagement that will create a community of meaning and shared values.
He maintains that individualism as a creed undermines social integration and community commitment and fosters a therapeutic culture in
which expressive individualism predominates.

The tight social integration and sense of commitment to the collective well-being that Bellah and colleagues (1985) maintain characterized
the earlier history of the United States were, as we know, based on relatively homogeneous populations integrated under patriarchal religion
and republican political structures that privileged white men of European descent at the expense of women and racial and ethnic minorities.
The social integration was also not just lodged in commonly held values
but in survival needs linked to the economic base structure of the times,
strict behavioral guidelines and roles, and highly restrictive options
based on gender, race, ethnicity, and class.

One comes away from Lasch (1978) and Bellah and colleagues
(1985) sensing that retrenchment, whether aimed at a return to and
reclaiming the biblical and republican traditions of a better past or
socialist revolution, implies that the power would continue to rest with
those who traditionally have written the dominant history and wielded
the power. Bellah and colleagues' contention that the majority of
middle-class Americans hold "expressive individualist" views that place
their own personal self-fulfillment as the highest value in their lives and
privilege private life and intimate relationships as the source for their
fulfillment is doubtless accurate in a very general way, but models of
individualism exemplified in the ideas and practices of Midwest college
students are more complex and nuanced than Lasch (1978) and Bellah
and colleagues (1985) theorize. In part, this may be because the privilege of white, middle-class, middle-age, male heterosexual life experience in their accounts, the interpretation of women's lives through that
lens and an ambivalence toward women's changing roles, and the relatively little attention given to young people, racial and ethnic minorities,
nonheterosexuals, or other nondominant groups (many of whom have
become increasingly significant in organizing social movements emerging out of identity issues and in shaping public culture), limit the range
of experiences of contemporary culture that they explore. Midwest
undergraduates are mostly young, women make up over half of the
population, and this sample was designed to ensure that people from
different class backgrounds and racial and ethnic groups in attendance

at Midwest were included in the research. It is therefore not altogether surprising that the ideas about individualism and identity expressed by many of the students in this book are not completely consistent with the patterns theorized by Lasch (1978) or Bellah and colleagues (1985).

Focusing on love, marriage, and friendship in *Love in America: Gender and Self-Development*, Cancian ([1987] 1990) argues that recent trends point to the emergence of two forms of "androgynous" intimate relationships characterized by a greater balance of autonomy (self-development) and attachment (love), which are replacing a "self" defined by rigid gender roles with a more whole and flexible "self." The two primary forms of androgynous relationships are an "independent blueprint," in which men and women pursue self-development and love separately rather than in relationship to each other, and an "interdependent blueprint," based on mutual development, recognizing that self-development can occur only in relation to others and values intimacy, support, trust, communication, and commitment. According to Cancian, the "independent blueprint" holds the danger of producing a "culture of narcissism," as described by Lasch. The "interdependent blueprint" left undetected by social critics such as Lasch, communitarians, and quasicommunitarians such as Bellah and colleagues (1985), which Cancian clearly finds preferable, is becoming a social, cultural, and psychological ideal. Cancian draws on the work of Guntrip (1961), whose psychoanalytical approach is concerned with the transition from dependency in infancy to adult interdependence, rather than placing a strong emphasis on autonomy as Freud did.

According to Cancian ([1987] 1990), the feminization of love, which occurred during the period of industrialization, results in lopsided and rigidly gendered constructions of "self" in which men and women are stunted in developing their full potential as individuals, intimates, and members of the larger community. It produces depression among women, physical abuse of dependent wives, early deaths of men, and marital conflict over communication of feelings, intimacy, and power. Cancian presents four "blueprints" of marriage. The first blueprint of "family duty" (prevalent in the United States from 1840 to 1880), associated with the Victorian ideal in which the woman is responsible to fulfill her duty to her family, and the second of "companionship," which gained prevalence in the 1920s and incorporated more emphasis on intimacy in marriage relying on rigid gender roles, are both based on "feminized love." The third (independent) and fourth (interdependent) blueprints are embedded in a conception of "androgynous love." The decline of the companionship model began in the 1960s. The trend to independent and interdependent blueprints has gone through changes in overlapping eras. For instance, the 1920s and the late 1960s were characterized by an acceleration of the trend, while the 1950s saw it reversed, with gender roles being more rigidly defined. The "independent" and "interdependent" blueprints emerged strongly in the 1970s.

For Cancian, the individual is related to others and society rather than in opposition to them. She agrees that economic security and security in relationships are important to a sense of self but maintains that constraining beliefs and expectations shared with others do not have to be hegemonic or experienced as external and embodied in superior authorities. Values and rules can be developed and changed by the participants themselves in a decentralized and democratized culture, where both the benefits of shared beliefs and minimum restriction and domination can exist. Additionally, she argues that there is a "rich social life" possible in modern society found in friendship networks, subcultures, voluntary associations, and neighborhoods. "The decline of community ties for most Americans has not been very large, and the decreasing authority of the national culture has been partly offset by the increasing authority of subcultures" (Cancian [1987]1990, 54).

Cancian acknowledges that many of Lasch's (1978) and Bellah and colleagues' (1985) criticisms of contemporary culture are partly valid, revealing the weaknesses of the "independent blueprint" and the need for commitment to other people and to moral standards. But she points out the dangers in the Durkheimian decline-of-community approach. It exaggerates the collapse of social ties, romanticizes the past, and underestimates the costs of patriarchal authority. Cancian holds that most people are not deluded and victimized by the system as Lasch, for instance, asserts, according to numerous studies of contemporary Americans. "Most seekers for self-development seem to be following the interdependence blueprint, and they are making small but substantial steps to a better private life" (Cancian [1987] 1990, 60). She believes "instead of looking back to traditional gender roles or way ahead to the distant possibility of revolutionary change, we should recognize and cultivate this positive development in American styles of love" (154). For her, this approach extends to all relationships and includes friends and relatives as well as couples.

Bellah and colleagues' analysis of the implications of individualist ideology and Cancian's blueprints of intimate relationships inform the typology of blueprints of individualism developed in this book out of the approaches to individualism and identity work found to be guiding the life trajectory plans of students.

IDENTITY CONSTRUCTION AND
RELATIONSHIPS IN LATE MODERNITY

Important to the findings of this research about the identity work and individualization process of college students are several broad theoretical works dealing with the changing patterns of individualization and identity development in late modernity in connection to economic and political conditions of late modernity. Key for this analysis are Bauman's work *The Individualized Society* (2001), which represents a macro-sociological alternative to Bellah and colleagues' perspectives on modernity and late modernity. Giddens's book, *Modernity and Self-Identity* (1991), deftly theorizes that the links between structural changes in late modernity and changes in the nature of identity construction also contribute to theory elaboration, particularly in developing the ideal-type blueprints of individualism found among Midwest students. Both theorize a new form of identity work demanded by structural and cultural changes occurring in the world.

According to Bauman (2001), the nature of interpersonal relations is changing dramatically in late modernity and is now unpredictable and transitory. He theorizes that there are two main influences in the network of human relations in late modernity, a trend toward "impersonalization" of relations and a shift away from paternalistic relations, and the rise of relations involving people in participation in citizenship and politics within nations as self-interested and vulnerable actors. Society is increasingly experienced as uncertain and insecure because of the failure of traditional state-centered institutions to provide stability in the global context; deregulation and the privileging of market competition and the freedom of capital and finance with little consideration of organizing society to enhance other types of freedom; the deconstruction of social safety nets; and the rising dominance of the market and the spirit of consumerism now shaping interpersonal relations so that they actually reflect the characteristics of the market. While individuals may be freed from ascribed identities, they are now constrained by the task of achieving an identity in a highly unstable and unpredictable world. In somewhat similar fashion, Beck and Beck-Gernsheim ([2001] 2002) argue that human identity, which was once prescribed and certain, now consists of an overlapping set of nonlinear tasks for individuals to complete on their own in order to make their way through life. Each life is full of risks and must be faced alone.

Giddens argues that these changes have potentially emancipatory implications. He maintains that in late modernity the self has become a "reflexively organized endeavor" (1991, 5) and is no longer primarily defined by custom, religion, family, or even occupation or guild membership, as was once the case. Late modernity implies, according to Giddens, who draws from Ulrich Beck in this part of his reasoning, risk by the "fact that modern social life introduces new forms of danger which humanity has to face" (28) and "living in the 'risk society' means living with a calculative attitude to the open possibilities of action, positive and negative, with which, as individuals and globally, we are confronted in a continuous way in our contemporary social existence" (28). Now people have to embrace a process of ongoing choice and self-determination. It is through the self-referential organizing lifestyle choices and actions that people in late modernity construct the "narrative of self-identity" (Giddens 1991, 81) that enables them to obtain a sense of ontological security.

Giddens points out that "in high modernity, we all not only follow lifestyles, but in an important sense are forced to do so—we have no choice but to choose. A lifestyle can be defined as a more or less integrated set of practices which an individual embraces, not only because such practices fulfill utilitarian needs, but because they give material form to a particular narrative of self-identity" (Giddens 1991, 81). They must do this in the face of a radically destabilized world. "The more posttraditional the settings in which an individual moves, the more lifestyle concerns the very core of self-identity, its making and remaking" (81). He turns to behaviorist psychology of child development to argue his points. He maintains that the predictable caretaking of infants that forms the basis for trust and security is replicated in adult life through the lifestyle choices and habitual actions that individuals adopt. Giddens's vision, more so than Bauman's, holds onto the idea that the Enlightenment's promise of autonomy, self-determination, and free agency for the individual may yet be fulfilled, though perhaps not in the way it was once envisioned.

Appendix 2.1

The data in Table 2.1 locate students based on the relationship theme that was most salient in their discussions about their relationships with their parents by FGC/PGC status, gender, and race/ethnicity minority or white status. Some students touched on more than one of these issues, but generally they talked about a set of things that gave priority to one aspect of their relationship with their parents that was of central concern to them.

TABLE 2.1

THEMES OF AUTONOMY, COMFORT, AND UNDERSTANDING IN STUDENT DESCRIPTIONS OF THEIR RELATIONSHIPS WITH THEIR PARENTS BY PARENTAL EDUCATION (PGC/FGC), GENDER, AND RACE/ETHNICITY MINORITY AND WHITE STATUS

	Minority PGC Females	White PGC Females	Minority PGC Males	White PGC Males	Minority FGC Females	White FGC Females	Minority FGC Males	White FGC Males
Autonomy	1	13		5		1		
Comfort	1	6	2	13	1	1	1	4
Understanding	1		1		3	3		3

PGC = Parent(s) Graduated College; FGC = First-Generation College Student

Appendix 2.2

Twenty-three of the thirty-one women and twenty-one of the twenty-nine men come from two-parent households in which both their parents are their birth parents. This fact was a source of pride for a number of these students, who made a point of mentioning it. Two women and one man have reconstituted families, and seven women and six men came to college from single-parent households. A higher number of students whose parents did not attend college lived in blended- or single-family households prior to coming to college.

TABLE 2.2
FAMILY STRUCTURE OF PGC AND FGC STUDENTS BY GENDER

	PGC		FGC		Totals	
	Female	Male	Female	Male	Female	Male
Never Divorced, Two Parent	18	21	4	1	22	22
Reconstituted	1		2	1	3	1
Single Parent	3		3	6	6	6
Totals	22	21	9	8	31	29

PGC = Parent(s) Graduated College; FGC = First-Generation College Student

Of the twenty-two women from never-divorced families, eighteen also had at least one parent who attended college. Twenty-one of the twenty-two men from two-parent, never-divorced families also had parent(s) who attended college.

Three of the twenty-two women whose parent(s) attended college came from single-parent households and one from a reconstituted family. One of the three who lived in a single-parent household is

201

Taylor, a black woman raised by her father. The other two are white women with single mothers. Three of the nine women who are first-generation college students come from single-parent households. Two are African American women, and one is white. Two FGC women come from reconstituted families. One is Asian American the other is American Indian. The American Indian woman lived many years with her single mother and views her as the primary parent. Four of the six women who lived with single mothers prior to coming to college are racial and ethnic minorities, and two are white.

None of the men with a living parent who graduated from college came from single-parent or reconstituted families. Though Roy's birth mother had gone to college, he came to college living with a father and stepmother who were not college graduates, so he was placed as a first-generation college student. The six men who were raised by a single parent and the man who came from a reconstituted family were all white first-generation college students. All of the racial and ethnic minority males in the sample came from two-parent, never-divorced families.

A PGC freshman woman who lived with her single mother prior to coming to college said she talks to her mother at least four times a day on the phone, and that her mother is her best friend. Further, she indicated, "When I go shopping I always call her and describe what I'm thinking of buying to find out if it will look good on me." One of the three white PGC females who lived with single mothers prior to college said that her mother is her best friend. She did not complain about wanting more independence or autonomy. The other white PGC woman from a single-mother household was very angry at her mother because her mother was in a relationship with a man she dislikes. Among the racial and ethnic minority females from single-parent families, one PGC African American woman from a single-father household and one FGC African American woman from a single-mother household had some degree of conflict with their parent. One African American woman from a single-mother household said that her mother is thoughtful, sometimes sending her cash for buying clothes, but she did not describe the constant contact and interaction that characterized the white PGC women's relationships with their single mothers.

Single-mother PGC households appear to result in close bonds between daughters and mothers, with little concern on the part of female students about struggling for more autonomy. For instance, three of the six white PGC women who indicated that they are comfortable in their relationships with their parent(s) were from single-mother households. Because there were no PGC men from single-parent or reconstituted families in the sample, no patterns regarding the influence of family structure for PGC males were identified. The FGC women (two racial and ethnic minority students and one white) from single-parent families did not report the intensely close relationships with their mothers that three of the white PGC women reported. Instead, they described relationships ranging from demanding to supportive.

Six of the eight men who are first-generation college students were raised by single parents. All are white. Two had lived with their fathers and four with their mothers. One of the men raised by their mothers expressed strong and positive feelings about his relationship. He was a nontraditional student who had not lived with his mother for many years, but he expressed great appreciation to her for raising him and his siblings in conditions of poverty. The other three raised by single mothers had more distant relationships with their mothers. The mother of one of these men had moved to Midwest City to make going to college financially easier and to be there to support him, which he was ambivalent about. Over time, he distanced from her, saying that they did not "get along well," and eventually he said that he rarely sees her. Another had lived independently a number of years prior to coming to college and felt that his mother had a dysfunctional lifestyle that had held him back in some ways. While he saw her on some special occasions, he said they were not "close."

One of the men who had lived with his father expressed very positive feelings for his father but also said he regretted that his father's financial status was not as good as his mother's, who had remarried. He explained that he had chosen not to live with his mother while his sisters had lived with her, and that he had been economically disadvantaged by his choice. He had contact with his mother and expressed some negative feelings about her. One of the men who had lived with his father indicated that he had moved out in order to have more "privacy" and did not express a close connection to his father.

Students from reconstituted families included one PGC white woman, who described a relationship with her parents similar to PGC white women from never-divorced families. The white FGC woman from a reconstituted family expressed similar concerns as the FGC women from never-divorced families. One of the FGC students from a reconstituted family who was largely raised by a single mother is Asian American. Though she now has a stepfather, her mother's remarriage occurred late in her development, and she identified strongly with her mother as the primary parent. She viewed her mother as the one pressuring her to succeed academically and as the source of parental financial and emotional support. Roy, the FGC man from a reconstituted family, mentioned feelings of distance from, and discomfort with, his family as he adjusted to the death of his mother and his father's remarriage to someone who also had children.

APPENDIX 2.3

TABLE 2.3
STUDENTS WHO WANT TO RETURN HOME TO LIVE AND THOSE WHO WANT TO
MOVE AWAY FROM HOME AFTER COLLEGE BY RACE/ETHNICITY, GENDER,
AND PARENTAL COLLEGE EDUCATIONAL ATTAINMENT

	White FGC		Racial/Ethnic Minority FGC		White PGC		Racial/Ethnic Minority PGC	
	Female	*Male*	*Female*	*Male*	*Female*	*Male*	*Female*	*Male*
Plan (Want) to Return "Home" to Live after College	1	3		1	6	8	1	1
Plan (Want) to Move "Away" after College	4	4	4		13	10	2	2
Totals	5	7	4	1	19	18	3	3

FGC = First-Generation College Student; PGC = Parent(s) Graduated College

APPENDIX 3

National Lampoon's Van Wilder (2002) stars Ryan Reynolds as Van Wilder and Tara Reid as his romantic interest, Gwen Pearson. Van Wilder, a fun-loving party animal who manipulates the college student social scene with Machiavellian finesse, is the hero. The female lead is studying journalism and works for the school newspaper. They meet because she is assigned to do a series of stories on Van for the school newspaper. The upper-middle-class white son of an affluent man, Van has been in college for seven years and is in no hurry to graduate until two things happen: his father cuts off his financing, and he meets Gwen, who rejects his overtures and quickly becomes the object of his lustful and romantic desires.

Early in the movie Van's father, played by Tim Matheson, confronts his son with the fact that he has been in college for seven years without earning a degree. Van says, "I've done a lot in seven years dad." Vance Wilder Sr., his father, replies, "If you don't have a doctorate you haven't done enough. You have wasted enough of my money and your time." And he tells Van that he is coming home. Van replies, "No I'm staying here with my friends," to which Vance Wilder Sr. responds, "Fine, maybe your friends can pay your tuition, because this morning I placed a stop payment on this semester's check. I'm sorry son, but sometimes in life you have to realize a poor investment and simply cut your losses."

Gwen is dating a fraternity boy, the villain of the movie, a pre-med grind who makes her help him study all the time. He demands sex to help him relax before exams. He cultivates the favor of adults, including her parents and university faculty and administrators, and he serves on student government. His snobby, careerist, and sexually inept ways are contrasted with Van's "easygoing," fun-loving, sexually knowledgeable nature.

Van is an independent who sees worthiness in everyone from nerds to Taj Mahal, the Indian personal assistant he hires to manage his social calendar. Van raises money for college programs and "hooks up" sexually frustrated men with beautiful, sexually available women he knows. He is sexually adept and is desired by women from the freshman who readily offers herself to him to assuage his pain when Gwen appears to be going to get engaged to someone else, to the grey-haired university administrator who bribes him to have sex with her in return for not being kicked out of college for nonpayment of tuition after his father cuts him off financially.

Van organizes fabulous parties for different groups of students on campus, and they pay him handsomely for doing it, because he is the best party organizer around. He is loved by women and men alike. His popularity rests on his rejection of the hypocrisy of institutional and social achievement within the public sphere, and his focus is on the private-pleasures sphere, where what really matters is having fun, making friends, parties, and heterosexual sex.

When Van is really opening up to Gwen he confides, "My dad just didn't see me as a sound investment anymore. But he gave up on me and my mom a long time before I ever came here." Gwen responds, "Maybe seven years of tuition is a good way to remind him that you're still angry?" Abruptly, Van switches topics, his face showing she has hit home with her comment. He asks, "So how long have you and pre-med Richard been together?" "Since my freshman year," Gwen says sweetly. "I bet he's a tidy-widy guy," notes Van. "Excuse me?" responds Gwen, a little exasperatedly. Van explains, "White elastic band, constrictive. You can tell a lot about a person by the kind of drawers they wear. Like you, granny panties I bet?" Gwen asks, "Does that allude to me being the plain, boring type?" "No, I just wanted a visual," counters Van. "Well I think it takes a lot more than the kind of underwear one wears to define them as a person" Gwen states emphatically. Incredulous, Van responds, "Like what???" "Like their actions. For instance, most people want to get out of school so they can make money, you're trying to make money to stay in school," notes Gwen. A little defensively, Van says, "I like it here." Gwen asks, "What about your future?" Van responds, "You take life way too seriously." "Life is serious," says Gwen. "You know," says Van," I used to party with this guy who once told me, 'Van don't take life too seriously, you'll never get out alive, . . . you think about the future too much, you kind of forget about the present."

Van eventually realizes that maybe he has been delaying graduation because he is afraid of real life and living for work the way his father does. Gwen ends up falling for Van and writes his father letting him know of Van's graduation and sends him a copy of her laudatory final story for the school newspaper about Van. Van's father shows up for the graduation party, as does Gwen, who has broken up with her former boyfriend. In the last scene, Van's father is proud of him, and Gwen is his. She enters the Hawaiian luau-themed party wearing a white bikini top and mini skirt. Van has on a grey sleeveless T-shirt and dark slacks. She approaches, smiling. Van says, "You look so, wow!" She responds, "I was hoping you'd say that." Then she reaches up to put a lei around his neck and says, "May I?" His father watches from a distance. Van quips, "As long as we cuddle afterwards, so much I have to say, the article, I was scared that you wouldn't come." She says, "I was trying to decide which panties to wear." He asks, "Which ones did you choose?" And the last word of the movie is Gwen's. She answers, "none," and they smile at each other and embrace and kiss as the camera pans away, showing them in a huge crowd of revelers.

Appendix 4

Table 4 shows the primary and secondary ideal-type college student cultural orientations of the students included in this research and indicates whether students are first-generation college students or their parent(s) attended college, as well as their sex, race, and ethnicity. This table shows that the highest number of students in the sample have embraced the careerist subculture, followed by, in order of most to least in frequency, the credentialist, collegiate, alternative, and academic primary orientations.

The majority of students who were studied at Midwest University hold primary orientations that are careerist or credentialist. Of those in the sample, 35 percent are careerist, 26.6 percent are credentialist, 21.6 percent are collegiate, 10 percent are alternative, and 6.6 percent are academic in their primary orientation.

Twenty-one people are careerist in orientation, and sixteen are strongly linked to credentialism. Fourteen women and seven men orient primarily toward careerism. Ten PGC women and four PGC men have primary careerist orientations. Four FGC women and three FGC men are careerist in their primary orientation. Eight of those defined by the university as racial or ethnic minority students are careerist in orientation.

TABLE 4

PRIMARY AND SECONDARY COLLEGE-STUDENT CULTURAL ORIENTATIONS BY PARENTAL COLLEGE EDUCATION, GENDER, AND RACE AND ETHNICITY

Secondary ↓	Parental College Education	Academic		Careerist		Collegiate		Credentialist		Alternative		Totals	
Primary →		F	M	F	M	F	M	F	M	F	M	F	M
Academic	PGC			3W, 1A	1W						1W	4	2
	FGC			1W, 2B	2W, 1B							3	3
Careerist	PGC					4W	1W					4	1
	FGC		2W			1W		1W, 1AI	1W	2W	1W	5	4
Collegiate	PGC			3W, 1ME	1W, 1H, 1B			3W, 1B	7W, 1AA			8	11
	FGC			1AA					1W			1	1
Credentialist	PGC					1W	6W			1W	1W	2	7
	FGC												
Alternative	PGC	2W		2W								4	
	FGC												
Totals		2	2	14	7	6	7	6	10	3	3	31	29

PGC = Parent(s) Graduated College; FGC = First-Generation College Student; F = Female; M = Male; A = African; AA = Asian American; AI = American Indian; B = Black; H = Hispanic; IA = Indian American; ME = Multiethnic; W = White

Two FGC women and two FGC men are credentialist in their primary orientation. Four PGC women and eight PGC men hold credentialist primary cultural orientations. Six women and ten men gravitate to credentialism. Three racial or ethnic minority students hold views and behaviors consistent with a credentialist approach in college. Thirteen students, six women and seven men, gravitate primarily to the collegiate culture. Five women with a collegiate primary subculture orientation are PGC students, and seven of the men are. One woman with a collegiate primary orientation is an FGC student. Six people, three women and three men, have an alternative primary orientation. Two women with alternative primary orientations are FGC, and one is PGC. Two men with alternative primary orientations are PGC, and one is FGC. Only four students, two women and two men, gravitate primarily to the academic cultural orientation. The two men with academic primary orientations are FGC students, and the two women are PGC students.

Notably the most frequent secondary orientation among students is collegiate. Twelve are male, and nine are female. All but two have parents who attended college. Six are racial- or ethnic-minority students. The frequency of other secondary orientations is from most to least frequent: careerist, academic, credentialist, and alternative. Fourteen people, nine women and five men, align with the careerist cultural orientation as a secondary orientation. Five of the women and four of the men in this group are first-generation college students. Four women and one man in this group have parent(s) with college educations.

Twelve students have secondary academic orientations. Seven women and five men are in this group. Three women and three men are first-generation college students, and four women and two men have parent(s) who graduated from college. Two first-generation black women and one FGC black man align with a secondary orientation consistent with the academic cultural orientation, as does an African woman whose parents hold college degrees.

Nine students, two women and seven men, all of whom are white and whose parent(s) attended college, hold secondary orientations consistent with credentialist values and behaviors. Seven of the nine have primary collegiate orientations, while two are alternative in their primary orientations. Four white women with college-educated parent(s) hold secondary alternative orientations. Two of these women gravitate strongly to the academic, while two hold careerist primary orientations.

APPENDIX 5

The ideal-type blueprints of individualism that students use as guides in their life trajectory projects are included in Table 5.1, with the students in the sample located by college- student cultural orientations, gender, and race ethnicity.

TABLE 5.1
BLUEPRINTS OF INDIVIDUALISM BY COLLEGE-STUDENT CULTURAL
ORIENTATIONS, GENDER, AND RACE AND ETHNICITY

Blueprints of Individualism	Traditional		Independent		Interdependent	
	F	M	F	M	F	M
Academic/Careerist				1W		1W
Academic/Alternative					2W	
Careerist/Academic	1W 1B 1A	1W 1B	2W	1W	1W 1B	1W
Careerist/Alternative			2W			
Careerist/Collegiate	1W	1B	2W 1ME 1AA	1W 1H		
Collegiate/Careerist			3W	1W	2W	
Collegiate/Credentialist			1W	6W		
Credentialist/Careerist	1W	1W			1AI	
Credentialist/Collegiate	1W	3W 1AA	2W 1B	5W		
Alternative/Academic		1W				
Alternative/Careerist	2W	1W				
Alternative/Credentialist				1W	1W	
Totals by Gender	8	10	15	17	8	2

F = Female; M = Male; A = African; AA = Asian American; AI = American Indian; B = Black; H = Hispanic; ME = Multiethnic; W = White

215

Table 5.2 shows the blueprints of individualism adopted by Midwest students in the sample by gender and parental educational attainment.

TABLE 5.2
BLUEPRINTS OF INDIVIDUALISM BY GENDER AND PARENTAL EDUCATIONAL ATTAINMENT

Blueprints of Individualism	Traditional Individualist	Independent Individualist	Interdependent Individualist
PGC Females	3	13	6
FGC Females	5	2	2
PGC Males	6	15	
FGC Males	4	2	2
Total	18	32	10

PGC=Parent(s) Graduated College; FGC=First Generation College Student

NOTES

CHAPTER 1

1. In 2003, the United States' racial and ethnic minority composition of the on-campus undergraduate student population at Midwest was 5.6 percent African American, 0.6 percent American Indian or Alaskan Native, 2.7 percent Asian or Pacific Islander, and 1.6 percent Hispanic.
2. These data were provided by the Office of Institutional Research and include all undergraduates, freshman through seniors, on campus for the years indicated.
3. These data were provided in a table titled "First-Generation FTC Students by AU Fall 2006" on the Web pages of the office of the registrar for fall of 2006. "AU" means academic unit.
4. Schwalbe's definition of identity work is this:

> By identity work I mean anything we do, alone or with others, to establish, change, or lay claim to meanings as particular kinds of persons. As individuals, we must do some kind of identity work in every encounter. We do this when we give signs through dress, speech, demeanor, posture—that tell others who and what we are, how we are likely to behave, and how we expect to be treated. We do it also when we reflect on the meanings of our identities and try to reshape those meanings. This can be done alone, in thought or writing. Most identity work is interactive, however, since it is by engaging with others that we create and affirm the meanings that matter. (1996, 105)

CHAPTER 2

1. Jane is a composite of two students, both of whom began college as pre-health professions majors, both of whom were in a sorority, and both of whom had parents who paid in full for their college educations.

2. In my introductory classes students were asked to list their social statuses in rank order. A social status is defined in the textbook *Sociology: A Global Perspective*, which is used in the course, as "a position in a social structure," and the social role associated with a status is the "behavior expected of a status in relationship to another status" (Ferrante 2006, 153–54). In these classes I have asked students to rank the importance of the social statuses they hold as college students, and each semester about 40 percent rank their status as son or daughter as being the most important one in their lives. When the second most important social status is included, the total moves to between 80 and 90 percent.

3. The educational levels achieved by parents are linked to the educational achievement levels of their children. Family structure is another factor that affects the likelihood of educational attainment, and it is a factor in shaping the types of relationships that students report having with their parents. Income also is linked to educational attainment, with the college educated earning far more than those with only high school educations (Spain and Bianchi 1996). For instance in 1992 "a college-educated woman earned 58 percent more than a high school-educated woman" and a "college-educated man earned more than a high school-educated man" (Spain and Bianchi 1996, 121). "And in an era of rising college tuitions, wealthy families are able to provide (or heavily subsidize) college costs and to forego childrens' earnings (Mare 1995, 177, 181; Steelman and Powell 1991)" (Spain and Bianchi 1996, 64). In keeping with this, college-educated parents of students at Midwest are, on average, more affluent than parents who do not have college degrees.

4. Estimate based on data on student financial need and aid provided by Institutional Research and Planning.

5. In some cases this appeared to be discursive identity work that claimed independence and control in the face of contradictory information provided by the same informant at other times during the interview, but most often it appeared to be consistent with other evidence.

6. "The Millennial generation" of relatively privileged youth, Howe

and Strauss point out, is the most supervised and scheduled generation ever. "For most, hardly an hour goes by in which they are not within sight of a parent, teacher, a coach, a relative, or a child-care provider—or strapped into a minivan, in supervised transit between various adult-watched activities" (2000, 134). They point to a study by the University of Michigan's Institute for Social Research that compared time diaries of Generation X children ages three to twelve in 1981 with the same age group of Generation Y children and found that there had been a 37 percent reduction in the amount of time Generation Y children spend in unstructured activities (Robinson and Godbey 1999). They also reference the University of Maryland's "Use of Time Project" and the Michigan time diaries research done at the Institute for Social Research and Population Studies Center at the University of Michigan to demonstrate that parents of Generation Y are spending more time with them than did previous cohorts of parents (Sandberg and Hofferth 2001). They note that the amount parents spent with their children each week fell sharply from 1965 to 1975, but that since then it has turned around and climbed steadily. Parents of the current cohort have spent more time with them. By 1995, the parents of Generation Y were spending about the same number of hours with their children as parents had done thirty years earlier (Howe and Strauss 2000, 135).

7. One of the Web pages of the University of Texas at Dallas Student Counseling Center is titled "How to Raise a Parent While at College." The tips provided there for college students are typical of other such resources for the college bound and mirror some of the behaviors described by students at Midwest University who said they were successful in negotiating a new, more adult relationship with their parents. The Web pages point out, "properly raising a parent requires attention and thought. . . . Teaching them that you can take care of yourself *and* have a life is difficult. Acknowledging and working with their problem of letting go is challenging." The way to make your life "easier in the long run" is to be "proactive and invest time in your parents now." Students are told to remember that they "are not the only one learning and growing," that "parents don't magically know how to relate to their grown children as adults," and that "most parent-child relationships have a certain level of dependency" (University of Texas, Dallas, 2005, emphasis in original). If you want to reduce your parents' "dependency," you need to tell them about your successes and failures and let them know that you are handling your mistakes responsibly. Doing this will help them accept your new level of independence.

8. Roy is a composite of two students, both of whom are white FGC students who joined fraternities.

9. Of the ten out-of-state women, eight have parents who attended college, and for seven of the eight women, their parents are paying a substantial part or all of their college costs. One woman in this group is on an athletic scholarship. Only two of the eleven women who are first-generation college students are from out of state. One is African American and works as well as receiving scholarship support. The other is white and works on campus and off campus for a total of about forty-five hours a week. She manages this by working at a job that involves working all night, two nights a week.

10. Two women and four men visit home weekly. Three women and one man visit every two weeks. Four women and six men visit monthly. Four women and two men visit every two months. Eleven women and seven men visit home, or see their families, on major holidays and breaks. Four men and one woman, all from families where parents did not attend college, report having already established an adult home separate from their parents. Five women and three men report working during breaks and summers at a location that is not near their parents. Of these, two, one man and one woman, report working near a "summer" home of their parents where they can live independently for much of the break and be visited briefly by their parents.

CHAPTER 3

1. An e-mail directive issued by a top university administrator after 9/11, for instance, cautioned faculty members not to discuss 9/11 in the classroom. Some students said that they wanted to be able to discuss it in classes. One student said in an exasperated tone, "We can't ever really discuss the important things in class!"

A public forum facilitated by trained personnel was held specifically to deal with 9/11. In the context of the social relations within which the university as an institution exists, this is the bureaucratically rational and safe approach to take and cannot be faulted. Still, the message received by college students over time is that issues that really matter to them, and that things that are really important in the "real world" are not discussed in class. This contributes to a superficial quality in the public and quasipublic "shared" college student culture. This points to a failure in our culture to create spaces where difference can be discussed and "better versions" of reality can be established for the collective [Lara 1998].

2. Trevor is a multicomposite.
3. According to Chris Hughes of Facebook, 21,210 undergraduates, almost all of the 21,551 undergraduates at Midwest, were on Facebook in June 2006 (Hughes 2006).
4. Trevor's Facebook profile is based on a synthesized multicomposite, not an actual individual Facebook profile.
5. In 2006, 45.8 percent of women and 28.5 percent of men living in residence halls chose single-gender floors (Purdie 2006b).
6. The African American student population, making up the largest racial or ethnic minority population at Midwest, though small, has 5.1 percent of its population pledged to the four fraternities and three sororities at Midwest that are in the National Pan-Hellenic Council. Of the 5.1 percent of African Americans in the Greek system, 5.3 percent are women and 4.8 percent are men (Condron 2006). The majority of white students in sororities pledge sororities in the Pan-Hellenic Conference. Most white men who join fraternities are in fraternities in the Interfraternity Council. As mentioned in chapter 1, about 21 percent of Midwest students were in sororities or fraternities at the time this research began.
7. Popular culture images, such as those depicted in *National Lampoon's Van Wilder* (2002), mentioned earlier in this chapter, also play a role in the construction of the generalized college student culture of Midwest. Racial and ethnic hierarchies are not directly structured as dominant and subordinate in the popular culture images, but by featuring token minorities at homecoming and other events and stereotyped minorities in movies, the idea of white dominance is reinforced as the norm, since white cultural norms and numbers are the givens in these movies.

CHAPTER 4

1. Bob is a composite.
3. Josephine's is a pseudonym for a local restaurant.

CHAPTER 5

1. Only three women, two who are straight and one who indicated that she is bisexual, said they do not plan to marry but were not

certain about wanting to have children. These women were romantically involved during college and expected to have intimate relationships but not to marry. A man who described himself as gay, who had been married to a woman and has children, did not describe a life trajectory that involved marriage or having children in the future.

2. For example, football games, homecoming, and basketball games, the authority of institutional actors, rules and regulations, and the importance of collegiate culture carried by fraternities and sororities across the generations and encouraged at the university generally as a way of integrating the undergraduate student population and encouraging them to identify with the university.

BIBLIOGRAPHY

Advisory Committee on Student Financial Assistance. 2002. *Empty Promises: The Myth of College Access in America*. Washington, DC: Advisory Committee on Student Financial Assistance.

Allahar, A., and James E. Côté. 1998. *Richer and Poorer: The Structure of Inequality in Canada*. Toronto, Canada: Lorimer.

Andres, Lesley, Paul Anisef, Harvey Krahn, Diane Looker, and Victor Thiessen. 1999. "The Persistence of Social Structure: Cohort, Class, and Gender Effects on the Occupational Aspirations and Expectations of Canadian Youth." *Journal of Youth Studies* 2 (3): 261–82.

Animal House. 1978/2003. DVD. Directed by John Landis.Universal City, CA.

Arnett, Jeffrey Jensen. 1997. "Young People's Conceptions of the Transition to Adulthood." *Youth & Society* 29:1–23.

———. 1998. "Learning to Stand Alone: The Contemporary American Transition to Adulthood in Cultural and Historical Context." *Human Development* 41: 295–315.

———. 2000. "Emerging Adulthood: A Theory of Development from the Late Teens through the Twenties." *American Psychologist* 55 (5): 469–80.

———. 2003. "Conceptions of the Transition to Adulthood among Emerging Adults in American Ethnic Groups." *New Directions for Child and Adolescent Development* 100 (Summer): 63–75.

Bae, Yupin, Susan Choy, Claire Geddes, Jennifer Sable, and Thomas Snyder. 2000. *Trends in Educational Equity of Girls and Women*. U.S. Department of Education, National Center for Education Statistics. Washington, DC: U.S. Government Printing Office.

Bank, Barbara J. 2003. *Contradictions in Women's Education: Traditionalism, Careerism, and Community at a Single-Sex College.* New York: Teachers College Press.

Bauman, Zygmunt. 2001. *The Individualized Society.* Cambridge, UK: Polity Press.

Beck, Ulrich. 1992. *Risk Society: Towards a New Modernity.* London: Sage.

———. 1997. *The Invention of Politics.* Cambridge, UK: Polity Press.

———. 1998. *Democracy without Enemies.* Cambridge, UK: Polity Press.

Beck, Ulrich, and Elisabeth Beck-Gernsheim. [2001] 2002. *Individualization.* Thousand Oaks, CA: Sage.

Becker, Gary S. 1964. *Human Capital: A Theoretical and Empirical Analysis, with Special Reference to Education.* New York: Columbia University Press.

Becker, Howard S., Blanch Greer, and Everett C. Hughes. 1995. *Making the Grade.* New Brunswick, NJ: Transaction.

Behrman, Jere R., Robert A. Pollak, and Paul Taubman. 1986. "Do Parents Favor Boys?" *International Economic Review* 27: 31–52.

Bellah, Robert N., Richard N. Madsen, William M. Sullivan, Ann Swidler, and Steven M. Tipton. 1985. *Habits of the Heart: Individualism and Commitment in American Life.* Berkeley and Los Angeles: University of California Press.

Blau, Peter M., and Otis D. Duncan. 1967. *The American Occupation Structure.* New York: John Wiley.

Bourdieu, Pierre. 1984. *Homo Academicus.* Stanford, CA: Stanford University Press.

———. 1986. "The Forms of Capital." In *Handbook of Theory and Research for the Sociology of Education*, ed. J. Richardson, 241–58. New York: Greenwood Press.

———. 1993. *The Field of Cultural Production.* New York: Columbia University Press.

Brown, Phillip. 1997. "The 'Third Wave': Education and the Ideology of Parentocracy." In *Education: Culture, Economy, Society*, ed. A. H. Halsey, Hugh Lauder, Phillip Brown, and Amy Stuart Wells, 393–408. New York: Oxford University Press.

Buchmann, Claudia, and Thomas A. DiPrete. 2006. "The Growing Female Advantage in College Completion: The Role of Family Background and Academic Achievement." *American Sociological Review* 71: 515–541.

Bugeja, Michael J. 2006. "Facing the Facebook." *The Chronicle of Higher Education* 52 (21): C1. Also available online at http://www.chroniile.com/jobs/2006/01/2006012301c.htm.

Bui, Khanh Van T. 2002. "First-Generation College Students at a Four-Year University: Background Characteristics, Reasons for Pursuing Higher Education, and First-Year Experiences." *College Student Journal* 36 (1): 3–11.

Burawoy, Michael, Alice Buton, Ann Arnett Ferguson, Kathryn J. Fox, Joshua Gamson, Nadine Gartrell, Leslie Hurst, Charles Kurzman, Leslie Salzinger, Joseph Schiffman, and Shiori Ui. 1991. *Ethnography Unbound: Power, and Resistance in the Modern Metropolis.* Berkeley: University of California Press.

Callahan, David. 2004. *The Cheating Culture: Why More Americans Are Doing Wrong to Get Ahead.* New York: Harcourt.

Cancian, Francesca M. [1987] 1990. *Love in America: Gender and Self-Development.* New York: Cambridge University Press.

Charles, Maria, and Karen Bradley. 2002. "Equal but Separate? A Cross-National Study of Sex Segregation in Higher Education." *American Sociological Review* 67: 573–99.

Chodorow, Nancy. 1978. *The Reproduction of Mothering: Psychoanalysis and the Sociology of Gender.* Berkeley: University of California Press.

Clark, Burton R., and Martin Trow. 1966. "The Organizational Context." In *College Peer Groups: Problems and Prospects for Research*, ed. Theodore M. Newcomb and Everett K. Wilson, 17–70. Chicago, IL: Aldine.

Coburn, Karen Levin, and Madge Lawrence Treeger. 2003. *Letting Go: A Parents' Guide to Understanding the College Years.* New York: Quill.

Collins, Patricia Hill. 1990. *Black Feminist Thought: Knowledge, Consciousness, and the Politics of Empowerment.* New York: Routledge.

———. 1993. "Toward a New Vision: Race, Class, and Gender as Categories of Analysis and Connection." *Race, Sex & Class* 1 (1): 213–23.

Collins, Randall. 1979. *The Credential Society: An Historical Sociology of Education and Stratification.* New York: Academic Press.

Condron, Steve. 2006. May 3. E-mail.

Connell, Robert W. 1987. *Gender and Power: Society, the Person, and Sexual Politics.* Stanford, CA: Stanford University Press.

Côté, James E. 2000. *Arrested Adulthood: The Changing Nature of Identity and Maturity in the Late-Modern World.* New York: New York University Press.

———. 2002. "The Role of Identity Capital in the Transition to Adulthood: The Individualization Thesis Examined." *Journal of Youth Studies* 5 (2): 117–34.

Delanty, Gerard. 2003. *Community*. New York: Routledge.

Denzin, Norman K., and Yvonne S. Lincoln, eds. [1994] 2005. *Handbook of Qualitative Research*. Thousand Oaks, CA: Sage.

Dinnerstein, Dorothy. 1976. *The Mermaid and the Minotaur: Sexual Arrangements and Human Malaise*. New York: Harper and Row.

DiPrete, Thomas A., and Claudia Buchmann. 2006. "Gender-Specific Trends in the Value of Education and the Emerging Gender Gap in College Completion." *Demography* 43: 1–24.

Downey, Douglas B., and Anastasia S. Vogt Yuan. 2005. "Sex Differences in School Performance during High School: Puzzling Patterns and Possible Explanations." *Sociological Quarterly* 46: 299–321.

Edgell, Penny. 2006. *Religion and Family in a Changing Society*. Princeton, NJ: Princeton University Press.

Eisenberg, Avigail. 1999. "Cultural Pluralism Today." In *Understanding Contemporary Society: Theories of the Present*, ed. Gary Browning, Abigail Halcli, and Frank Webster, 385–401. London: Sage.

Evans, Karen, and Walter R. Heinz. 1994. *Becoming Adults in England and Germany*. London: Anglo-German Foundation.

Feagin, Joe R., Hernan Vera, and Nikitah Imani. 1996. *The Agony of Education: Black Students at White Colleges and Universities*. New York: Routledge.

Ferrante, Joan. 2006. *Sociology: A Global Perspective*. Belmont, CA: Thomson Wadsworth.

Foley, Douglas E. 1994. *Learning Capitalist Culture: Deep in the Heart of Texas*. Philadelphia: University of Pennsylvania Press.

Frank, Leonard Roy, ed. 1999. *Random House Webster's Quotationary*. New York: Random House.

Freedman, Samuel G. 2004. "Weaning Parents from Children As They Head Off to College." *New York Times*. September 15, reprinted online at http://www.samuelfreedman.com/articles/education/nyt091152004.html.

Frenette, Marc. 2000. "Overqualified? Recent Graduates and the Needs of Their Employers." *Education Quarterly Review* (Statistics Canada) 7 (1): 6–20.

Fuligni, Andrew J., Vivian Tseng, and May Lam. 1999. "Attitudes toward Family Obligations among American Adolescents with Asian, Latin American, and European Backgounds." *Child Development* 70 (4): 1030–44.

Furlong, Andy, and Fred Cartmel. 1997. *Young People and Social Change: Individualization and Risk in Late Modernity*. Buckingham, UK: Open University Press.

Galinsky, Ellen. 1999. *Ask the Children: What America's Children Really Think about Working Parents.* New York: William Morrow.

Giddens, Anthony. 1991. *Modernity and Self-Identity: Self and Society in the Late Modern Age.* Stanford, CA: Stanford University Press.

———. 1992. *The Transformation of Intimacy: Sexuality, Love, and Eroticism in Modern Societies.* Stanford, CA: Stanford University Press.

Glaser, Barney G., and Anselm L. Strauss. 1967. *The Discovery of Grounded Theory: Strategies for Qualitative Research.* Chicago, IL: Aldine.

Goldin, Claudia. 1992. "The Meaning of College in the Lives of American Women: The Past 100 Years." *Working Paper No. 4099.* Chicago, IL: National Bureau of Economic Research.

———. 1995. "Career and Family: College Women Look to the Past." *Working Paper No. 5188.* Chicago, IL: National Bureau of Economic Research.

Goldman, Marion S. 1999. *Passionate Journeys: Why Successful Women Joined a Cult.* Ann Arbor: University of Michigan Press.

Goldscheider, Francis Kobrin, and Julie Davanzo. 1986. "Semiautonomy and Leaving Home during Early Adulthood." *Social Forces* 65: 187–201.

Goldscheider, Francis Kobrin, and Calvin Goldscheider. 1994. "Leaving and Returning Home in 20th-Century America." *Population Bulletin* 48 (4): 1–35.

Greene, A. L., Susan M. Wheatley, and John F. Aldava, IV. 1992. "Stages on Life's Way: Adolescents' Implicit Theories of the Life Course." *Journal of Adolescent Research* 7: 364–81.

Grigsby, Mary. 2004. *Buying Time and Getting By: The Voluntary Simplicity Movement.* Albany: State University of New York Press.

Guntrip, Harry. 1961. *Personality Structure and Human Interaction.* New York: International Universities Press.

Hall, John, and Mary Jo Neitz. 1993. *Culture: Sociological Perspectives.* Englewood Cliffs, NJ: Prentice Hall.

Harding, Sandra. 1986. *The Science Question in Feminism.* Ithaca, NY: Cornell University Press.

———. 1987. *Feminism and Methodology: Social Science Issues.* Bloomington: Indiana University Press.

Hauser, Robert M., and Daphne H. Kuo. 1997. "How Does Size of Sibship Matter: Family Configuration and Family Effects on Educational Attainment." *Social Science Research* 26: 69–94.

Heining, Andres. 2005. "Facebook Follies." *Christian Science Monitor SciTechBlogr.* November 20. http://www.blogs.csmonitor.com/scitechblog/2005/11/ (accessed March 2, 2006), 1.

Henderson, Joan. 1999. "African Literary Giant Comes to St. Louis to Accept Prize." *St. Louis Post Dispatch.* October 27, E1.

Holland, Dorothy C., and Margaret A. Eisenhart. 1990. *Educated in Romance: Women, Achievement, and College Culture.* Chicago, IL: University of Chicago Press.

hooks, bell. 1984. *Feminist Theory: From Margin to Center.* Boston, MA: South End Press.

Horowitz, Helen Lefkowitz. 1987. *Campus Life: Undergraduate Cultures from the End of the Eighteenth Century to the Present.* Chicago, IL: University of Chicago Press.

Howe, Neil, and William Strauss. 2000. *Millennials Rising: The Next Great Generation.* New York: Vintage Books.

Hubbard, Elbert. (1856–1915). Citation. Http://www.en.wikipedia.org/wiki/Elbert_Hubbard; http://www.theotherpages.org/topic14.html #life. "Do not take life too seriously. You will never get out of it alive."

Hughes, Chris. 2006. June 9. E-mail.

Jacob, Brian A. 2002. "Where the Boys Aren't: Noncognitive Skills, Returns to School, and the Gender Gap in Higher Education." *Economics of Education Review* 21: 589–98.

Jacobs, Jerry A. 1995. "Gender and Academic Specialties: Trends among College Degree Recipients in the 1980s." *Sociology of Education* 68: 81–98.

———. 1996. "Gender Inequality and Higher Education." *Annual Review of Sociology* 22: 153–85.

———. 1999. "Gender and the Stratification of Colleges." *Journal of Higher Education* 70: 161–87.

Jencks, Christopher. 1972. *Inequality: A Reassessment of the Effect of Family and Schooling in America.* New York: Basic Books.

Johnson, Helen E., and Christine Schelhas-Miller. 2000. *Don't Tell Me What to Do, Just Send Money: The Essential Parenting Guide to the College Years.* New York: St. Martin's Press.

Johnson, Miriam. 1988. *Strong Mothers, Weak Wives: The Search for Gender Equity.* Berkeley: University of California Press.

Kalmijn, Matthijs. 1994. "Mother's Occupational Status and Children's Schooling." *American Sociological Review* 59 (April): 257–75.

Kelly, Karen, Linda Howatson-Leo, and Warren Clark. 1997. "I Feel Overqualified for My Job." *Canadian Social Trends* 47 (Winter): 11–16.

Korupp, Sylvia, Harry B. G. Ganzeboom, and Tanja Van Der Lippe. 2002. "Do Mothers Matter? A Comparison of Models of the Influence of Mothers' and Fathers' Educational and Occupational Status on Children's Educational Attainment." *Quality and Quantity* 36: 17–42

Krahn, Harvey, and Jeffrey W. Bowlby. 2000. *Education-Jobs Skills Match: An Analysis of the 1990 and 1995 National Graduates Surveys*. Ottawa: Human Resources Development Canada and Center for Education Statistics, Statistics Canada.

Lara, Maria Pia. 1998. *Moral Textures: Feminist Narratives in the Public Sphere*. Berkeley: University of California Press.

Lasch, Christopher. 1978. *The Culture of Narcissism: American Life in an Age of Diminishing Expectations*. New York: Norton.

Lichterman, Paul. 1996. *The Search for Political Community: American Activists Reinventing Commitment*. Cambridge, UK: Cambridge University Press.

Mare, Robert D. 1995. "Changes in Education and School Enrollment." In *The State of the Union*, ed. Reynolds Farley. New York: Russell Sage Foundation.

McPherson, Michael S., and Morton O. Schapiro. 1997. *The Student Aid Game: Meeting Need and Rewarding Talent in American Higher Education*. Princeton, NJ: Princeton University Press.

Mead, Margaret. 1928. *Coming of Age in Samoa: A Psychological Study of Primitive Youth for Western Civilization*. New York: William Morrow.

Milner, Murray, Jr. 2004. *Freaks, Geeks, and Cool Kids: American Teenagers, Schools, and the Culture of Consumption*. New York: Routledge.

Moffatt, Michael. 1989. *Coming of Age in New Jersey: College and American Culture*. New Brunswick, NJ: Rutgers University Press.

Morrow, Raymond Allan, and Carlos Alberto Torres. 1995. *Social Theory and Education: A Critique of Theories of Social and Cultural Reproduction*. Albany: State University of New York Press.

Nathan, Rebekah. 2005. *My Freshman Year: What a Professor Learned by Becoming a Student*. Ithaca, NY: Cornell University Press.

National Survey of Student Engagement (NSSE). 2005. *Exploring Different Dimensions of Student Engagement: 2005 National Survey Results*. Bloomington, IN: Center for Postsecondary Research.

———. 2006. *Engaged Learning: Fostering Success for All Students*. Bloomington, IN: Center for Postsecondary Research.

Neitz, Mary Jo. 1985. "Resistances to Feminist Analysis." *Teaching Sociology* 12 (3): 339–53.

Newcomb, Theodore M., and Everett K. Wilson, eds. 1966. *College Peer Groups: Problems and Prospects for Research.* Chicago, IL: Aldine.

Nobert, Lucie, Ramona McDowell, and D. Goulet. 1992. *Profile of Post-Secondary Education in Canada 1991 Edition.* Ottawa: Minister of Supply and Services.

Pahl, Ray. 1995. *After Success: Fin-de-Siécle Anxiety and Identity.* Cambridge, UK: Polity Press.

Pascarella, Ernest T., Christopher T. Pierson, Gregory C. Wolniak, and Patrick T. Terenzini. 2004. "First-Generation College Students: Additional Evidence on College Experiences and Outcomes." *The Journal of Higher Education* 75 (3) (May–June) 249–84.

Phinney, Jean S., Anthony Ong, and Tanya Madden. 2000. "Cultural Values and Intergenerational Value Discrepancies in Immigrant and Nonimmigrant Families." *Child Development* 71 (2): 528–39.

Polanyi, Karl. 1944. *The Great Transformation: The Political and Economic Origins of Our Time.* Boston, MA: Beacon Press.

Powell, Brian, and Douglas B. Downey. 1997. "Living in Single-Parent Households: An Investigation of the Same-Sex Hypothesis." *American Sociological Review* 62: 521–39.

Purdie, John. 2006. March 22. Phone conversation.

———. 2006b. May 8. E-mail.

Putnam, Robert D. 2000. *Bowling Alone: The Collapse and Revival of American Community.* New York: Simon & Schuster.

Robbins, Alexandra. 2004. *Pledged: The Secret Life of Sororities.* New York: Hyperion.

Robinson, John P., and Geoffrey Godbey. 1999. *Time for Life: The Surprising Ways Americans Use Their Time.* 2nd ed. University Park: Pennsylvania State University Press.

St. John, Edward P., and Michael D. Parsons. 2005. *Public Funding of Higher Education: Changing Contexts and New Rationales.* Baltimore, MD: Johns Hopkins University Press.

Sandberg, John F., and Sandra L. Hofferth. 2001. *Change in Parental Time with Children, U.S. 1981–1997.* Town, MI: Institute for Social Research and Population Studies Center, University of Michigan.

Schwalbe, Michael. 1996. *Unlocking the Iron Cage: The Men's Movement, Gender Politics, and American Culture.* New York: Oxford University Press.

Selingo, Jeffrey, and Jeffrey Brainard. 2006. "The Rich-Poor Gap Widens for Colleges and Students." *The Chronicle of Higher Education* LII (31): A1, A13.

Sewell, Willaim H., Archibald O. Haller, and Alejandro Portes. 1969. "The Educational and Early Occupational Attainment Process." *American Sociological Review* 34: 82–92.

Shellenbarger, Sue. 2005. "In Defense of Hovering Parents: Parents Explain Their Meddling at College." *The Wallstreet Journal Online*. August 25.

Sommers, Christian H. 2000. *The War against Boys: How Misguided Feminism Is Harming Our Young Men*. New York: Touchstone.

Spain, Daphne, and Suzanne M. Bianchi. 1996. *Balancing Act: Motherhood, Marriage, and Employment among American Women*. New York: Russell Sage Foundation.

Steelman Lal Carr, and Brian Powell. 1991. "Sponsoring the Next Generation: Parental Willingness to Pay for Higher Education." *American Journal of Sociology* 96 (6): 1505–29.

Swidler, Ann. 1986. "Culture in Action: Symbols and Strategies." *American Sociological Review* 51: 273–86.

Talisha. 2006. July 1. E-mail.

Terenzini, Patrick T., Leonard Springer, Patricia M. Yaeger, Ernest T. Pascarella, and Amaury Nora. 1996. "First-Generation College Students: Characteristics, Experiences, and Cognitive Development." *Research in Higher Education* 37: 1–22.

Thompson, E. P. 1963. *The Making of the English Working Class*. New York: Vintage Books.

Tönnies, Ferdinand. [1887] 2002. *Community and Society*. New York: Dover.

Turner, Ralph. 1976. "The Real Self: From Institution to Impulse." *American Journal of Sociology* 81: 989–1016.

Turner, Sarah E., and William G. Bowen. 1999. "Choice of Major: The Changing (Unchanging) Gender Gap." *Industrial and Labor Relations Review* 52: 289–313.

Twenge, Jean M. 2006. *Generation Me: Why Today's Young Americans Are More Confident, Assertive, Entitled—and More Miserable Than Ever Before*. New York: Free Press.

University of Texas, Dallas. 2005. Student Counseling Center. "How to Raise Your Parents While at College." http://www.utdallas.edu/counseling/selfhelp/raising-parents.html (accessed June 1, 2005).

U.S. Department of Education. National Center for Education Statistics. 2004. *Digest of Education Statistics 2004*. Washington, DC: U.S. Government Printing Office.

Van Wilder. 2002. DVD. Directed by Walt Becker. Van Nuys, CA: Artisan Home Entertainment.

Walby, Sylvia. 1990. *Theorizing Patriarchy*. Cambridge, MA: Basil Blackwell.

Wallace, Claire and Suhja Kovatcheva. 1996. "Youth Cultures and Consumption in Eastern and Western Europe." *Youth and Society* 28 (2): 189–214.

———. 1998. *Youth in Society: The Construction and Deconstruction of Youth in East and West Europe*. London: Macmillan Press.

Weber, Max. [1904] 1958. *The Protestant Ethic and the Spirit of Capitalism*. New York: Charles Scribner's Sons.

Wilson, Robin. 2007. "The New Gender Divide." *Chronicle of Higher Education* January 26, LII (21): A37–A39.

INDEX

233